DUNGEONS & DRAGONS

FORGOTTEN REALMS

C U T T E R

Credits

Written by	**R.A. Salvatore** **Geno Salvatore**
Art by	**David Baldeon**
Colors by	**David Garcia Cruz**
Letters by	**Neil Uyetake**
Series Edits by	**John Barber**
Collection Edits by	**Justin Eisinger** **Alonzo Simon**
Collection Design by	**Neil Uyetake**
Collection Cover by	**Steve Ellis**

Special thanks to Hasbro's Michael Kelly and Ed Lane, and Wizards of the Coast's Jon Schindehette, James Wyatt, Chris Perkins, Liz Schuh, Nathan Stewart, Laura Tommervik, Shelly Mazzanoble, Hilary Ross, and Chris Lindsay.

IDW founded by Ted Adams, Alex Garner, Kris Oprisko, and Robbie Robbins |

ISBN: 978-1-61377-792-3

16 15 14 13   1 2 3 4

Ted Adams, CEO & Publisher
Greg Goldstein, President & COO
Robbie Robbins, EVP/Sr. Graphic Artist
Chris Ryall, Chief Creative Officer/Editor-in-Chief
Matthew Ruzicka, CPA, Chief Financial Officer
Alan Payne, VP of Sales
Dirk Wood, VP of Marketing
Lorelei Bunjes, VP of Digital Services

Become our fan on Facebook **facebook.com/idwpublishing**
Follow us on Twitter **@idwpublishing**
Check us out on YouTube **youtube.com/idwpublishing**
www.IDWPUBLISHING.com

Welcome to a world where adventurers delve into the depths to win great treasures of old, heroes stave off the insidious plots of shadowborn fiends, undead necromancers vie for absolute mastery of life, and voracious dragons hunt. Welcome to a land whose magic-soaked bedrock has spawned millennia of eye-popping wonders and heart-stopping threats.

Welcome... to the Forgotten Realms.

Art by Steve Ellis

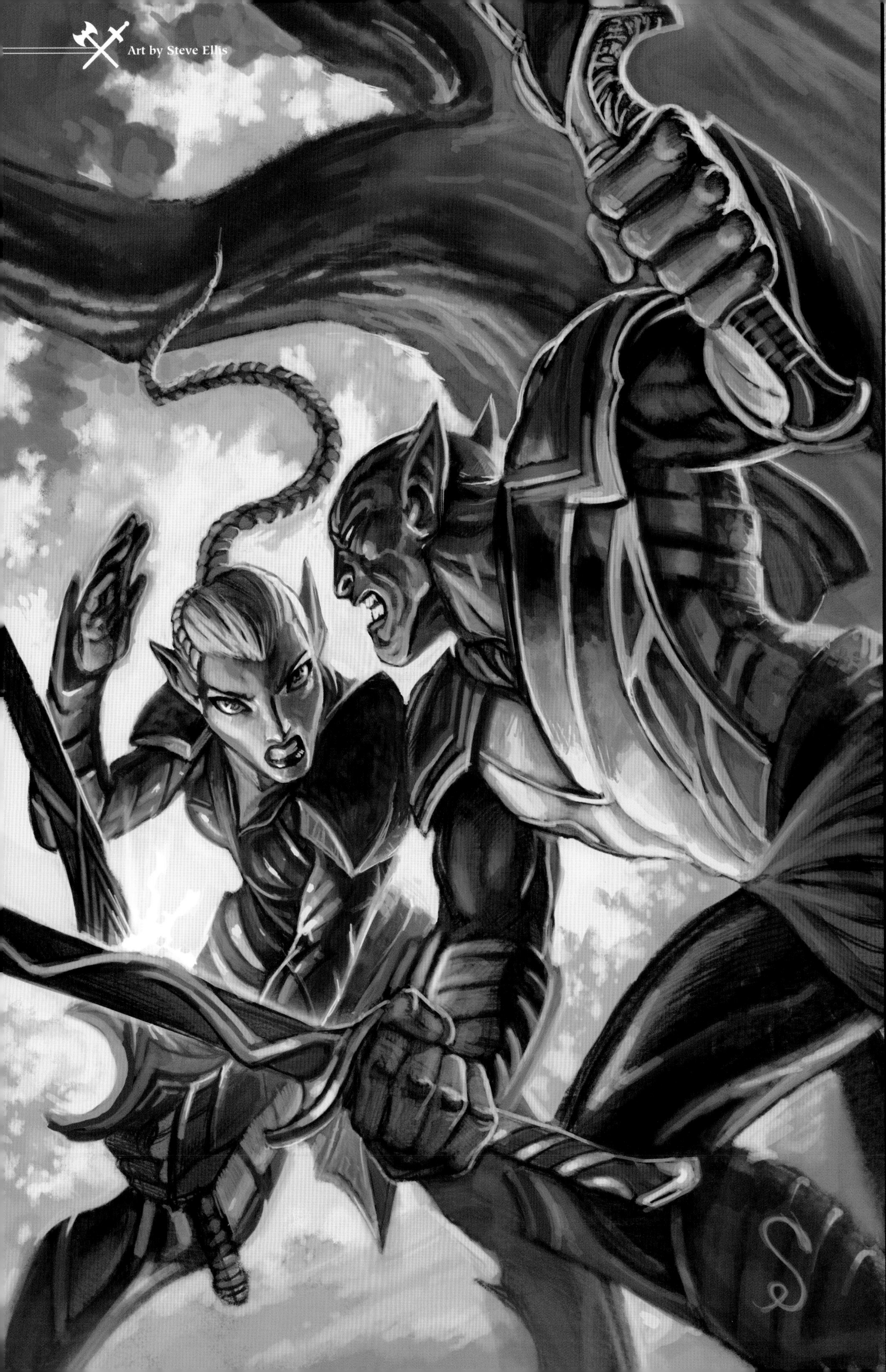

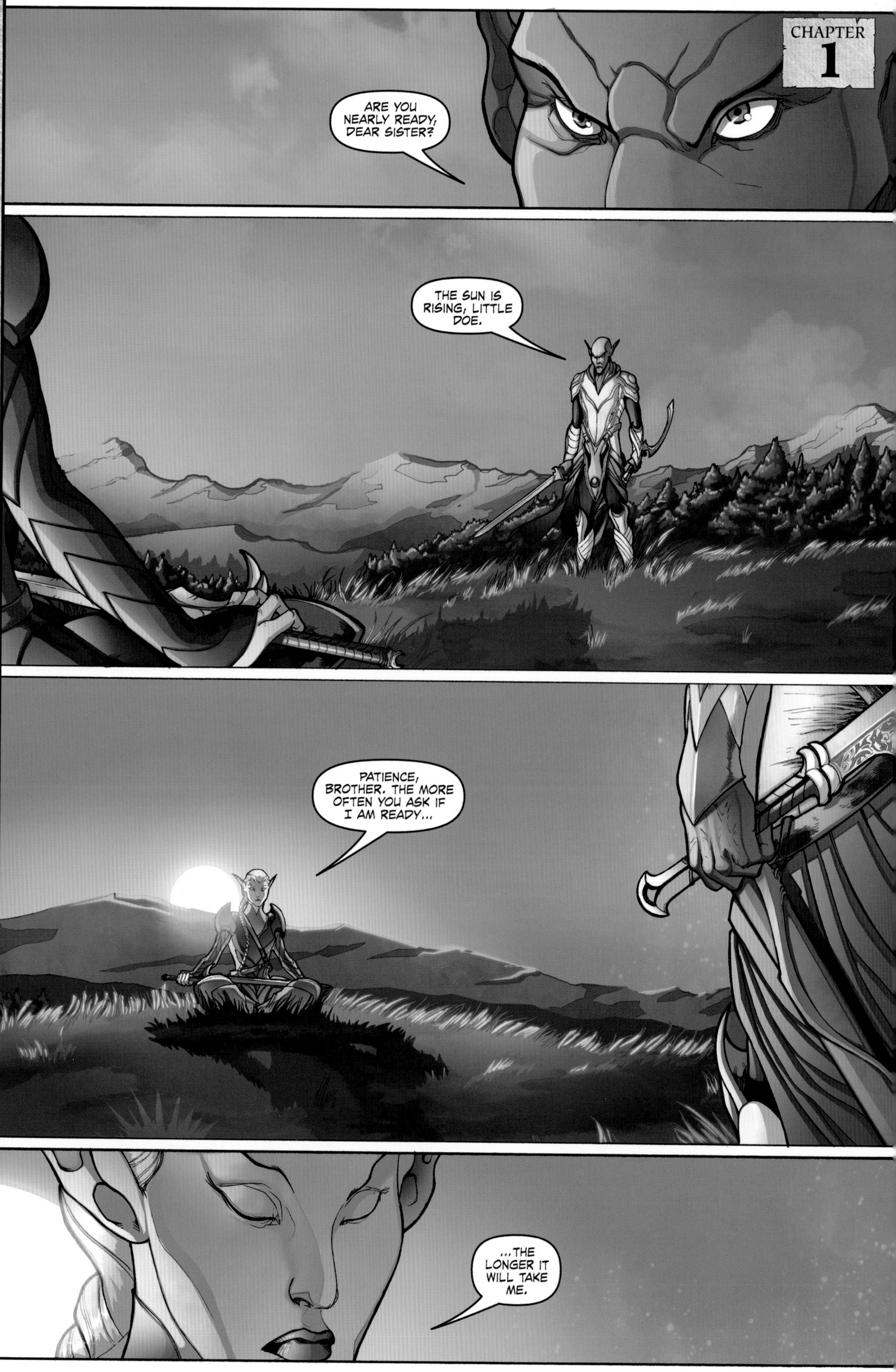
CHAPTER 1
ARE YOU NEARLY READY, DEAR SISTER?
THE SUN IS RISING, LITTLE DOE.
PATIENCE, BROTHER. THE MORE OFTEN YOU ASK IF I AM READY...
...THE LONGER IT WILL TAKE ME.

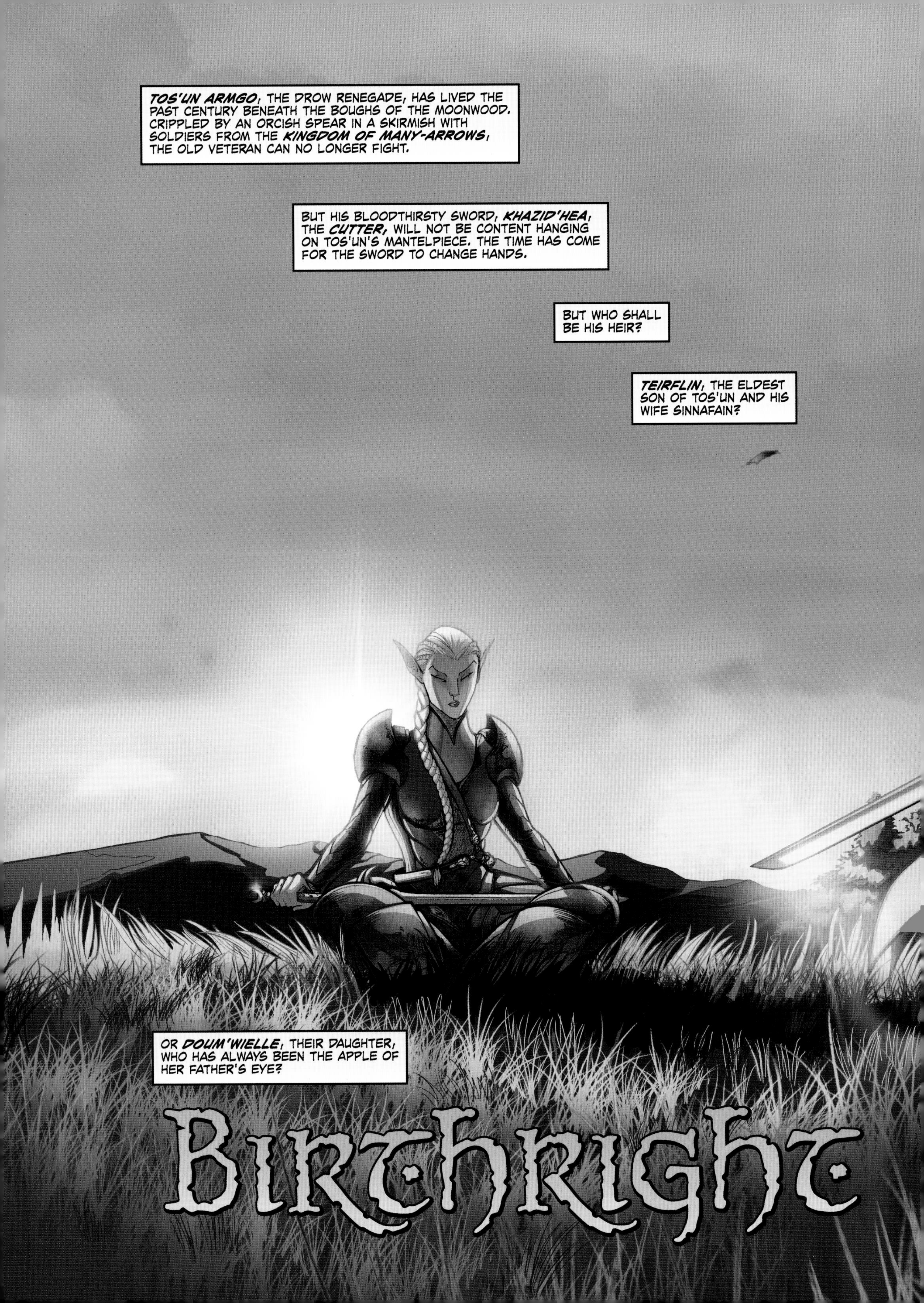
TOS'UN ARMGO, THE DROW RENEGADE, HAS LIVED THE PAST CENTURY BENEATH THE BOUGHS OF THE MOONWOOD. CRIPPLED BY AN ORCISH SPEAR IN A SKIRMISH WITH SOLDIERS FROM THE KINGDOM OF MANY-ARROWS, THE OLD VETERAN CAN NO LONGER FIGHT.
BUT HIS BLOODTHIRSTY SWORD, KHAZID'HEA, THE CUTTER, WILL NOT BE CONTENT HANGING ON TOS'UN'S MANTELPIECE. THE TIME HAS COME FOR THE SWORD TO CHANGE HANDS.
BUT WHO SHALL BE HIS HEIR?
TEIRFLIN, THE ELDEST SON OF TOS'UN AND HIS WIFE SINNAFAIN?
OR DOUM'WIELLE, THEIR DAUGHTER, WHO HAS ALWAYS BEEN THE APPLE OF HER FATHER'S EYE?
BIRTHRIGHT

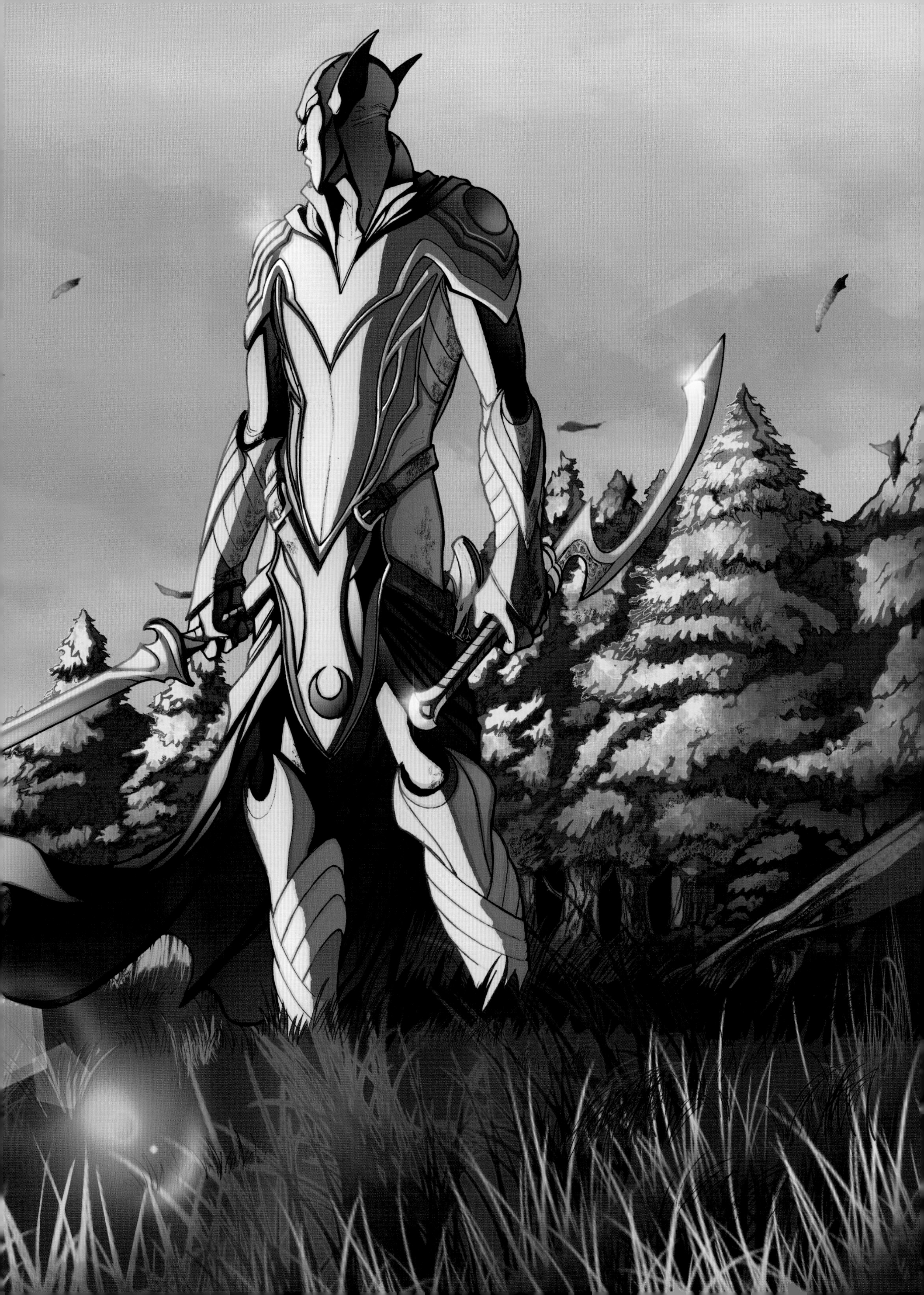

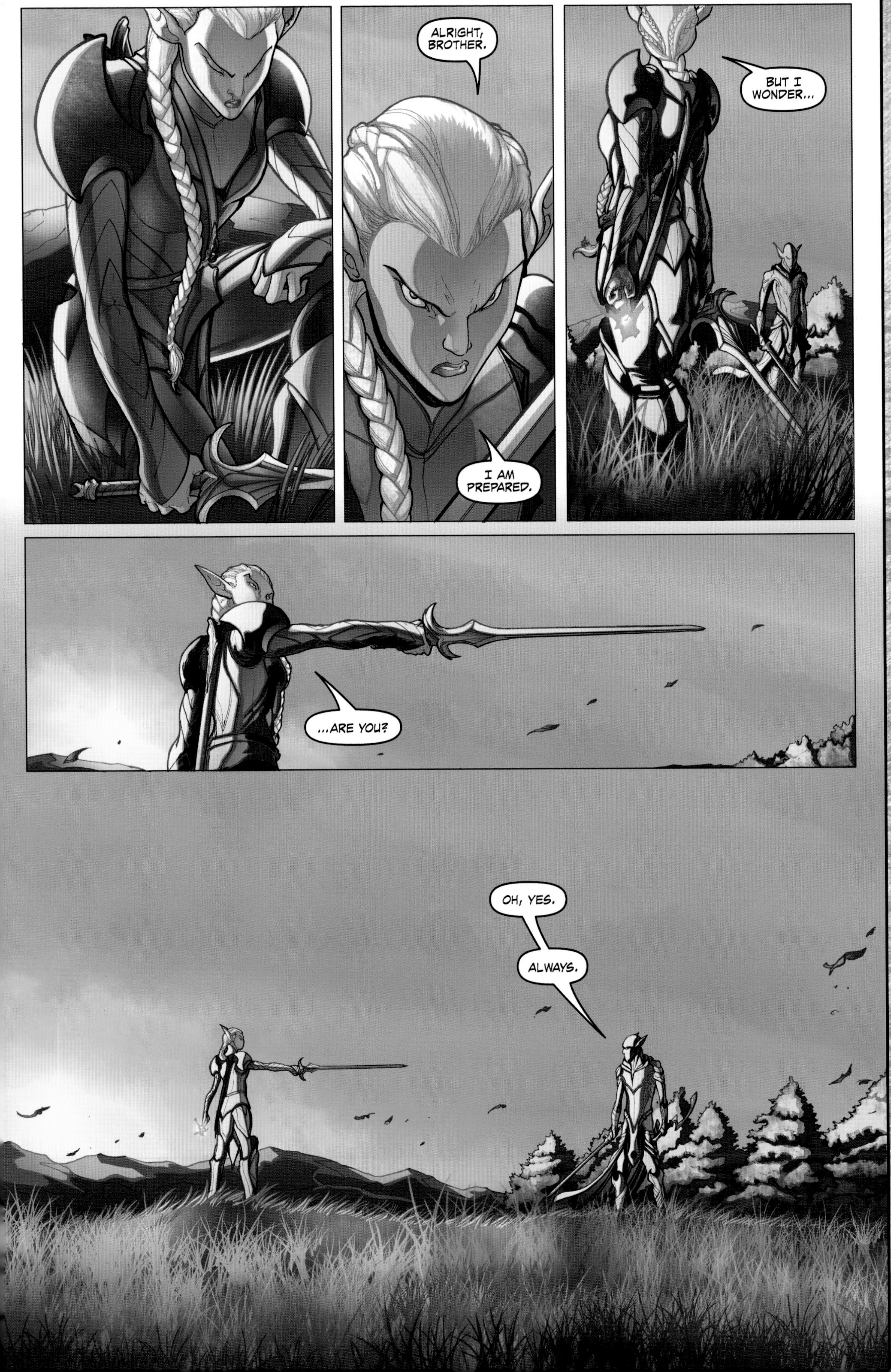
ALRIGHT, BROTHER.
I AM PREPARED.
BUT I WONDER...
...ARE YOU?
OH, YES.
ALWAYS.

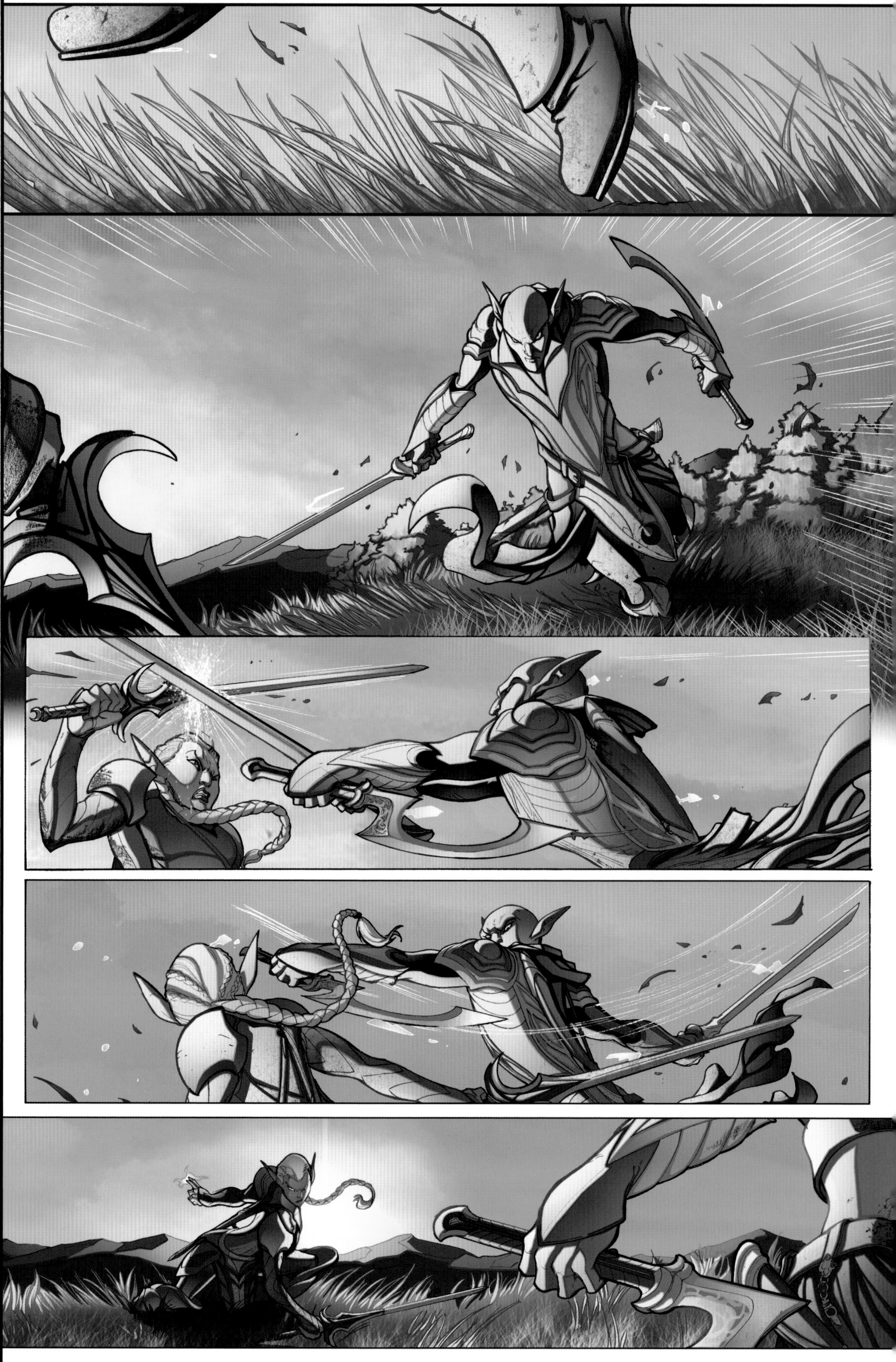

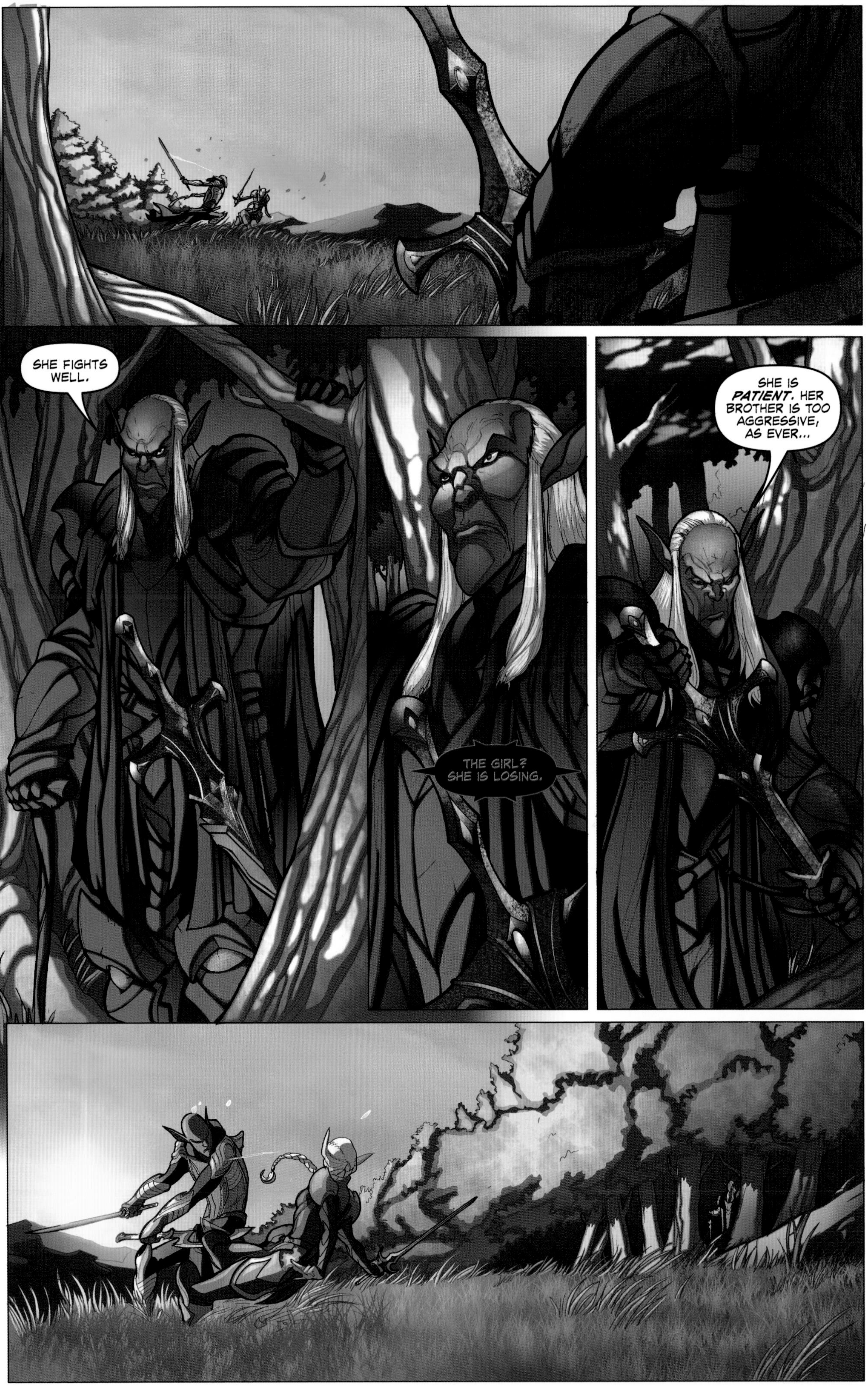
SHE FIGHTS WELL.
THE GIRL? SHE IS LOSING.
SHE IS *PATIENT*. HER BROTHER IS TOO AGGRESSIVE, AS EVER...

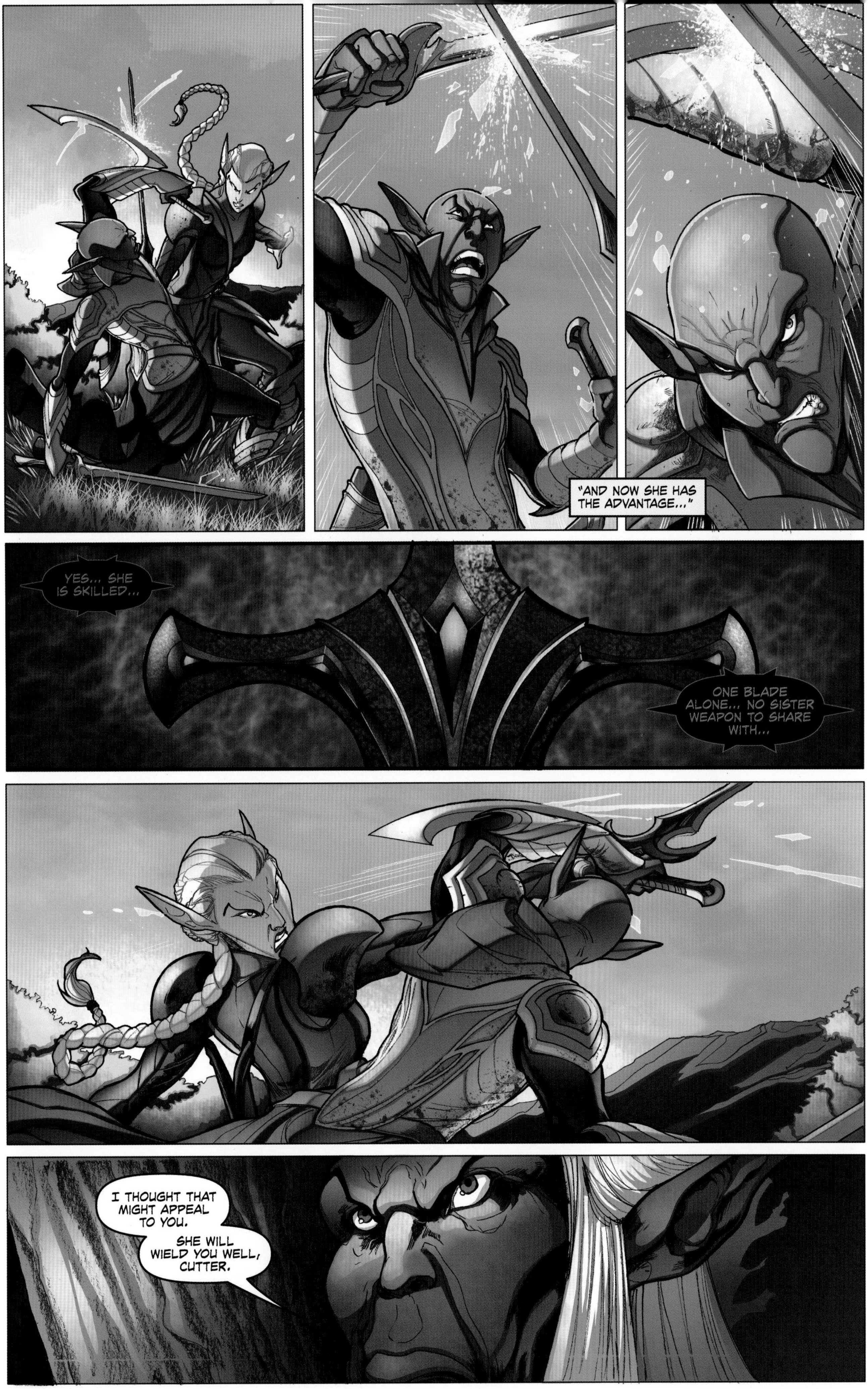
"AND NOW SHE HAS THE ADVANTAGE..."
YES... SHE IS SKILLED...
ONE BLADE ALONE... NO SISTER WEAPON TO SHARE WITH...
I THOUGHT THAT MIGHT APPEAL TO YOU.
SHE WILL WIELD YOU WELL, CUTTER.

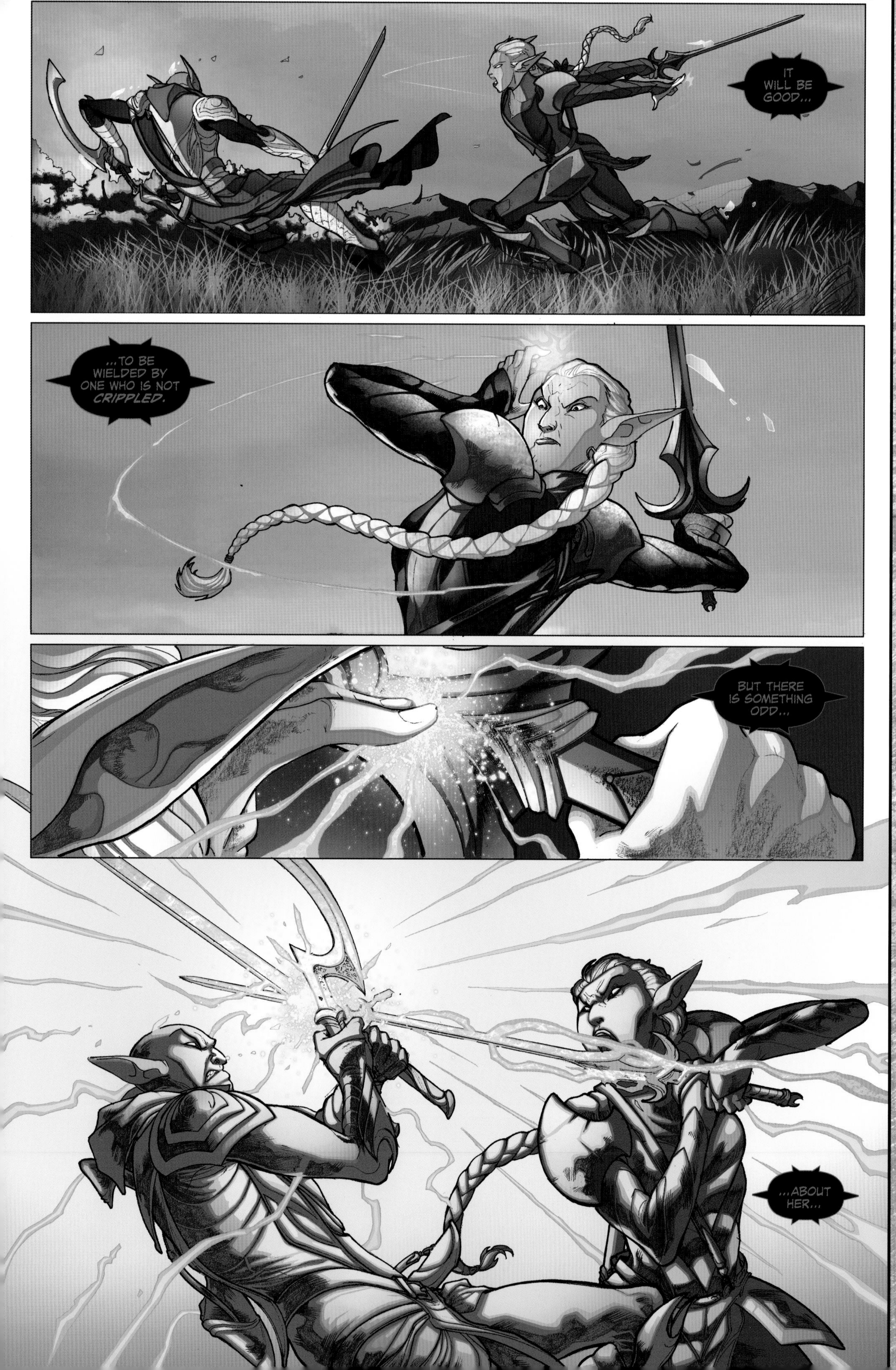
IT WILL BE GOOD...
...TO BE WIELDED BY ONE WHO IS NOT *CRIPPLED*.
BUT THERE IS SOMETHING ODD...
...ABOUT HER...

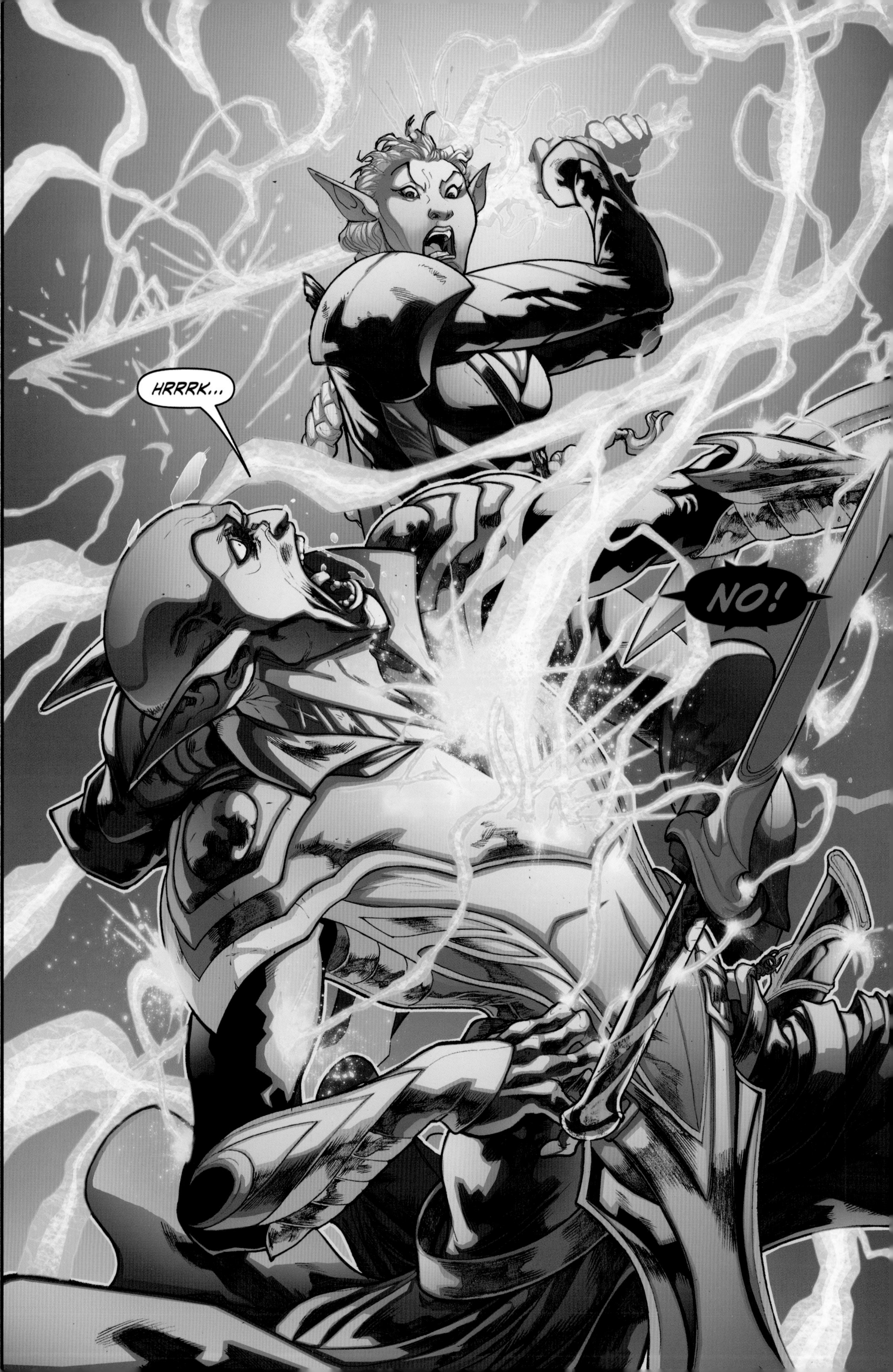
HRRRK...
NO!

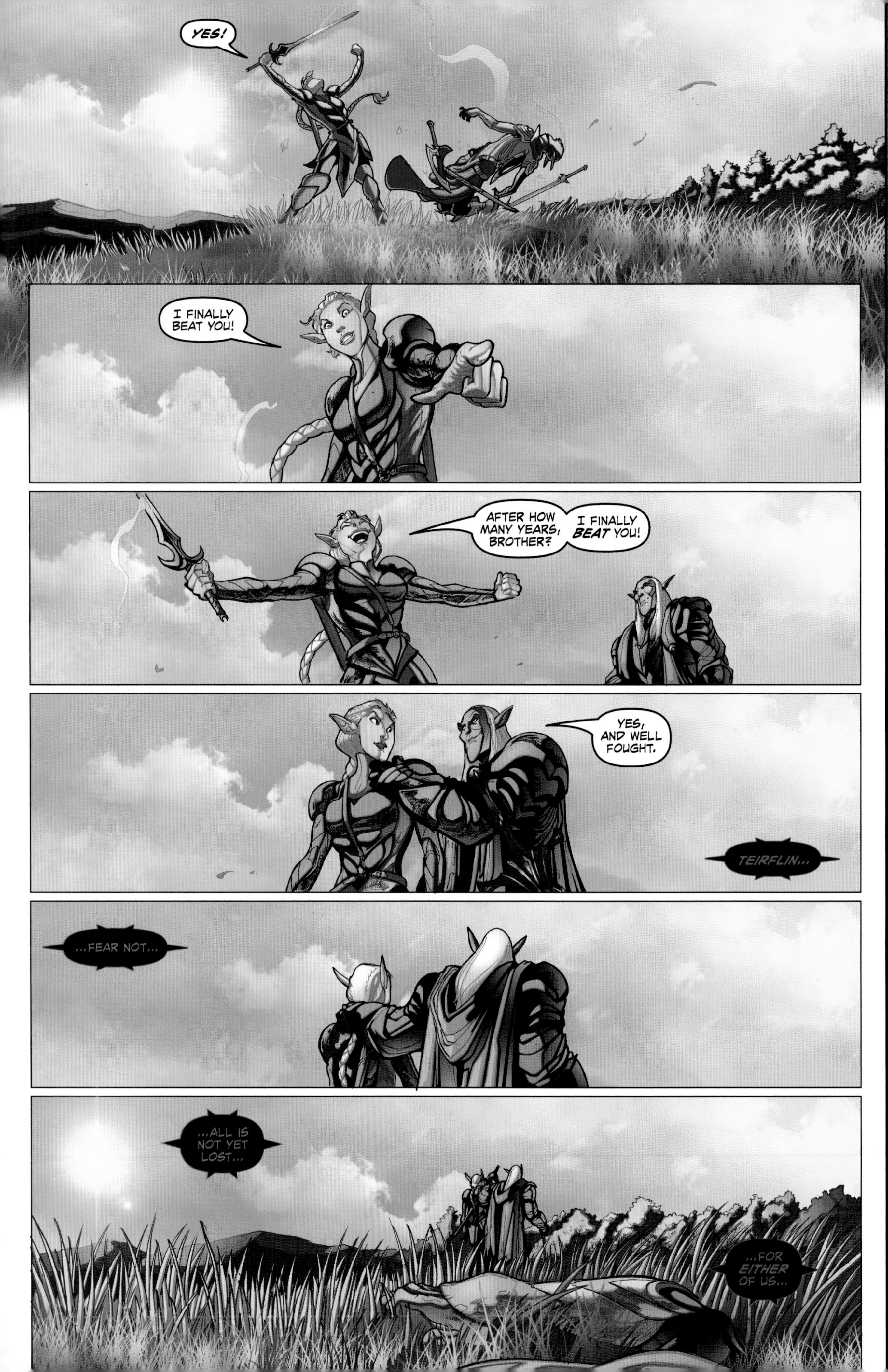
YES!
I FINALLY BEAT YOU!
AFTER HOW MANY YEARS, BROTHER?
I FINALLY BEAT YOU!
YES, AND WELL FOUGHT.
TEIRFLIN...
...FEAR NOT...
...ALL IS NOT YET LOST...
...FOR EITHER OF US...

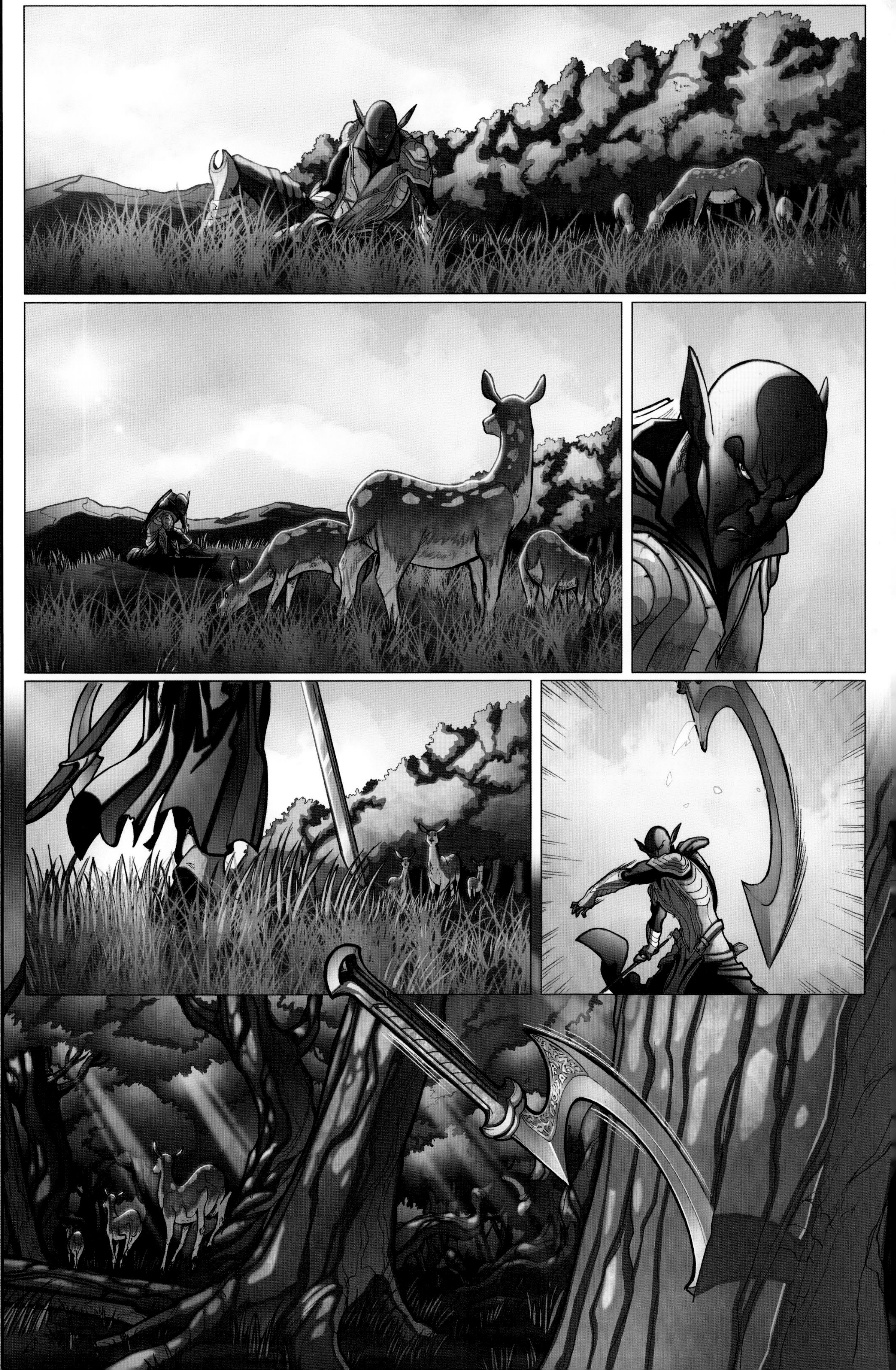

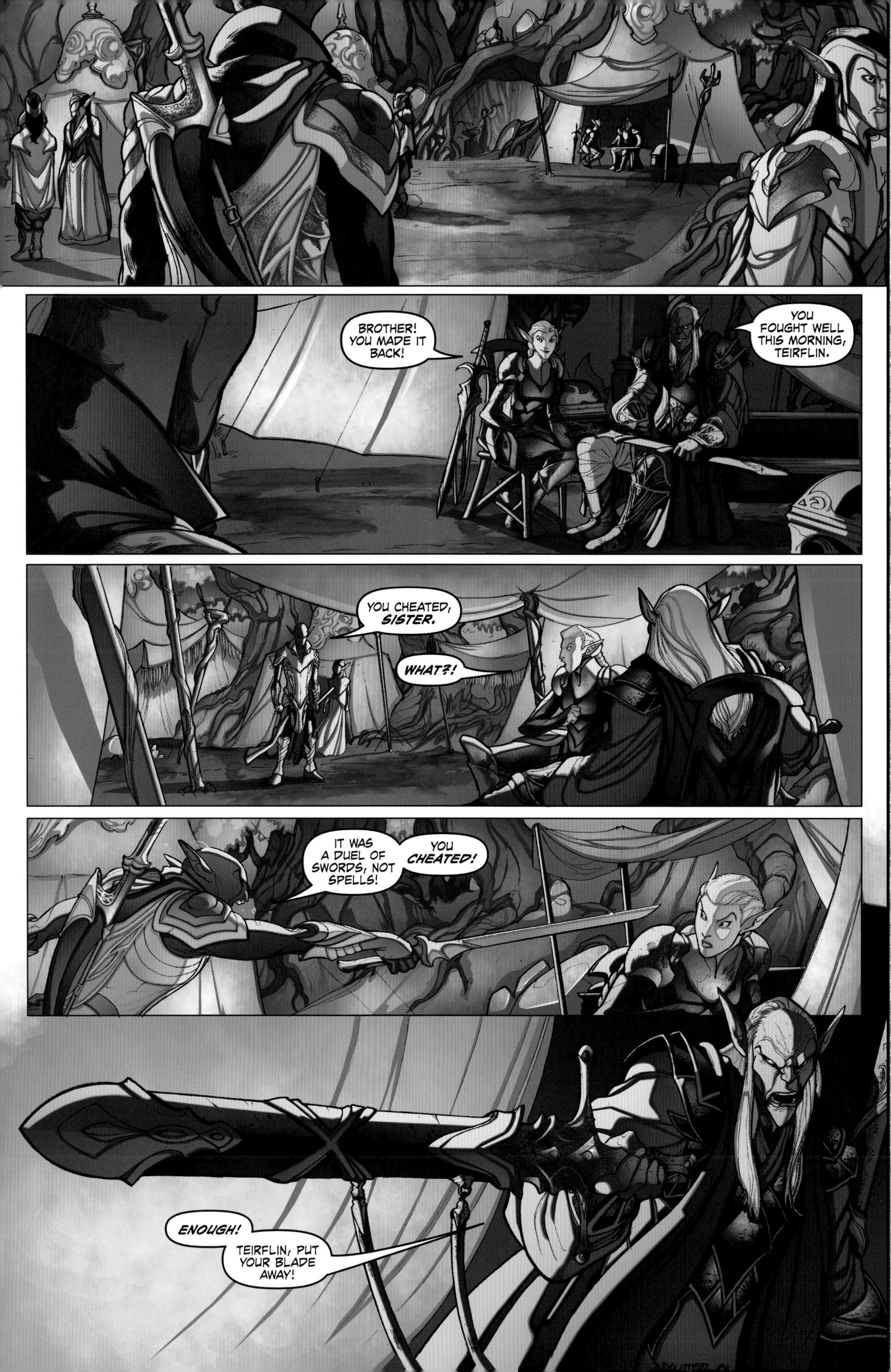
BROTHER! YOU MADE IT BACK!
YOU FOUGHT WELL THIS MORNING, TEIRFLIN.
YOU CHEATED, SISTER.
WHAT?!
YOU CHEATED!
IT WAS A DUEL OF SWORDS, NOT SPELLS!
ENOUGH!
TEIRFLIN, PUT YOUR BLADE AWAY!

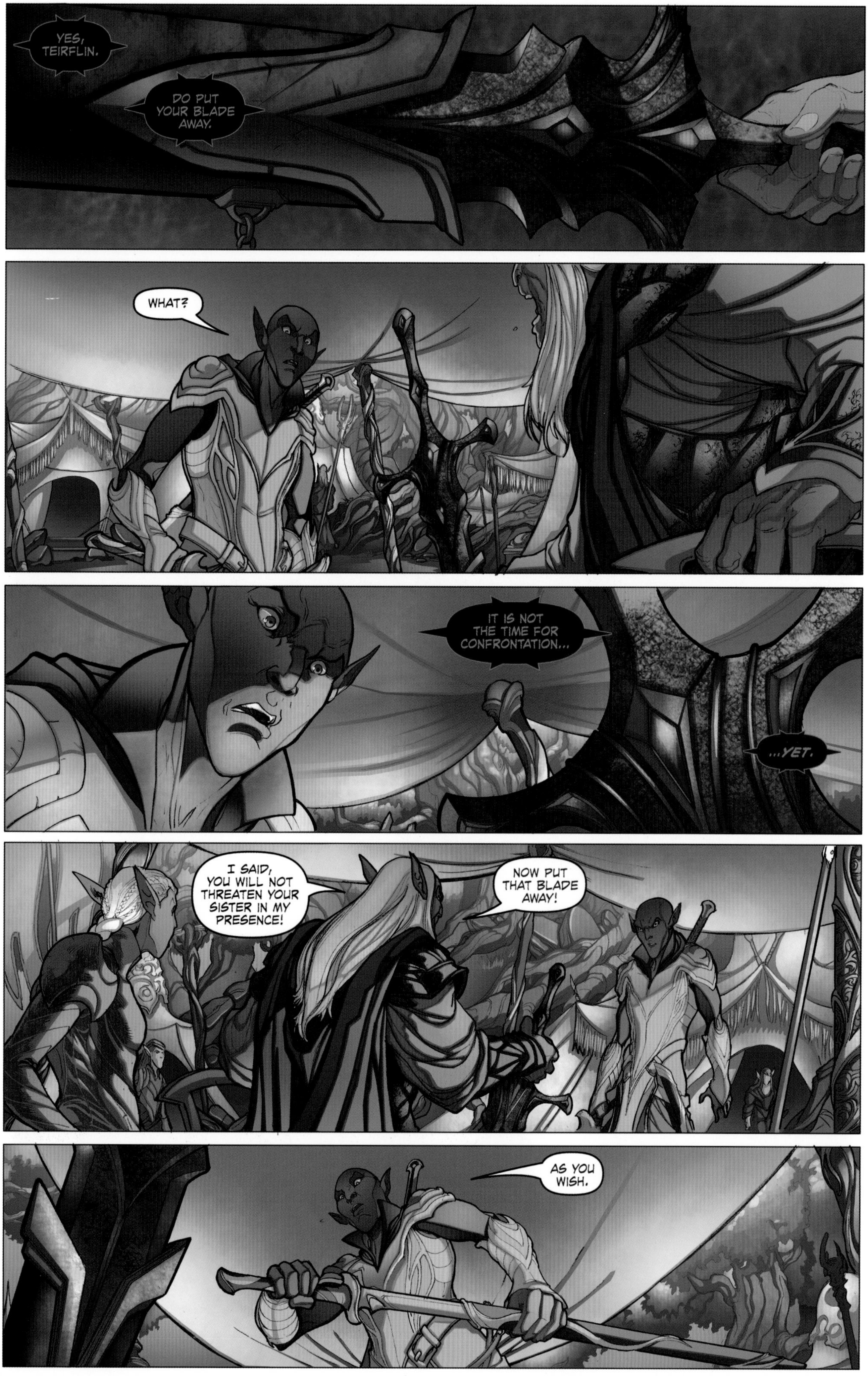
YES, TEIRFLIN.
DO PUT YOUR BLADE AWAY.
WHAT?
IT IS NOT THE TIME FOR CONFRONTATION...
...YET.
I SAID, YOU WILL NOT THREATEN YOUR SISTER IN MY PRESENCE!
NOW PUT THAT BLADE AWAY!
AS YOU WISH.

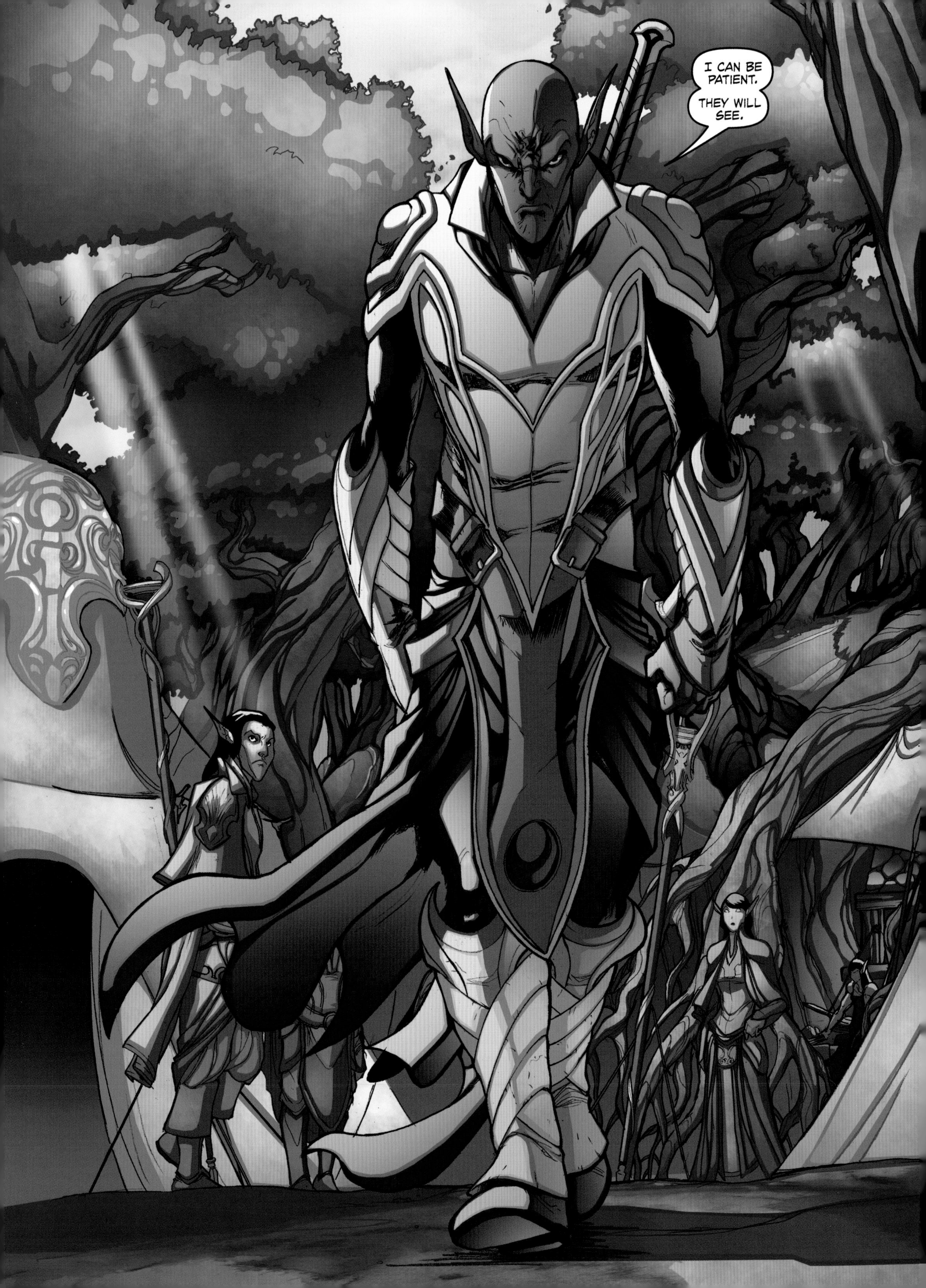
I CAN BE PATIENT.
THEY WILL SEE.

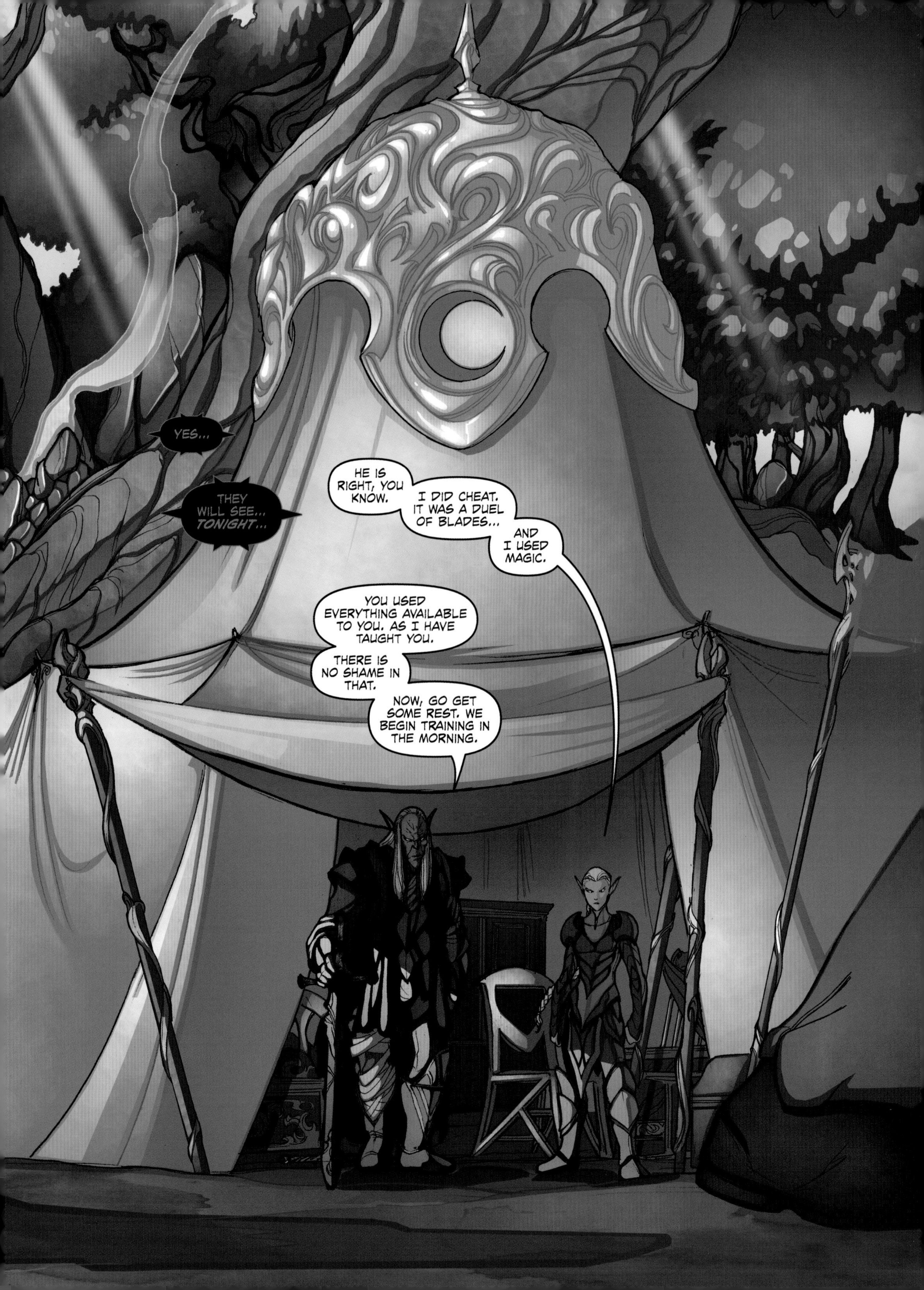
YES...
THEY WILL SEE... TONIGHT...
HE IS RIGHT, YOU KNOW.
I DID CHEAT. IT WAS A DUEL OF BLADES...
AND I USED MAGIC.
YOU USED EVERYTHING AVAILABLE TO YOU. AS I HAVE TAUGHT YOU.
THERE IS NO SHAME IN THAT.
NOW, GO GET SOME REST. WE BEGIN TRAINING IN THE MORNING.

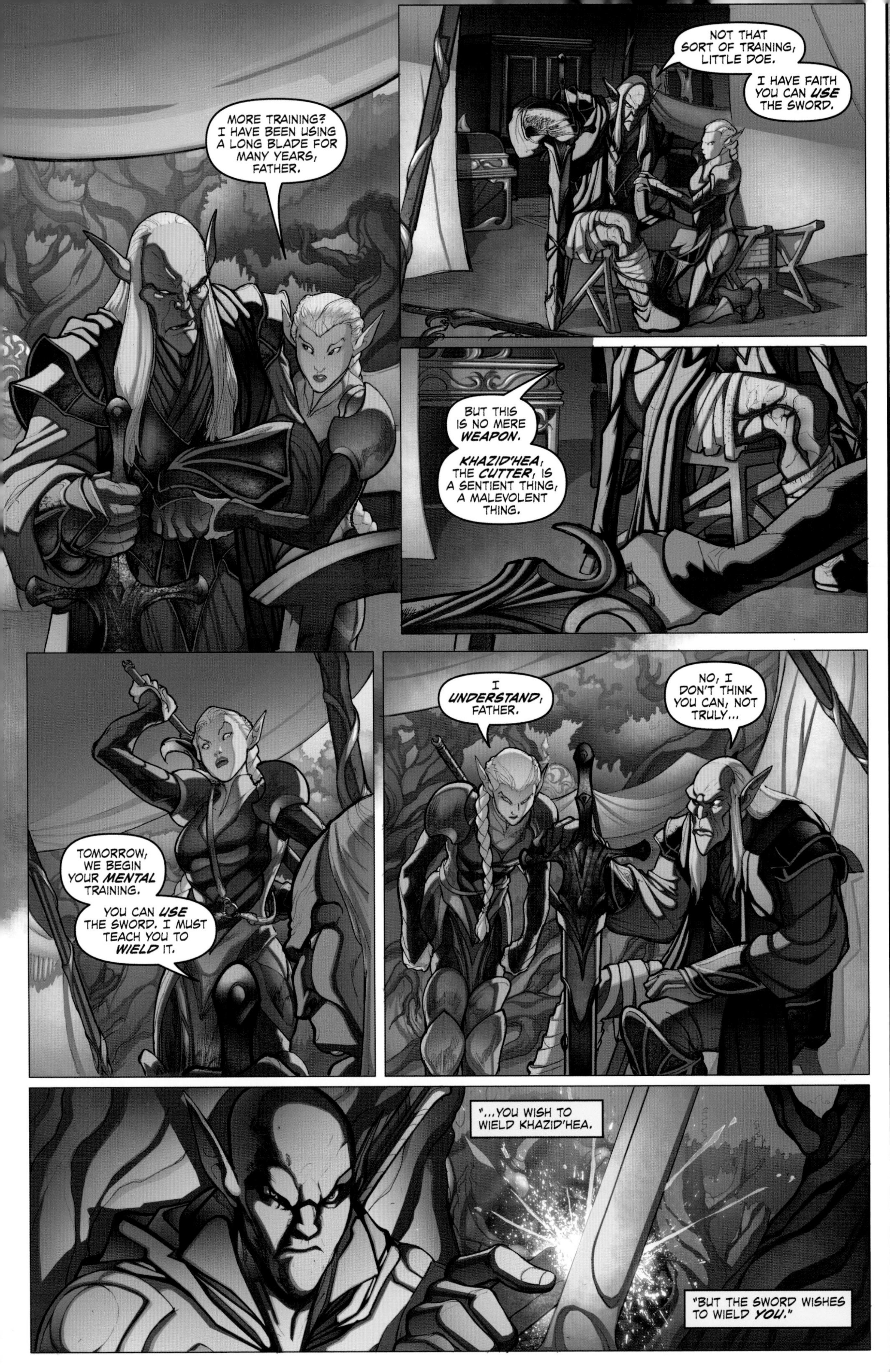

MORE TRAINING? I HAVE BEEN USING A LONG BLADE FOR MANY YEARS, FATHER.
NOT THAT SORT OF TRAINING, LITTLE DOE.
I HAVE FAITH YOU CAN USE THE SWORD.
BUT THIS IS NO MERE WEAPON.
KHAZID'HEA, THE CUTTER, IS A SENTIENT THING, A MALEVOLENT THING.
TOMORROW, WE BEGIN YOUR MENTAL TRAINING.
YOU CAN USE THE SWORD. I MUST TEACH YOU TO WIELD IT.
I UNDERSTAND, FATHER.
NO, I DON'T THINK YOU CAN, NOT TRULY...
"...YOU WISH TO WIELD KHAZID'HEA.
"BUT THE SWORD WISHES TO WIELD YOU."

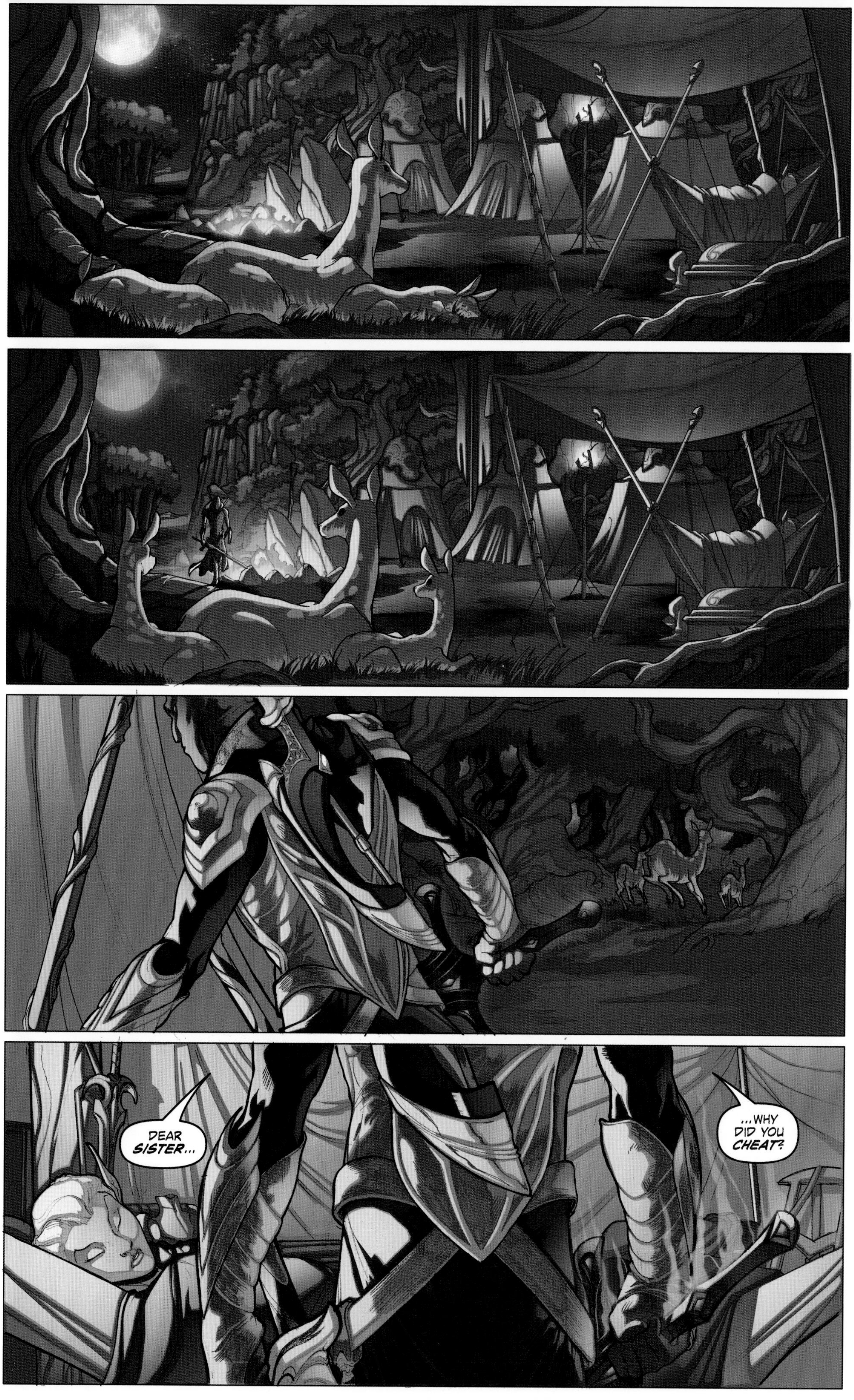
DEAR SISTER...
...WHY DID YOU CHEAT?

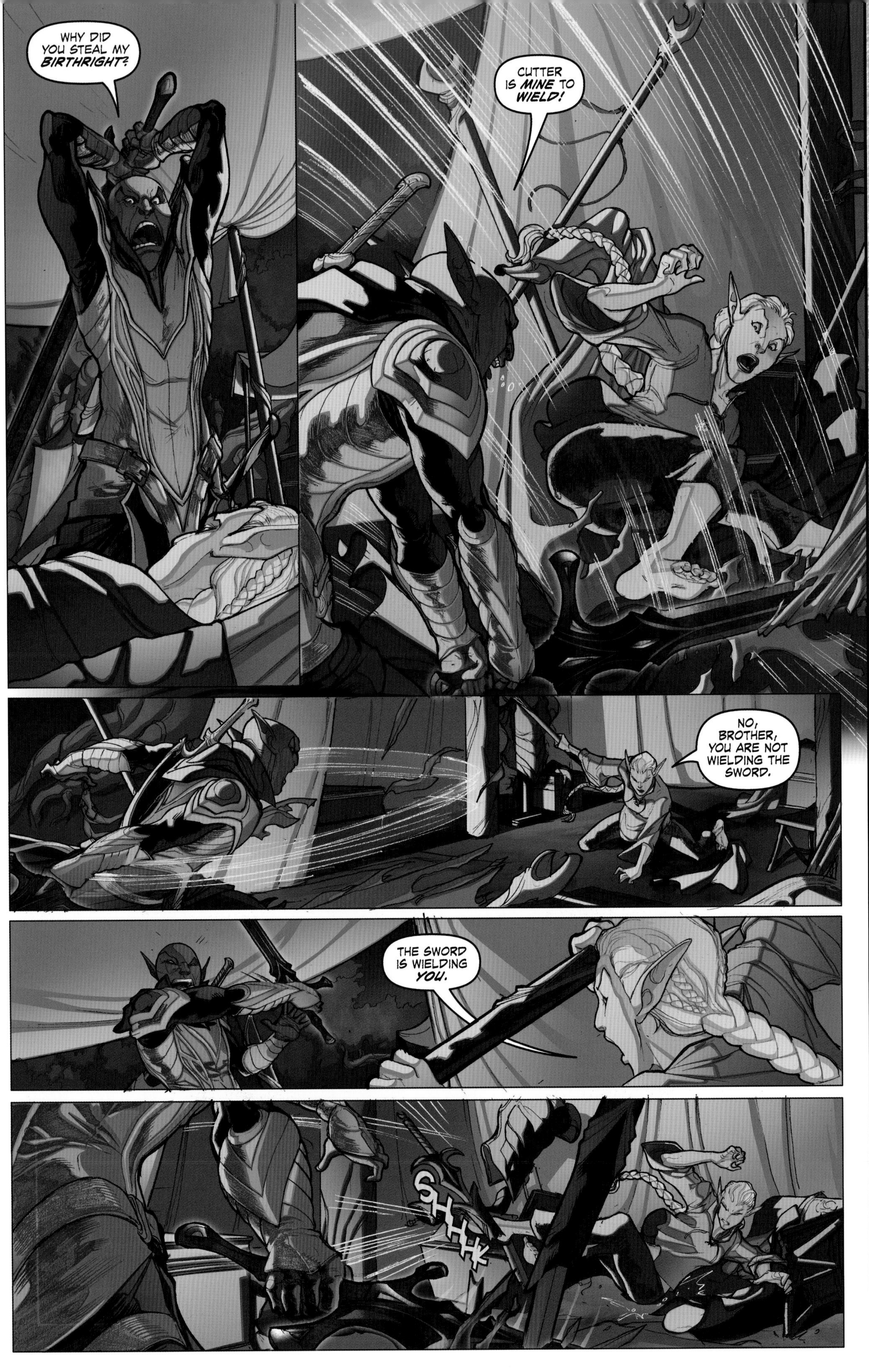
WHY DID YOU STEAL MY BIRTHRIGHT?
CUTTER IS MINE TO WIELD!
NO, BROTHER, YOU ARE NOT WIELDING THE SWORD.
THE SWORD IS WIELDING YOU.
SHHHK

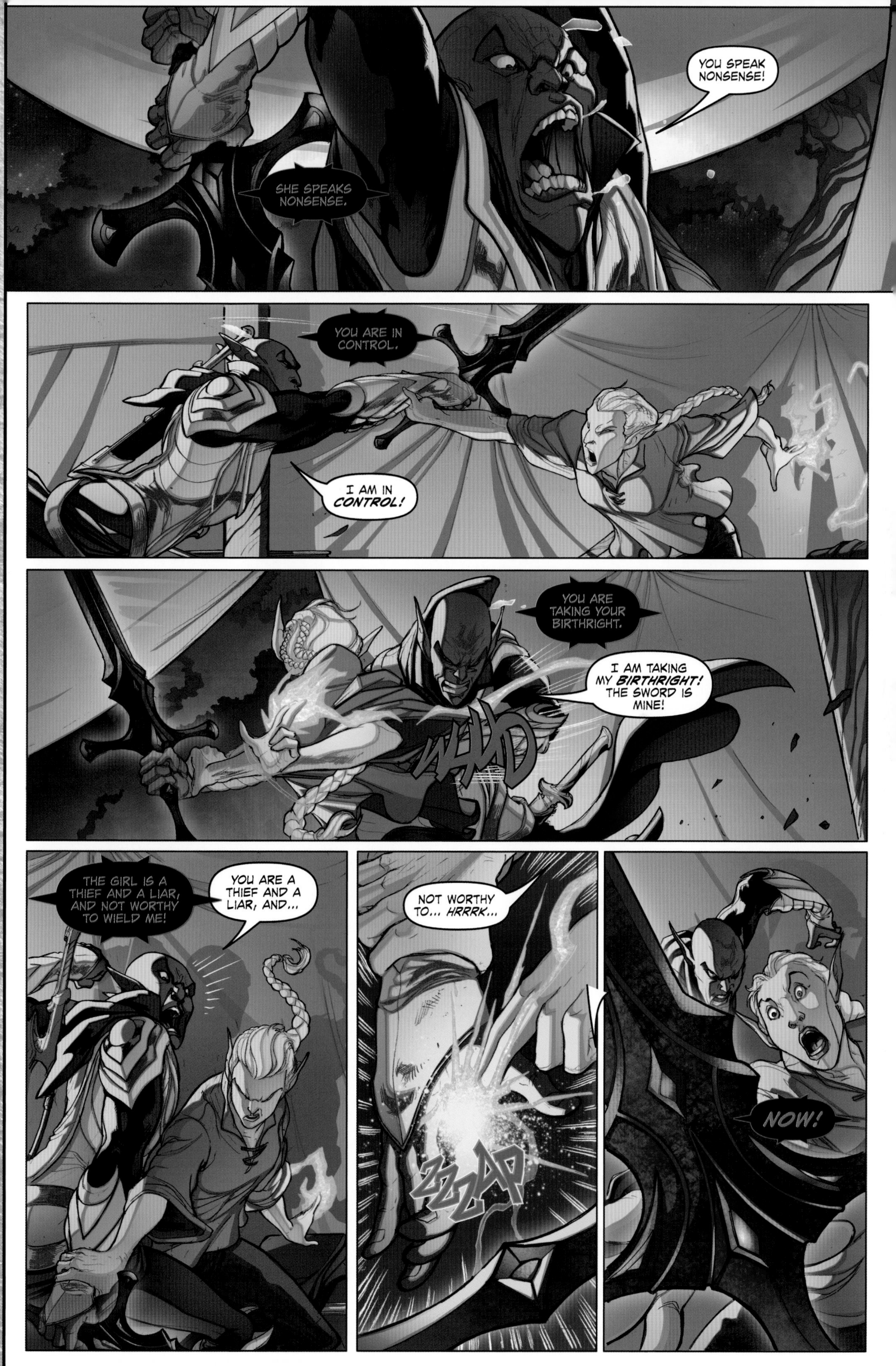

YOU SPEAK NONSENSE!
SHE SPEAKS NONSENSE.
YOU ARE IN CONTROL.
I AM IN CONTROL!
YOU ARE TAKING YOUR BIRTHRIGHT.
I AM TAKING MY BIRTHRIGHT! THE SWORD IS MINE!
WHUD
THE GIRL IS A THIEF AND A LIAR, AND NOT WORTHY TO WIELD ME!
YOU ARE A THIEF AND A LIAR, AND...
NOT WORTHY TO... HRRRK...
ZZZAP
NOW!

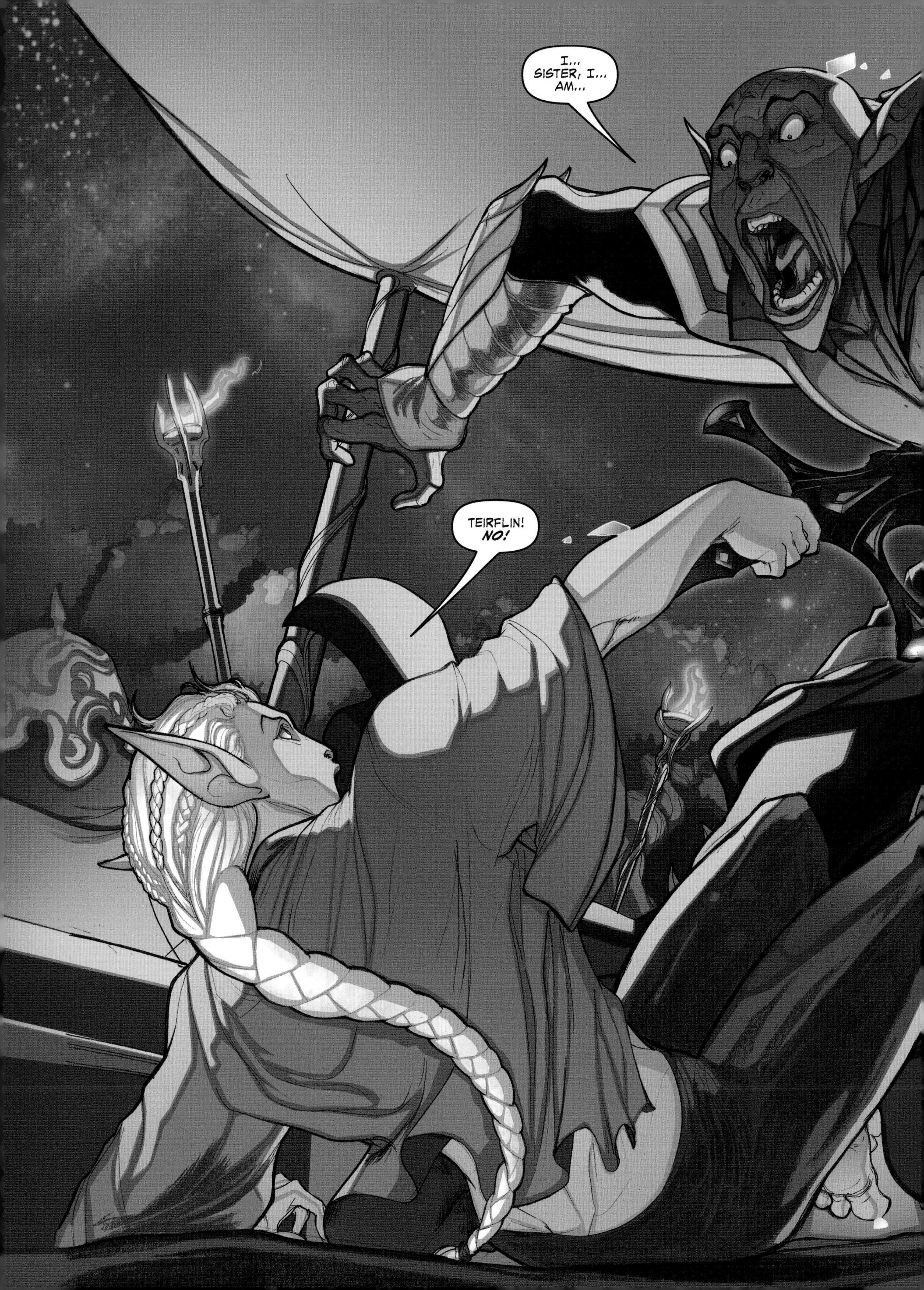
I... SISTER, I... AM...
TEIRFLIN! NO!

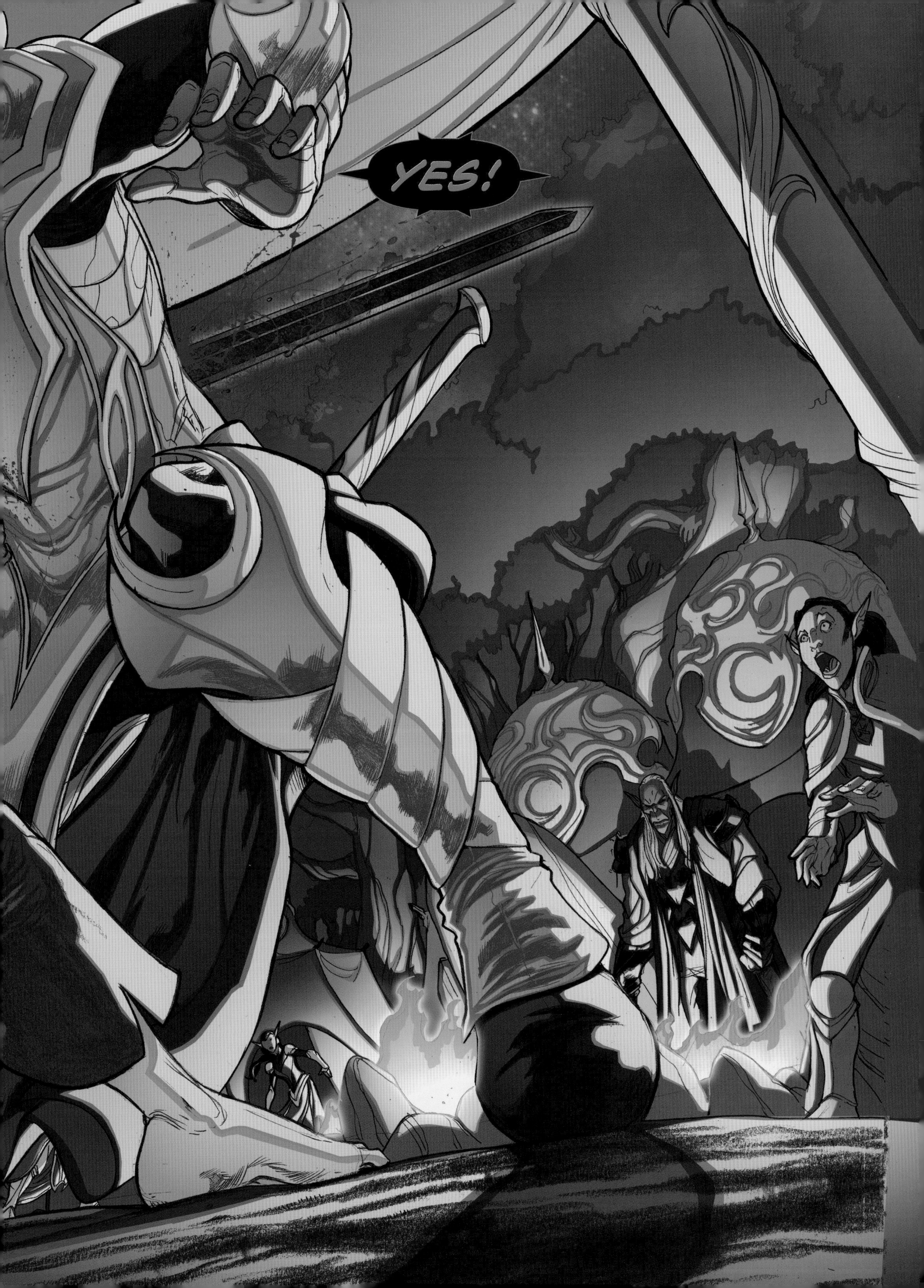
YES!

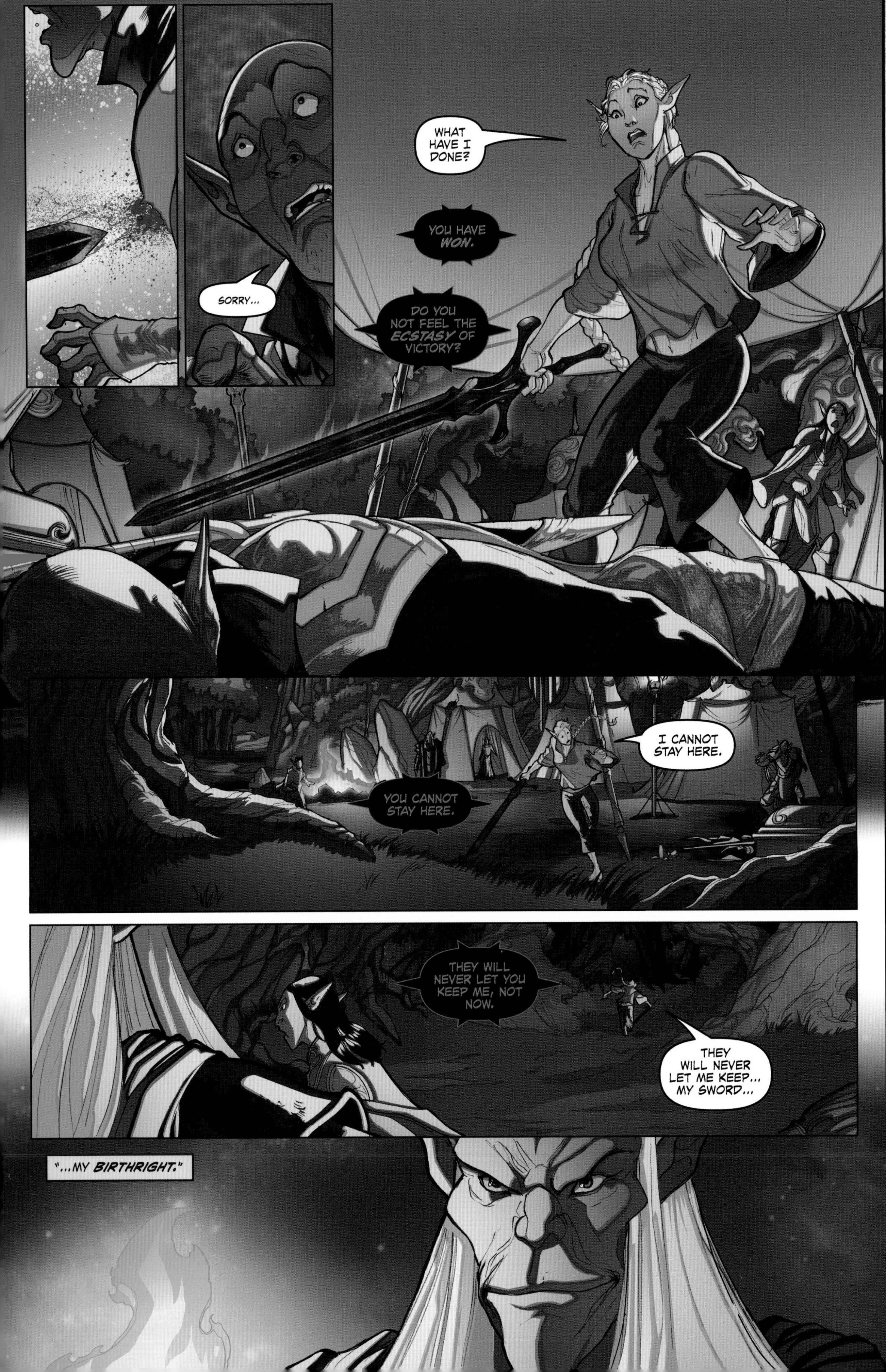
SORRY...
WHAT HAVE I DONE?
YOU HAVE WON.
DO YOU NOT FEEL THE ECSTASY OF VICTORY?
I CANNOT STAY HERE.
YOU CANNOT STAY HERE.
THEY WILL NEVER LET YOU KEEP ME, NOT NOW.
THEY WILL NEVER LET ME KEEP... MY SWORD...
"...MY BIRTHRIGHT."

Art by David Baldeon

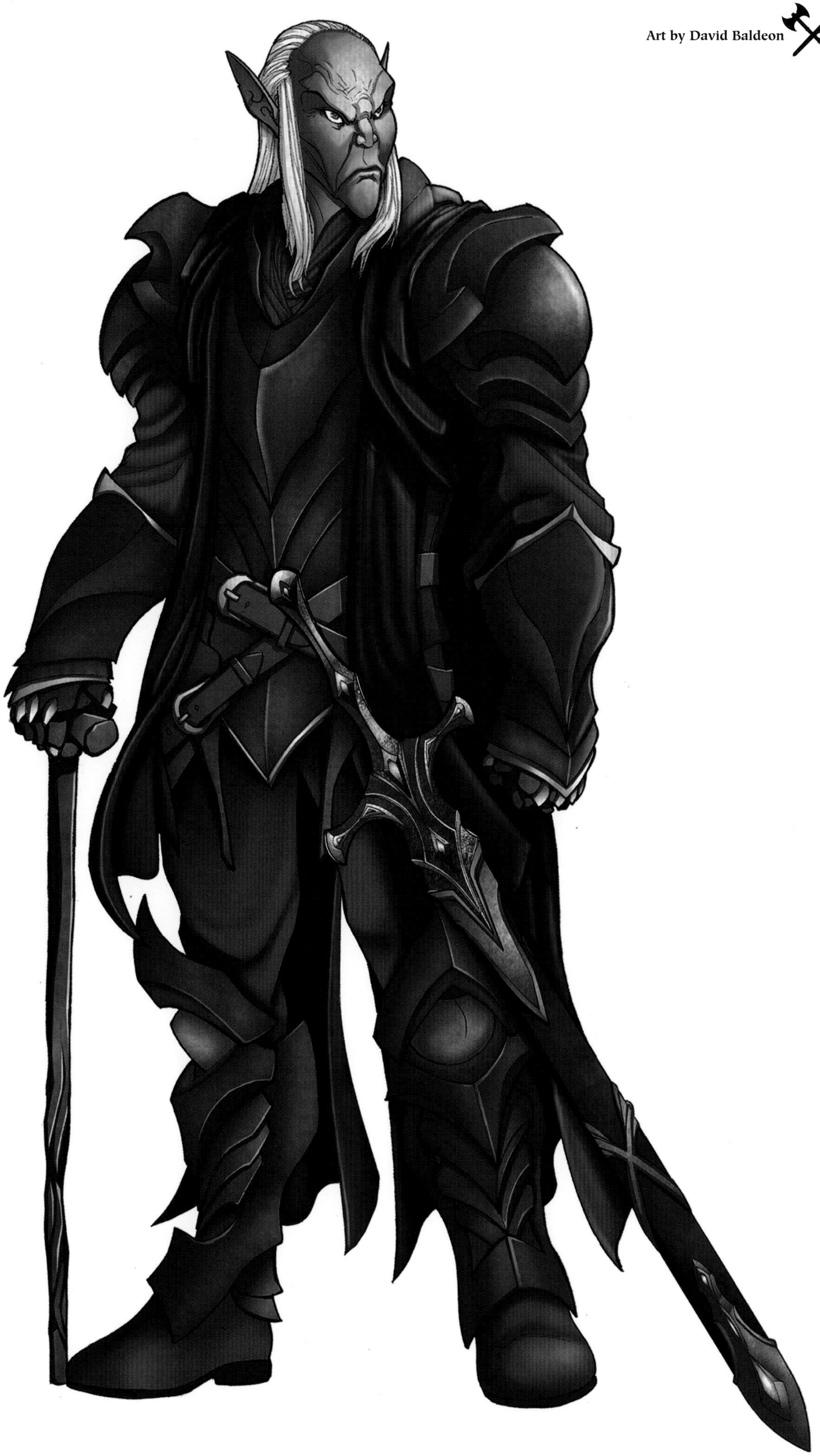

Art by Steve Ellis

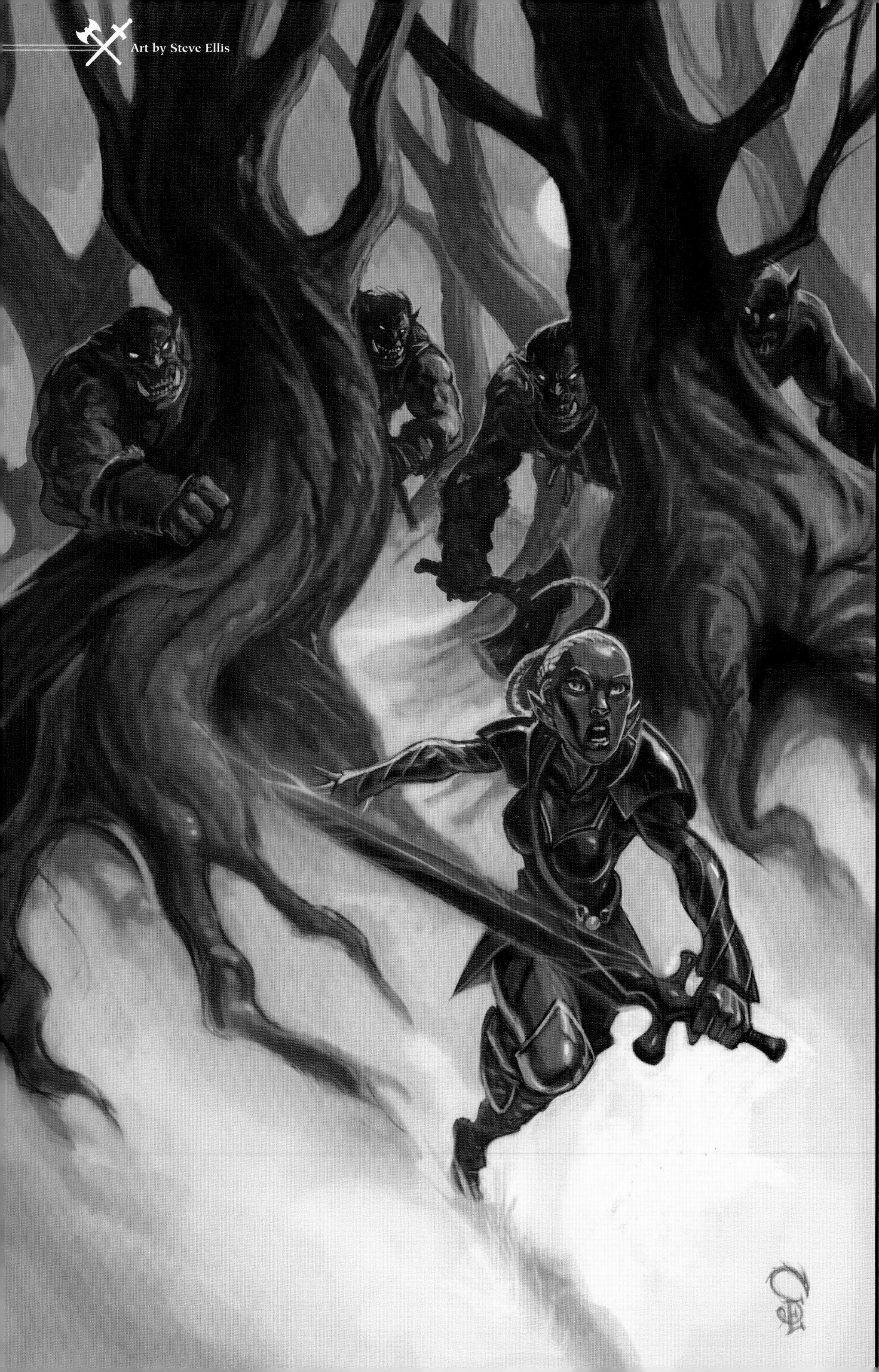

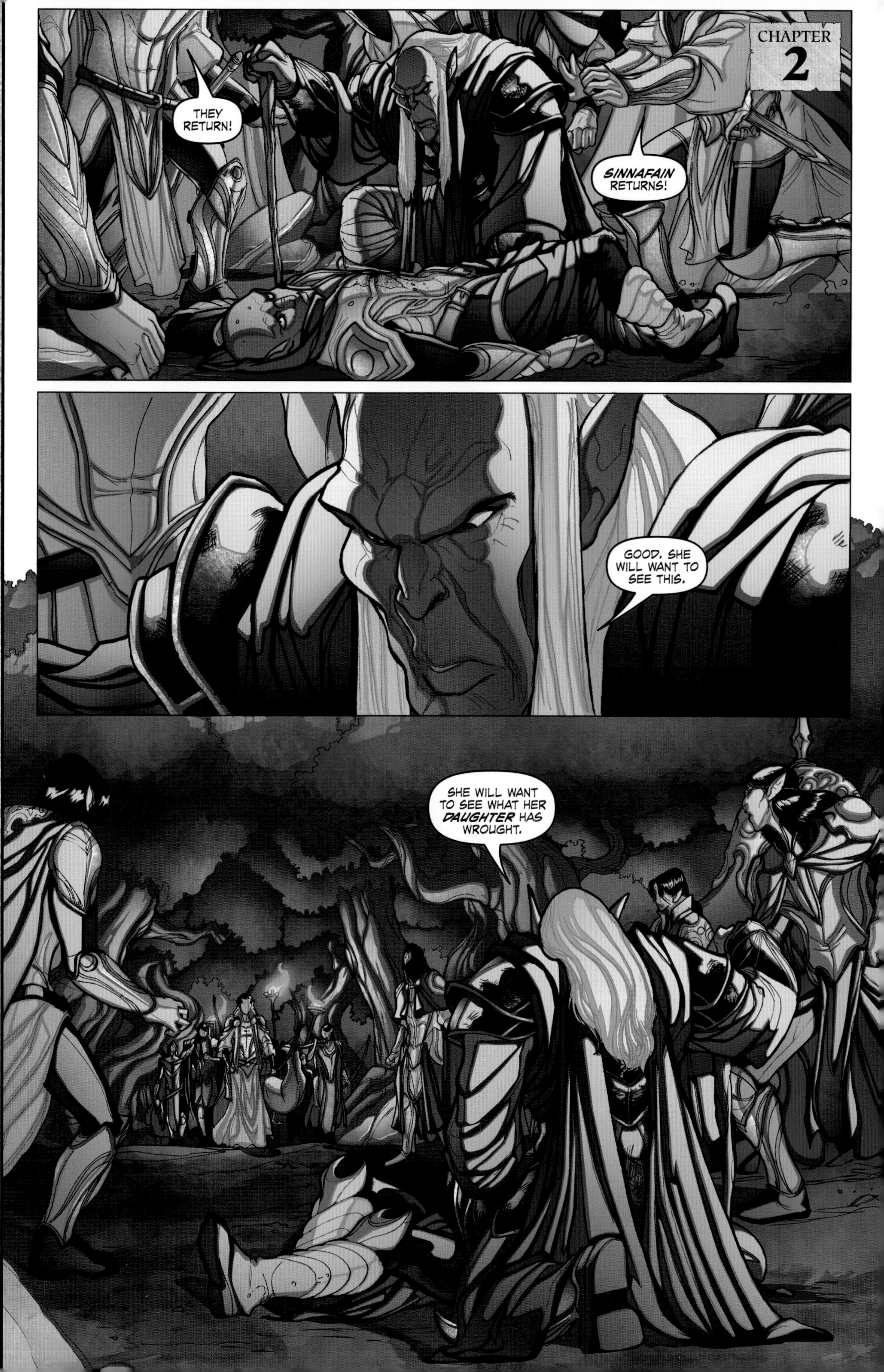
CHAPTER 2
THEY RETURN!
SINNAFAIN RETURNS!
GOOD. SHE WILL WANT TO SEE THIS.
SHE WILL WANT TO SEE WHAT HER DAUGHTER HAS WROUGHT.

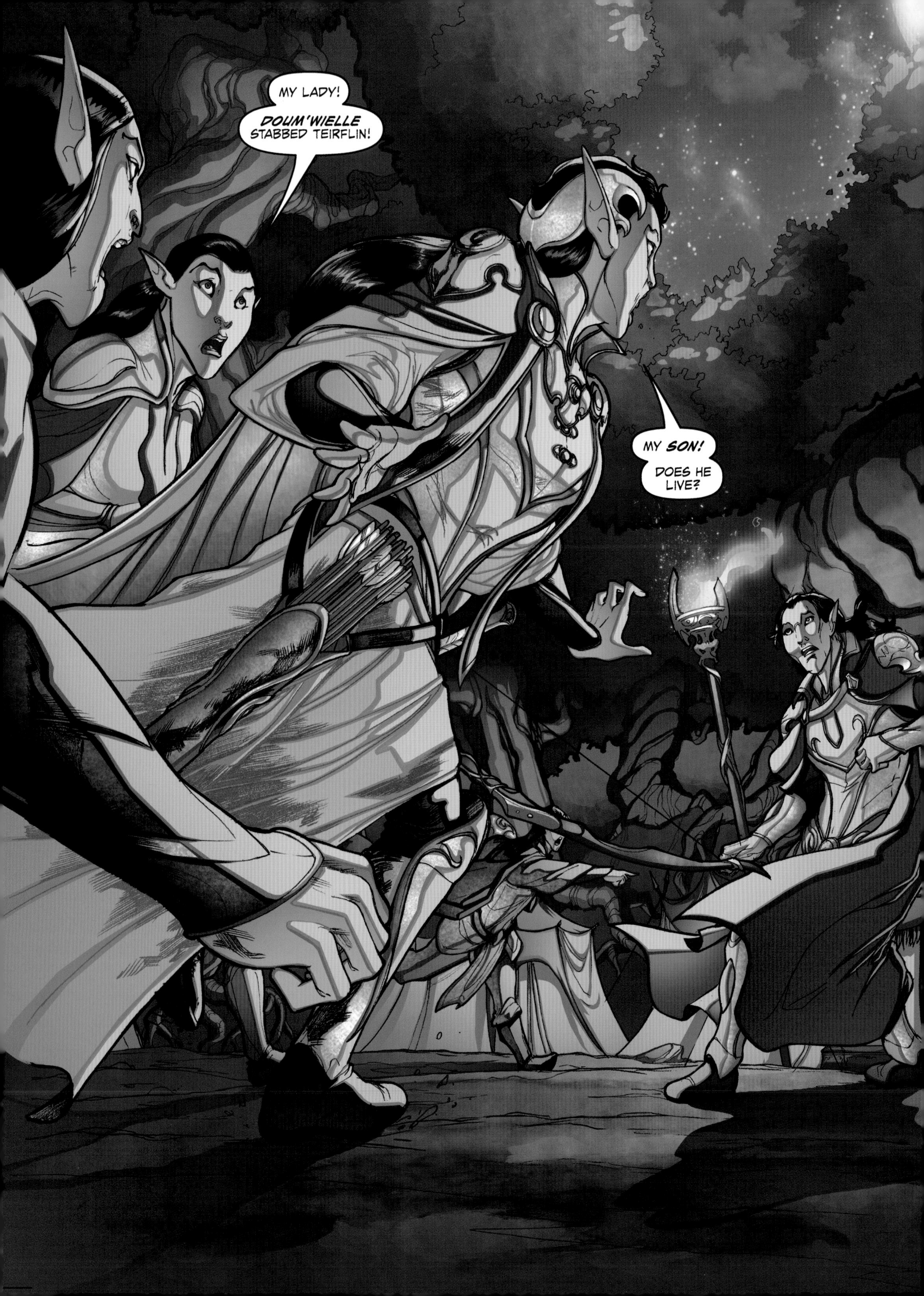
MY LADY!
DOUM'WIELLE STABBED TEIRFLIN!
MY SON!
DOES HE LIVE?

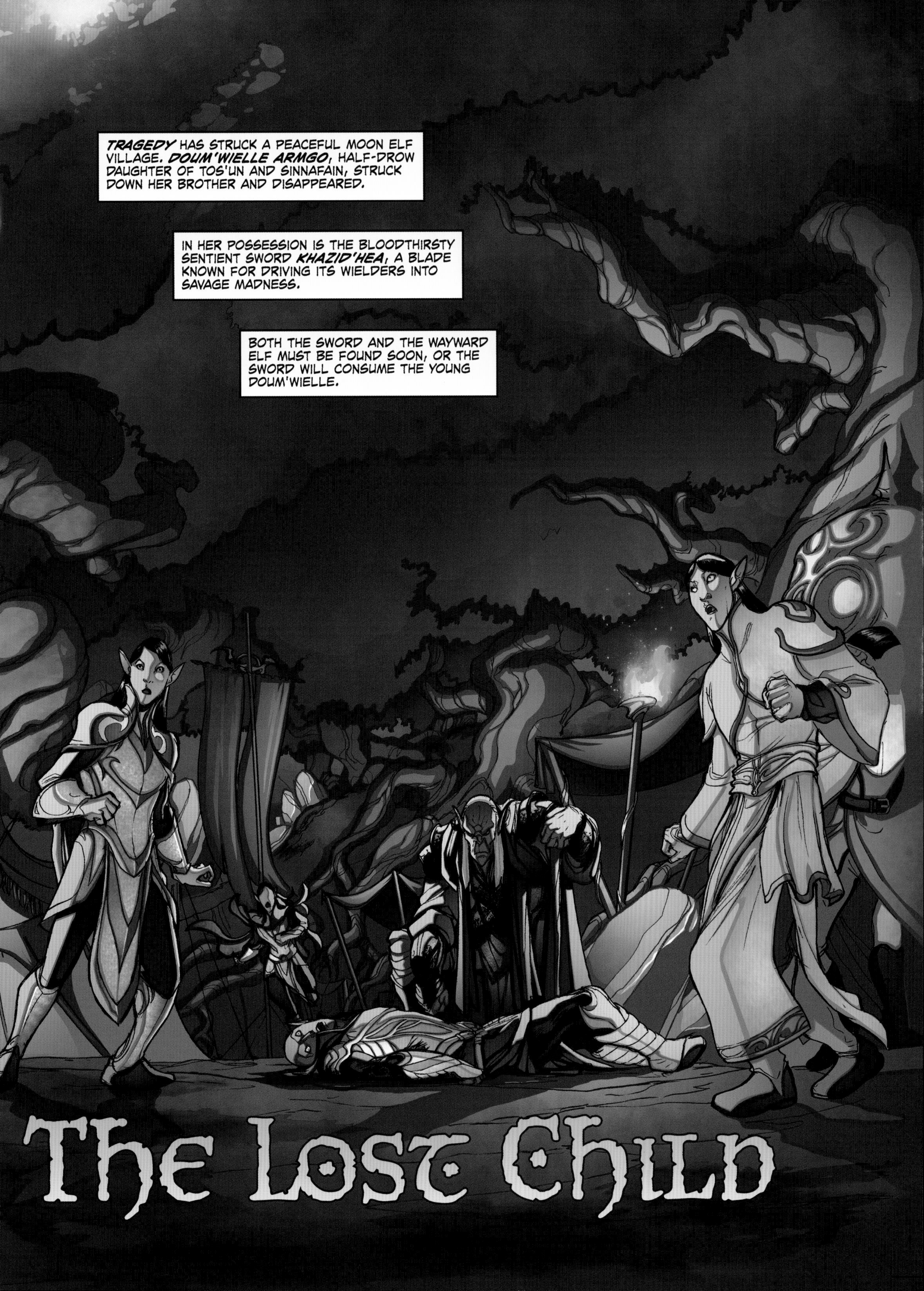
TRAGEDY HAS STRUCK A PEACEFUL MOON ELF VILLAGE. DOUM'WIELLE ARMGO, HALF-DROW DAUGHTER OF TOS'UN AND SINNAFAIN, STRUCK DOWN HER BROTHER AND DISAPPEARED.
IN HER POSSESSION IS THE BLOODTHIRSTY SENTIENT SWORD KHAZID'HEA, A BLADE KNOWN FOR DRIVING ITS WIELDERS INTO SAVAGE MADNESS.
BOTH THE SWORD AND THE WAYWARD ELF MUST BE FOUND SOON, OR THE SWORD WILL CONSUME THE YOUNG DOUM'WIELLE.
THE LOST CHILD

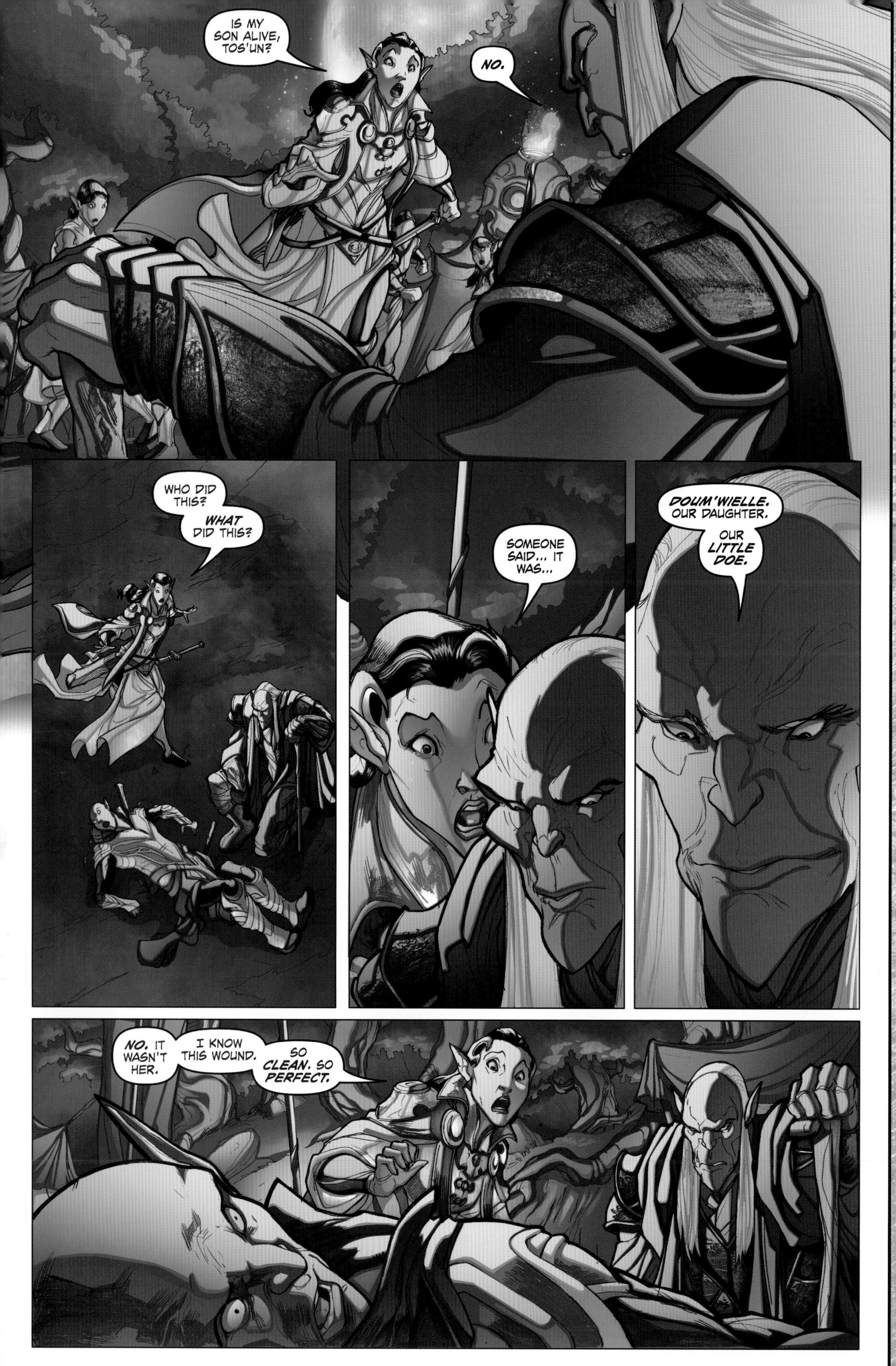
IS MY SON ALIVE, TOS'UN?
NO.
WHO DID THIS? WHAT DID THIS?
SOMEONE SAID... IT WAS...
DOUM'WIELLE. OUR DAUGHTER.
OUR LITTLE DOE.
NO. IT WASN'T HER.
I KNOW THIS WOUND.
SO CLEAN. SO PERFECT.

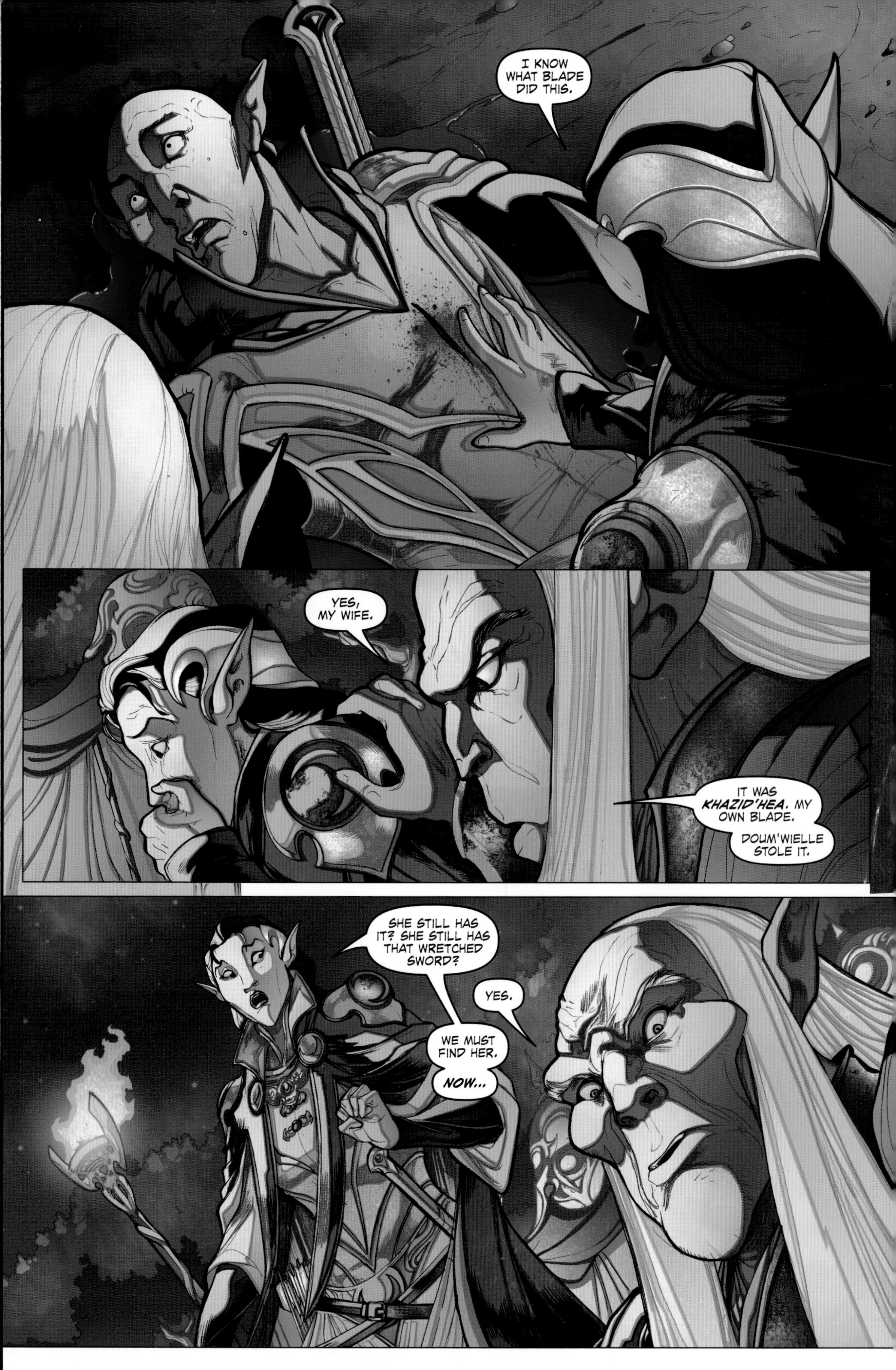

I KNOW WHAT BLADE DID THIS.
YES, MY WIFE.
IT WAS **KHAZID'HEA.** MY OWN BLADE.
DOUM'WIELLE STOLE IT.
SHE STILL HAS IT? SHE STILL HAS THAT WRETCHED SWORD?
YES.
WE MUST FIND HER.
NOW...

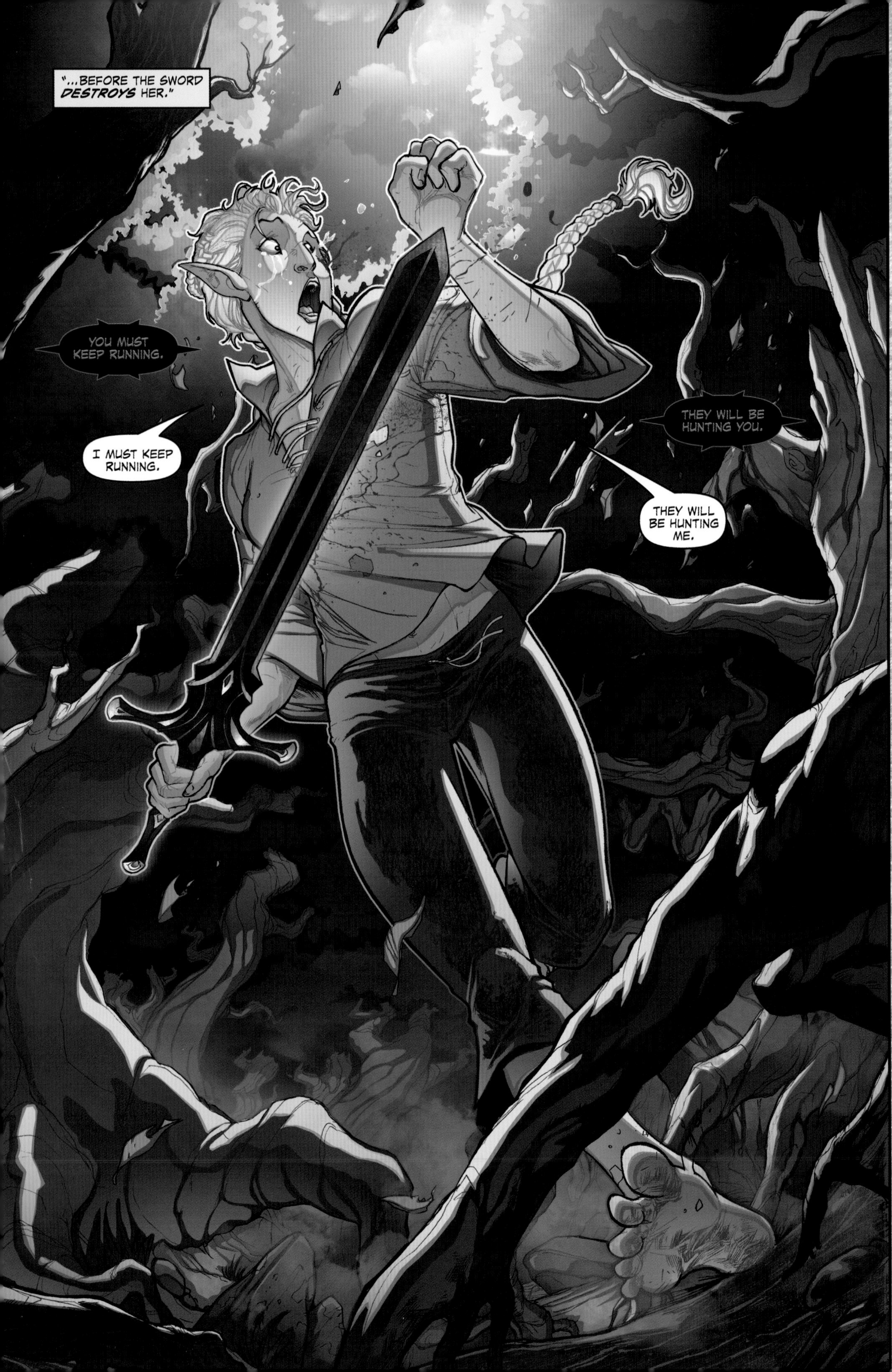
"...BEFORE THE SWORD DESTROYS HER."
YOU MUST KEEP RUNNING.
I MUST KEEP RUNNING.
THEY WILL BE HUNTING YOU.
THEY WILL BE HUNTING ME.

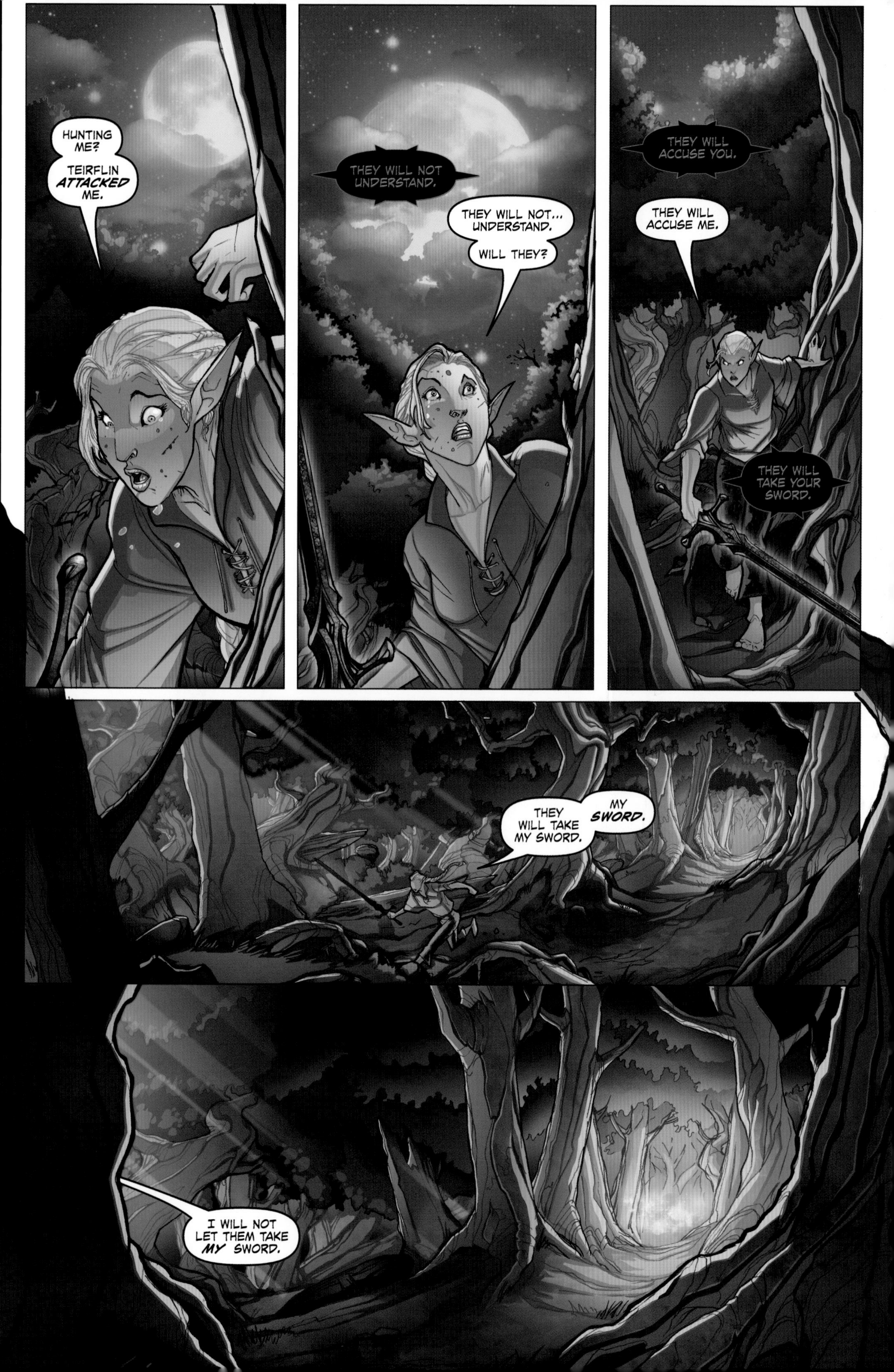
HUNTING ME?
TEIRFLIN ATTACKED ME.
THEY WILL NOT UNDERSTAND.
THEY WILL NOT... UNDERSTAND.
WILL THEY?
THEY WILL ACCUSE YOU.
THEY WILL ACCUSE ME.
THEY WILL TAKE YOUR SWORD.
THEY WILL TAKE MY SWORD.
MY SWORD.
I WILL NOT LET THEM TAKE MY SWORD.

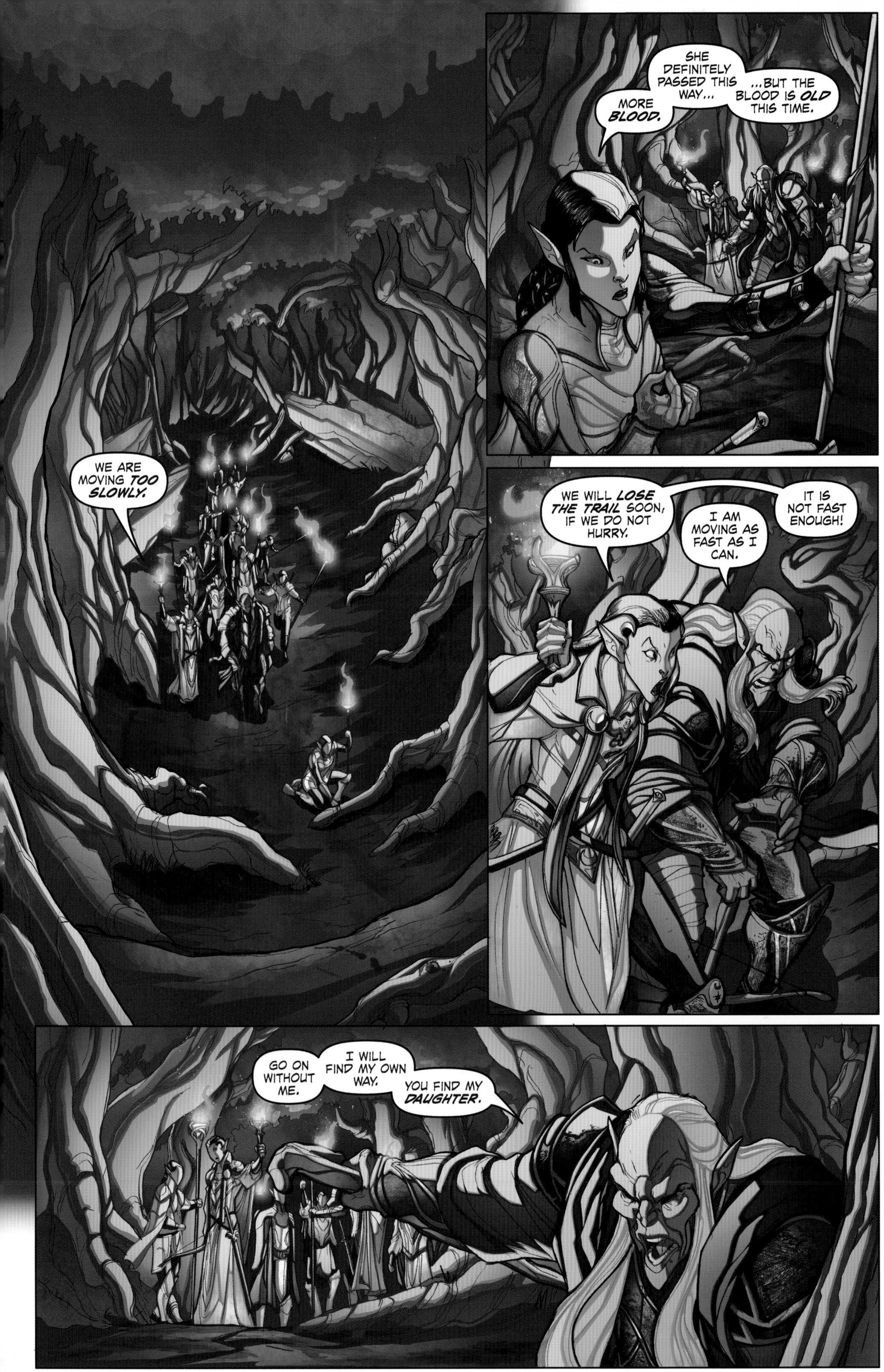
MORE BLOOD.
SHE DEFINITELY PASSED THIS WAY...
...BUT THE BLOOD IS OLD THIS TIME.
WE ARE MOVING TOO SLOWLY.
WE WILL LOSE THE TRAIL SOON, IF WE DO NOT HURRY.
I AM MOVING AS FAST AS I CAN.
IT IS NOT FAST ENOUGH!
GO ON WITHOUT ME.
I WILL FIND MY OWN WAY.
YOU FIND MY DAUGHTER.

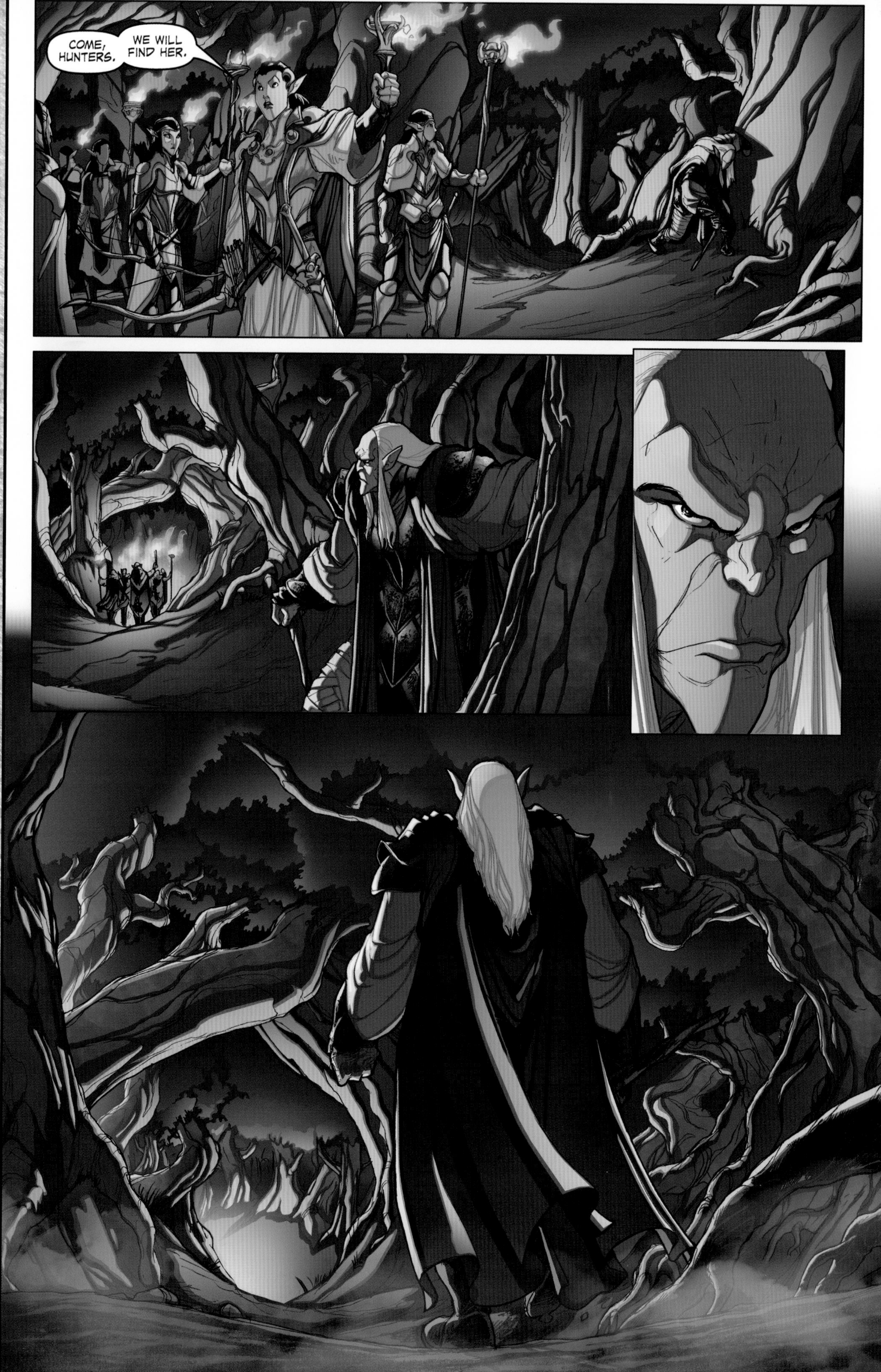
COME, HUNTERS.
WE WILL FIND HER.

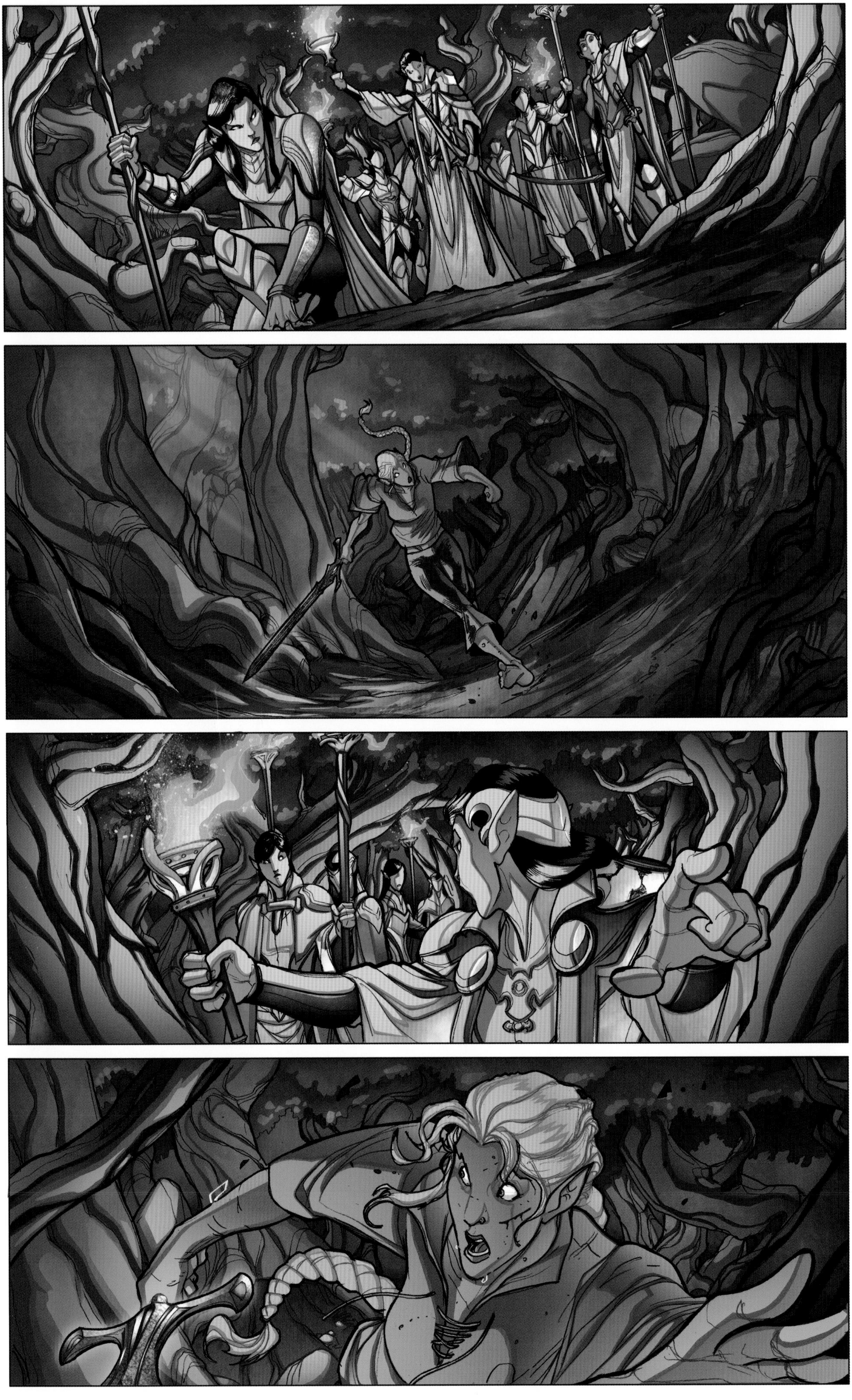

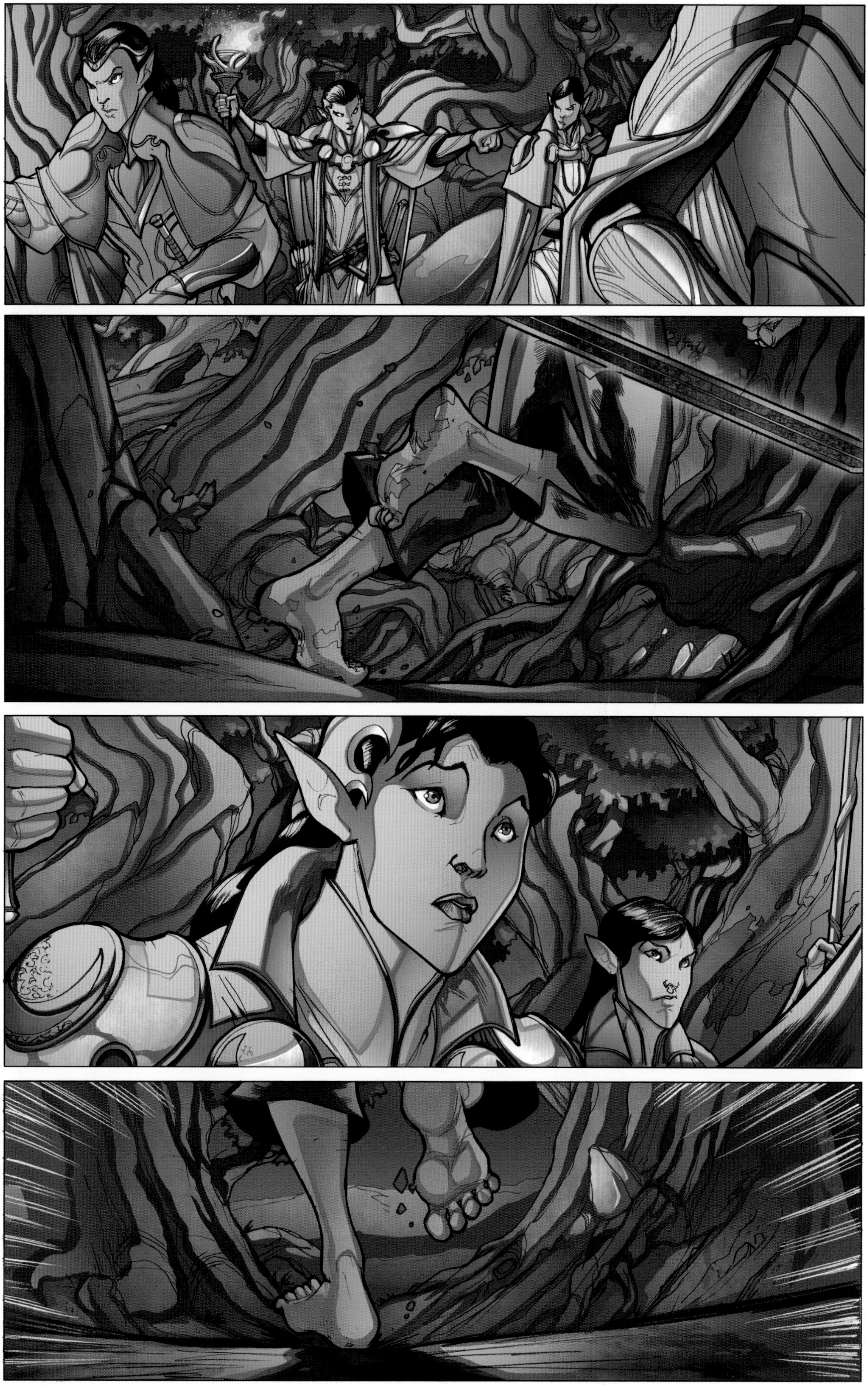

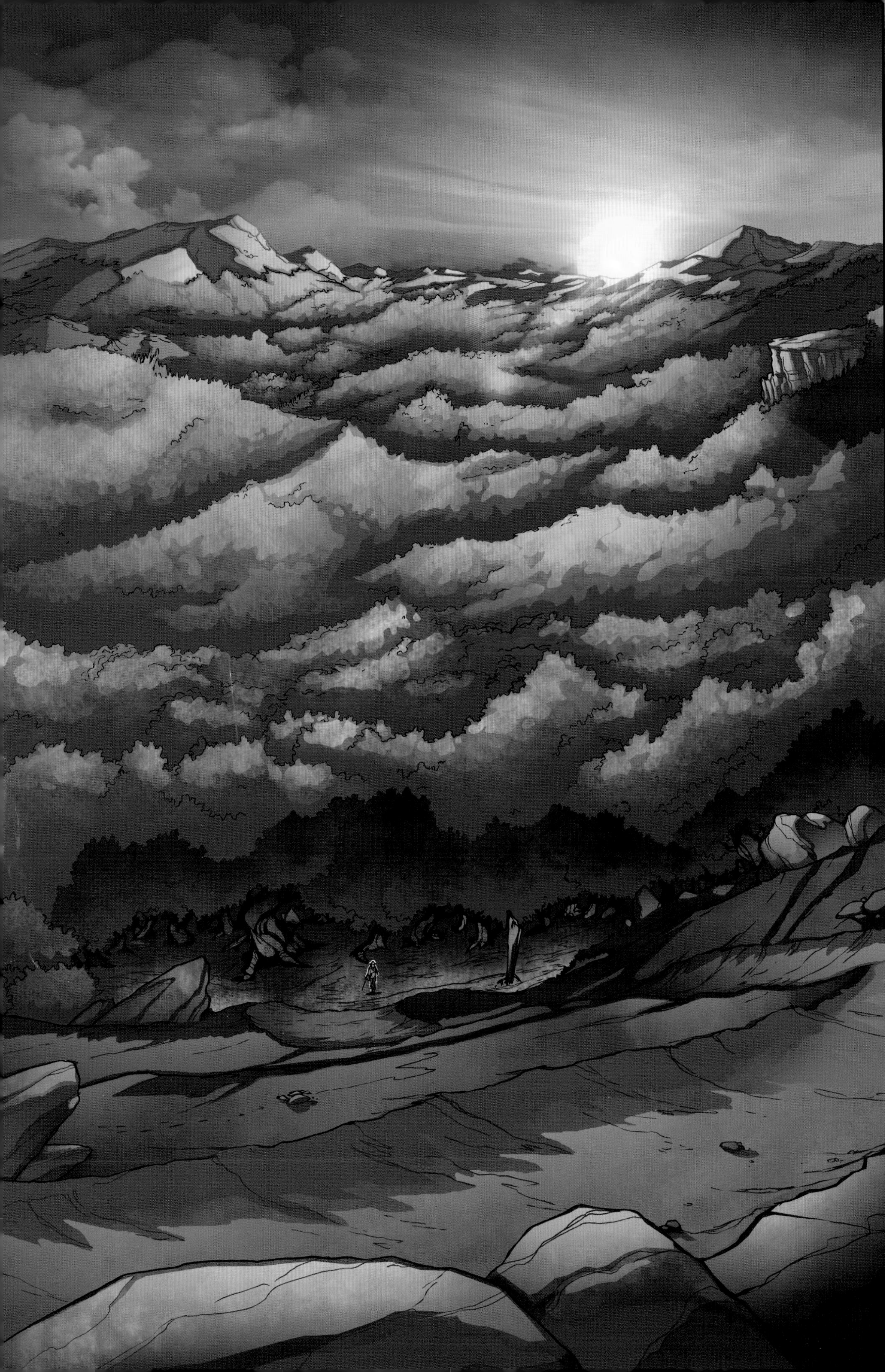

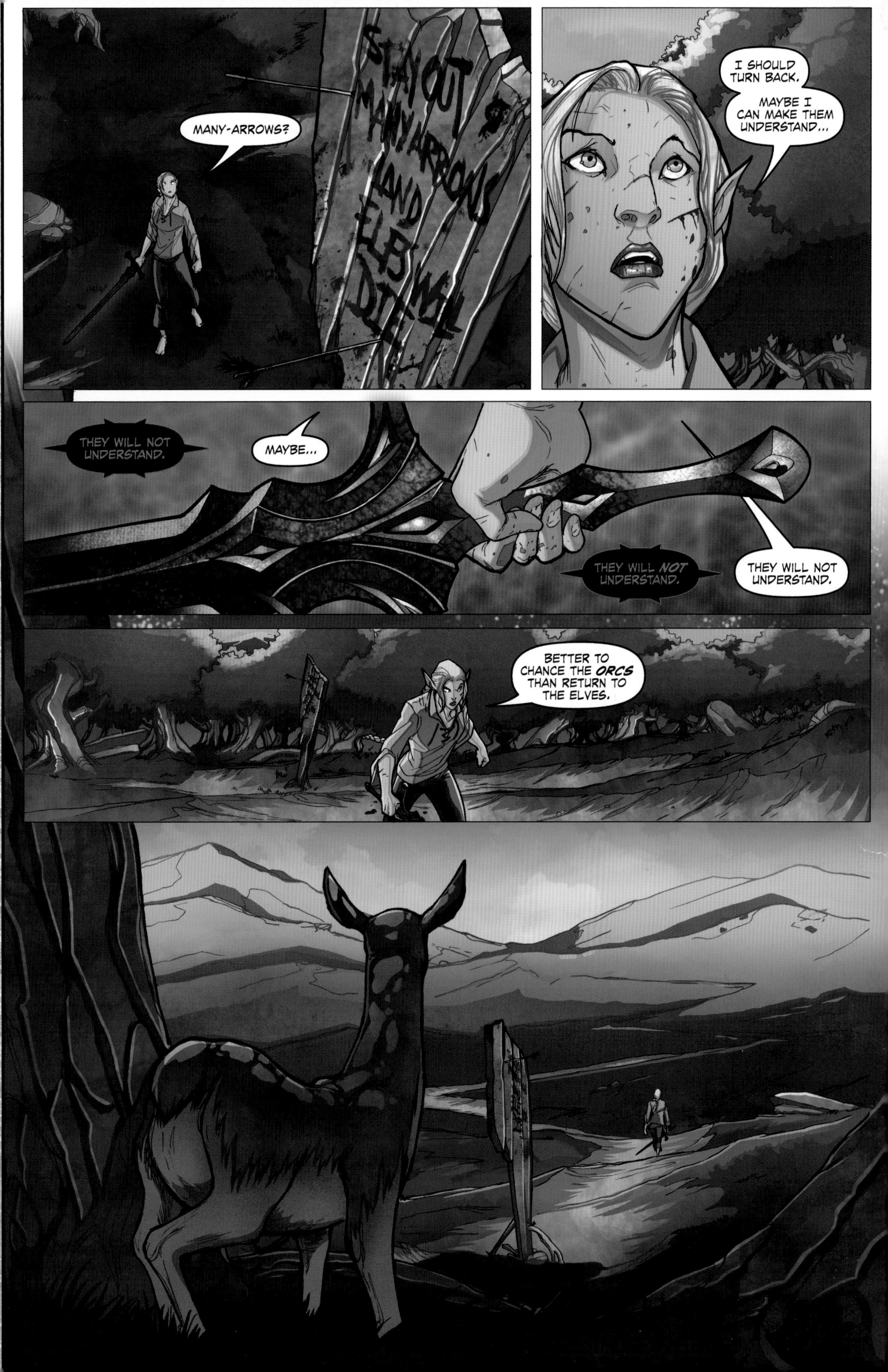
MANY-ARROWS?
I SHOULD TURN BACK.
MAYBE I CAN MAKE THEM UNDERSTAND...
THEY WILL NOT UNDERSTAND.
MAYBE...
THEY WILL *NOT* UNDERSTAND.
THEY WILL NOT UNDERSTAND.
BETTER TO CHANCE THE ***ORCS*** THAN RETURN TO THE ELVES.

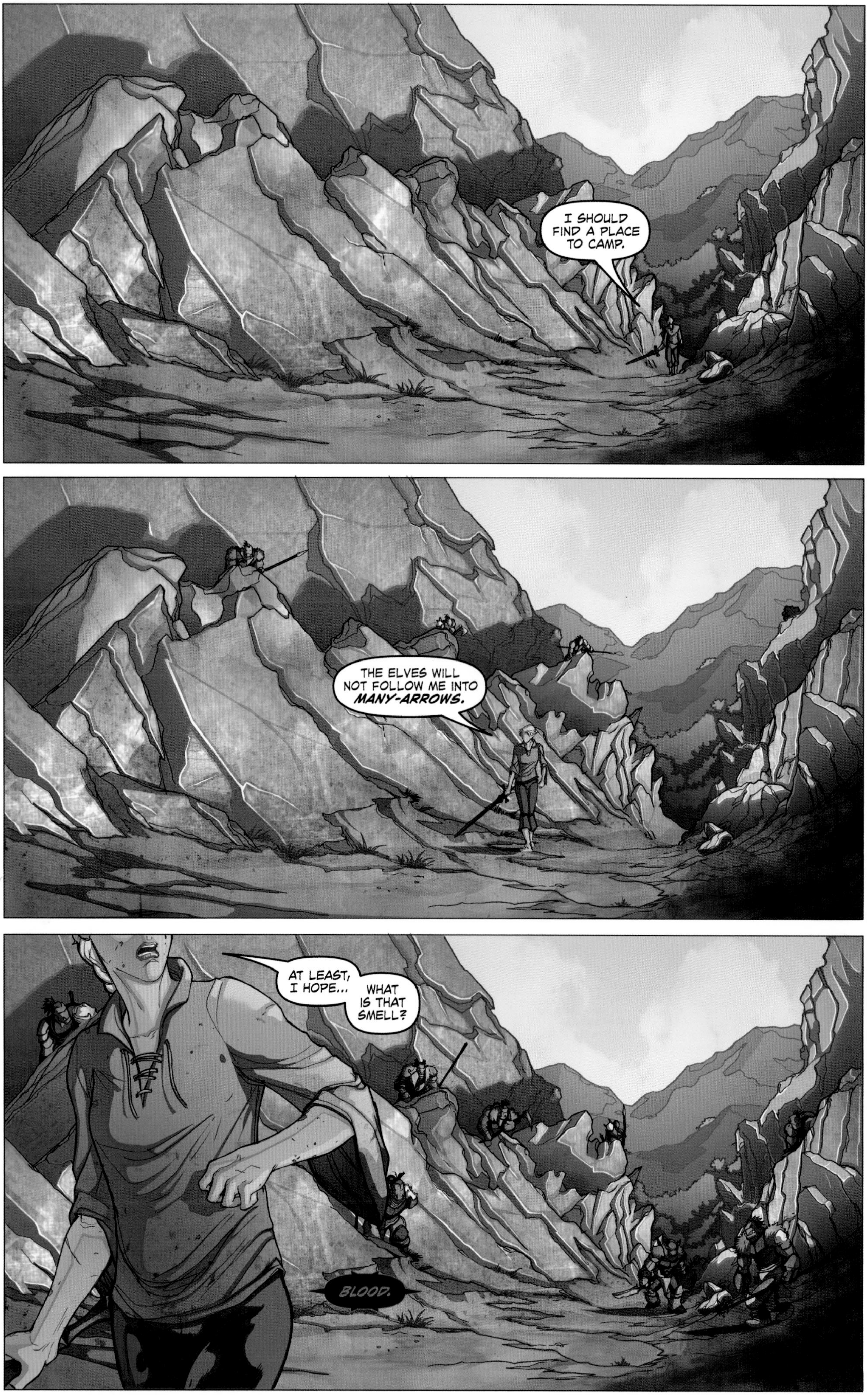
I SHOULD FIND A PLACE TO CAMP.
THE ELVES WILL NOT FOLLOW ME INTO MANY-ARROWS.
AT LEAST, I HOPE...
WHAT IS THAT SMELL?
BLOOD.

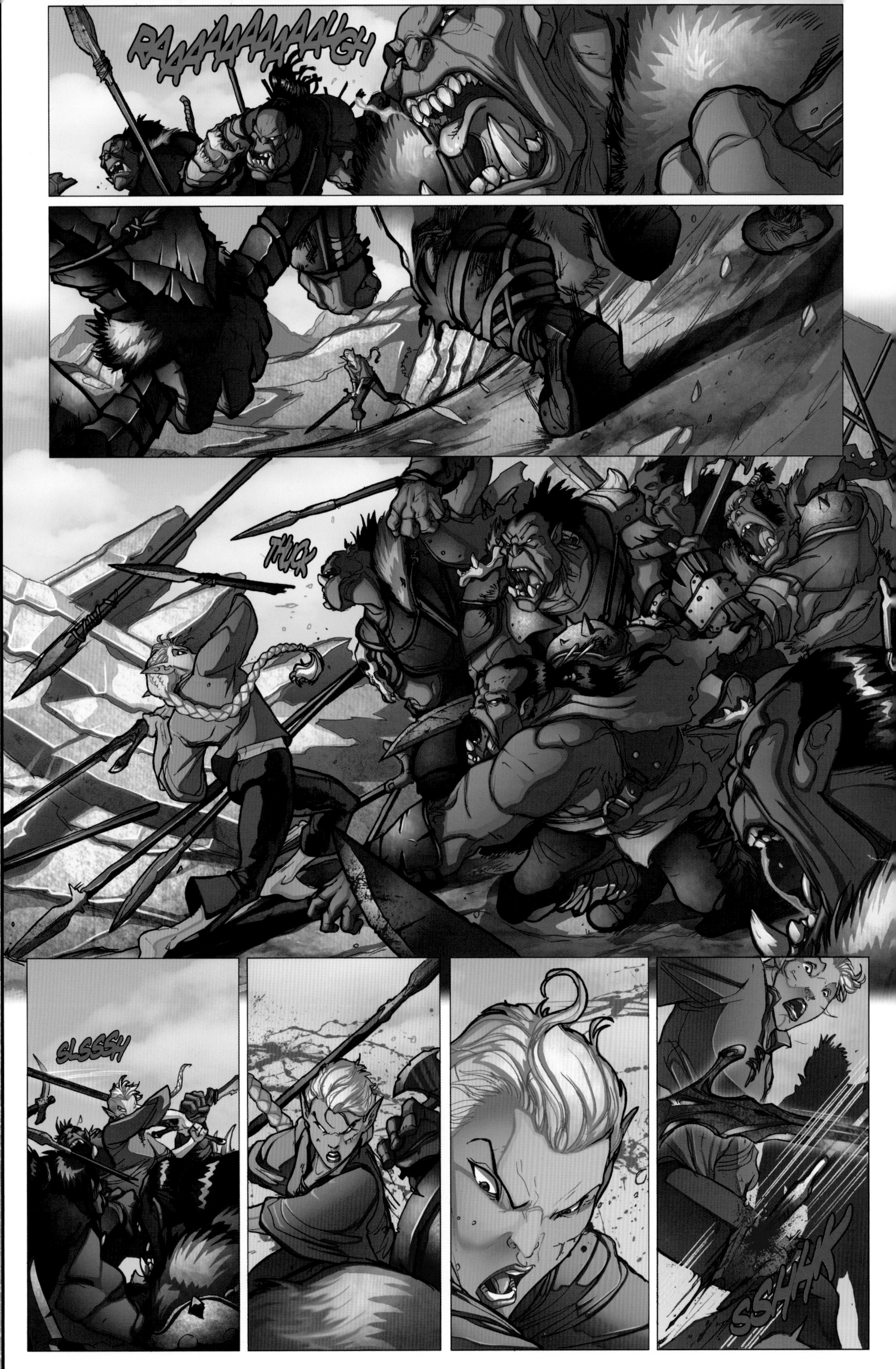
RAAAAAAAAAUGH
THUCK
SLSSSH
SSHHK

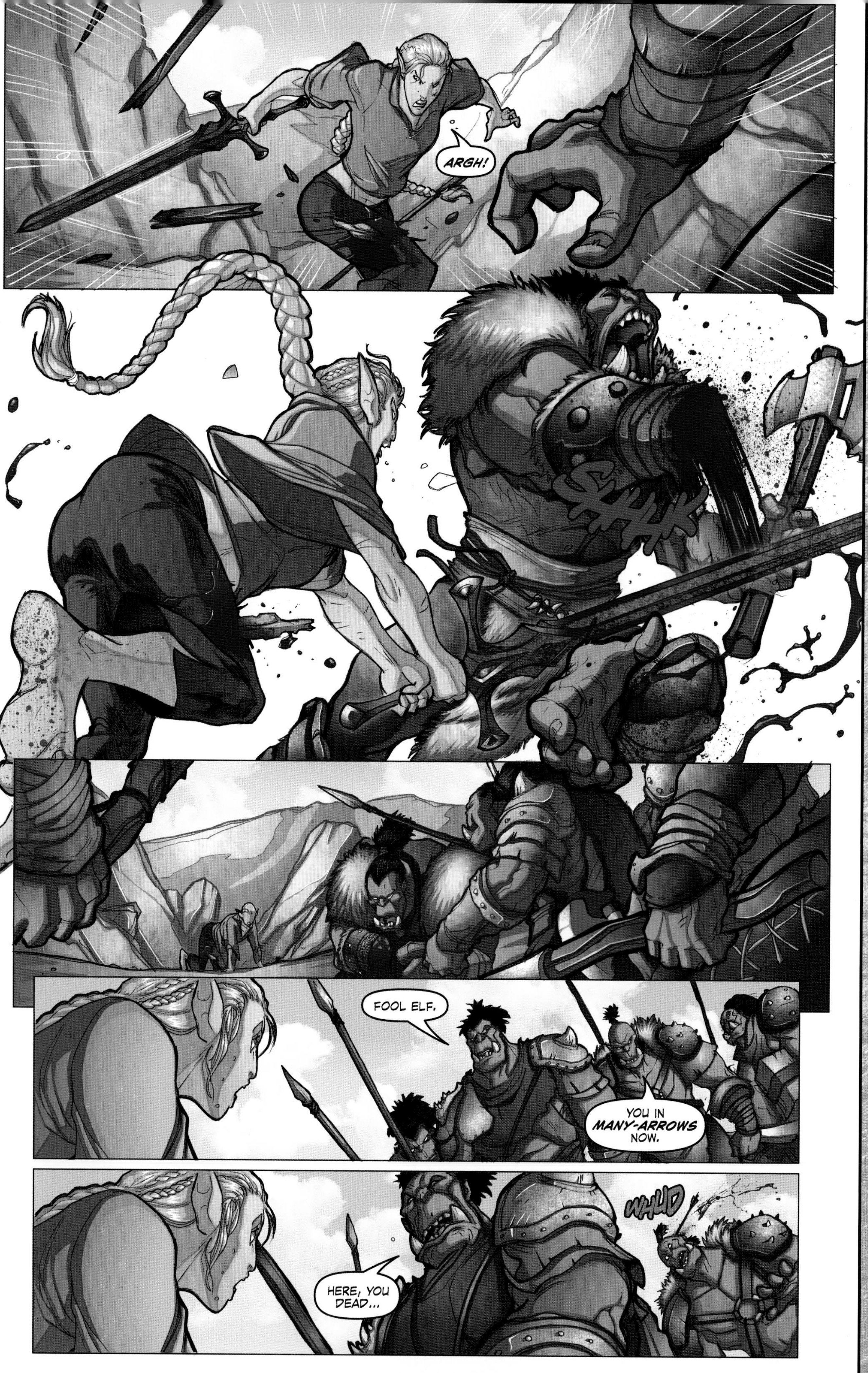
ARGH!
SHHK
FOOL ELF.
YOU IN *MANY-ARROWS* NOW.
WHUD
HERE, YOU DEAD...

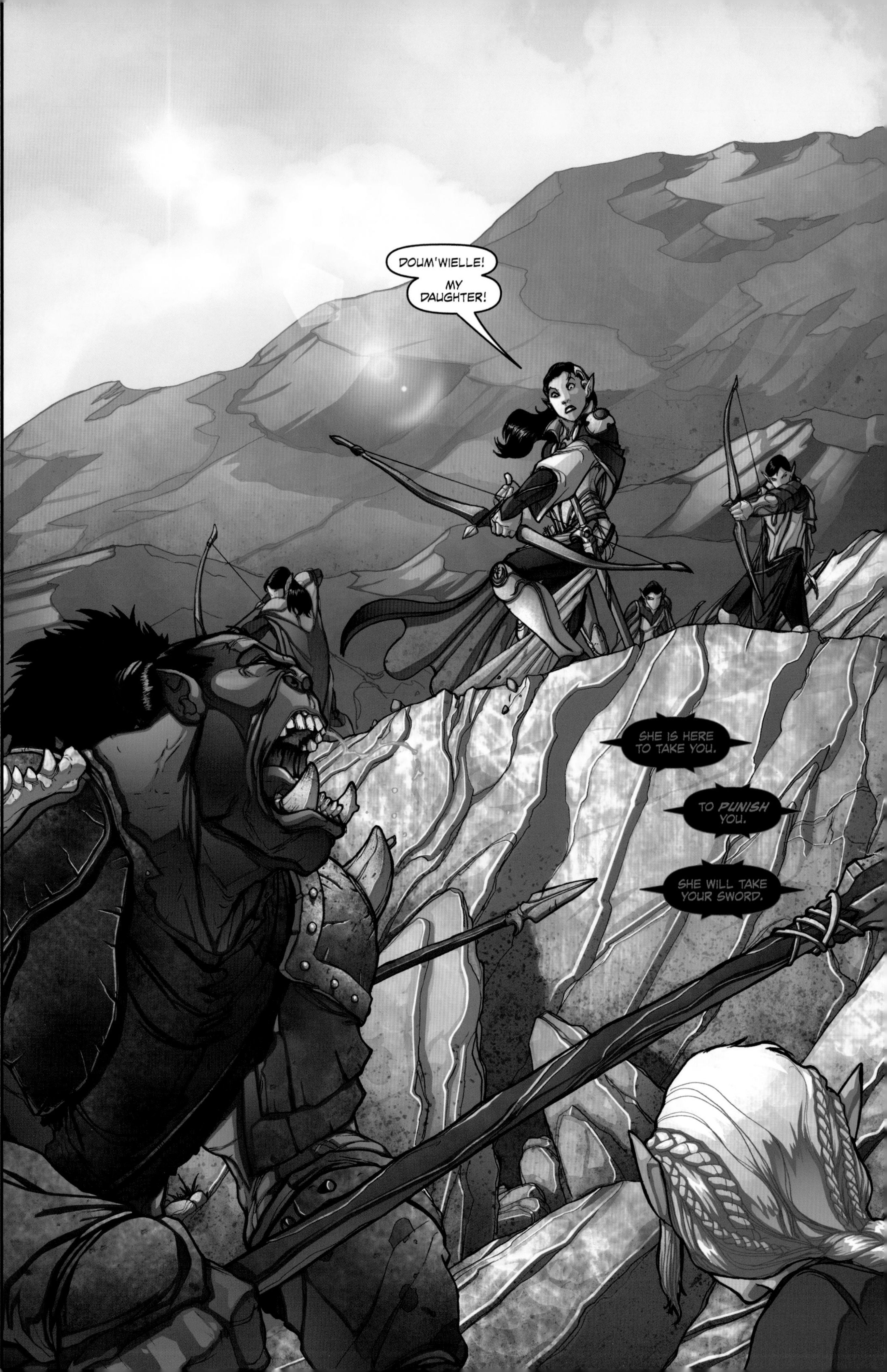
DOUM'WIELLE! MY DAUGHTER!
SHE IS HERE TO TAKE YOU.
TO PUNISH YOU.
SHE WILL TAKE YOUR SWORD.

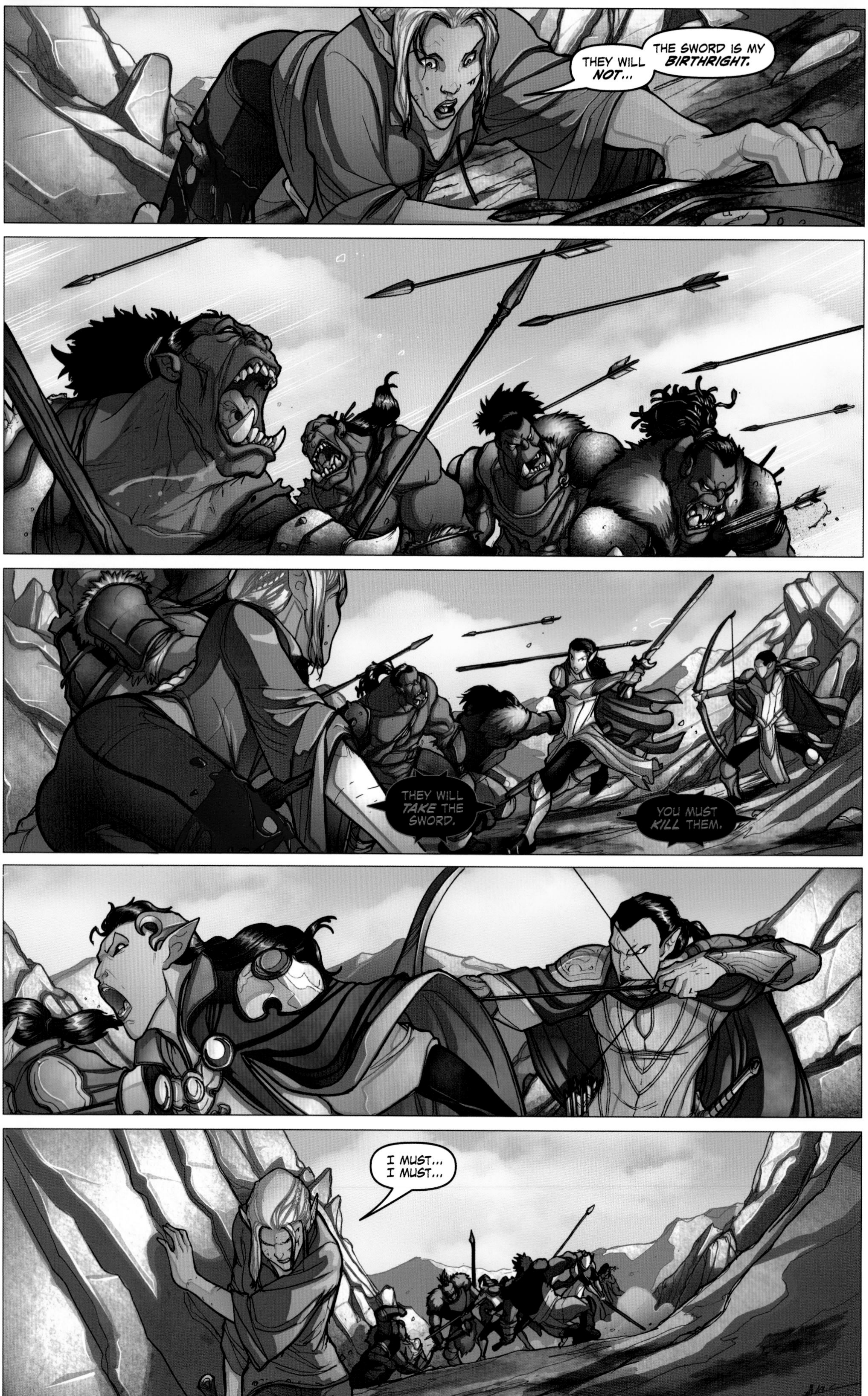
THEY WILL NOT...
THE SWORD IS MY BIRTHRIGHT.
THEY WILL TAKE THE SWORD.
YOU MUST KILL THEM.
I MUST... I MUST...

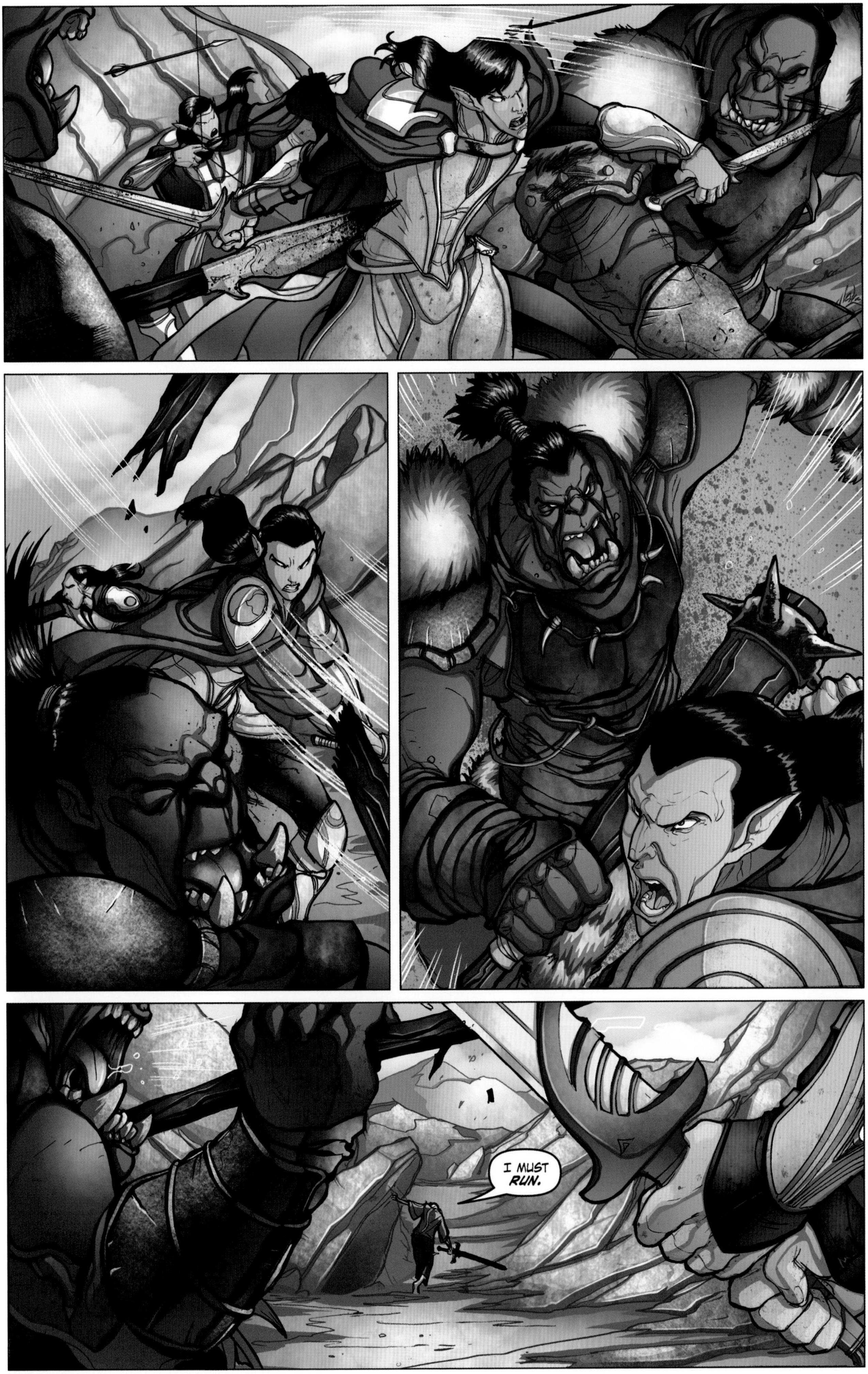
I MUST RUN.

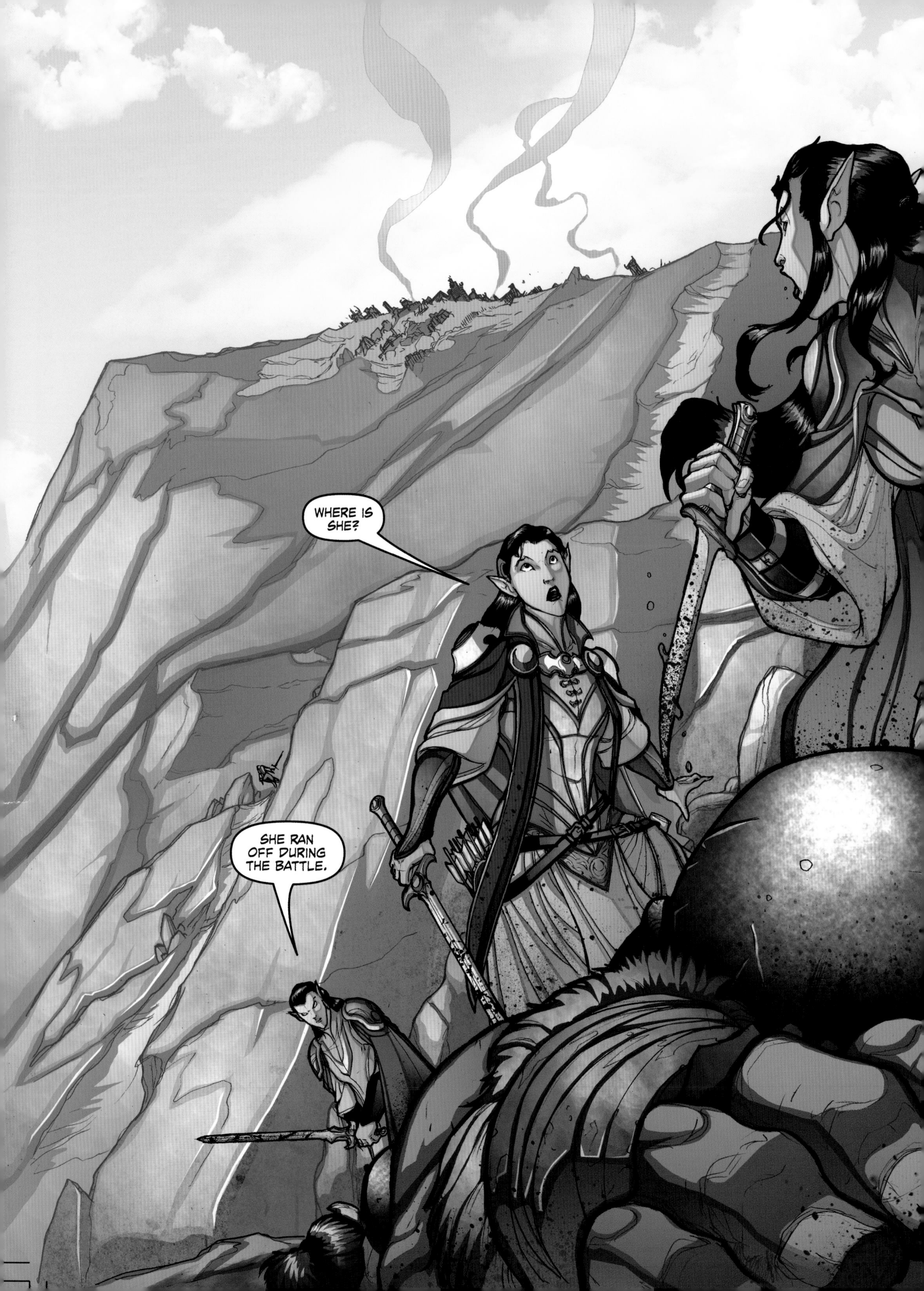
WHERE IS SHE?
SHE RAN OFF DURING THE BATTLE.

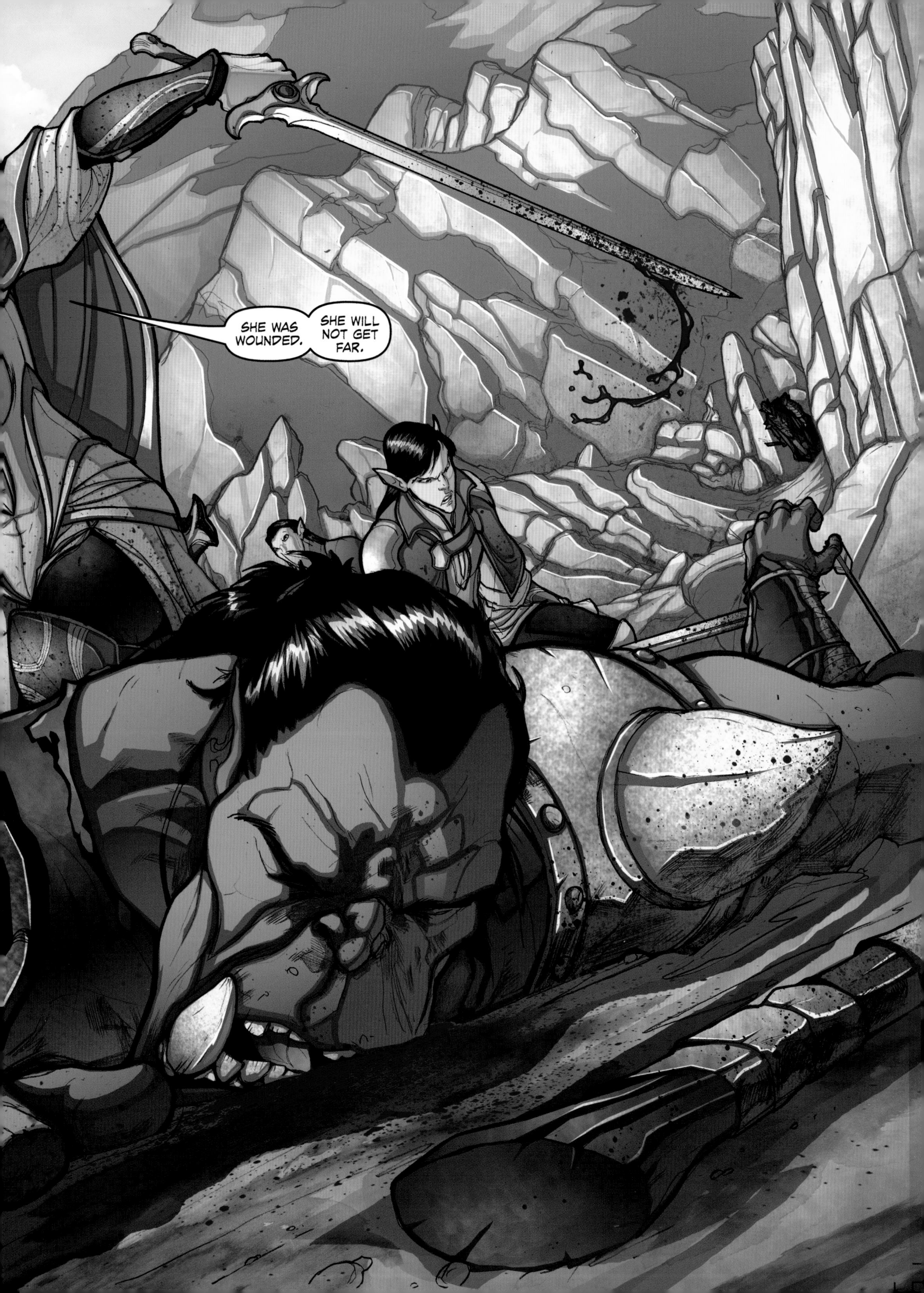
SHE WAS WOUNDED.
SHE WILL NOT GET FAR.

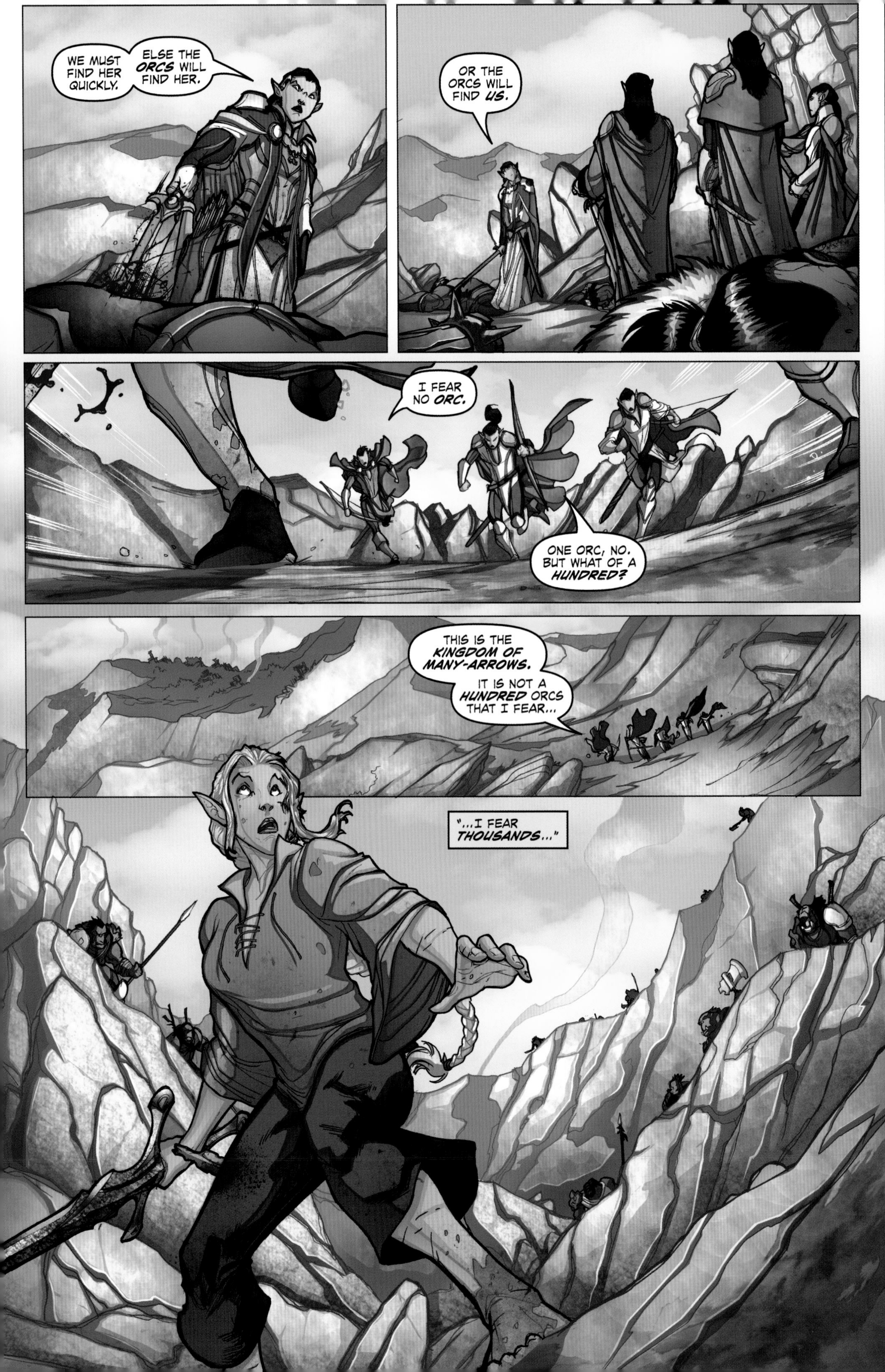
WE MUST FIND HER QUICKLY.
ELSE THE ORCS WILL FIND HER.
OR THE ORCS WILL FIND US.
I FEAR NO ORC.
ONE ORC, NO. BUT WHAT OF A HUNDRED?
THIS IS THE KINGDOM OF MANY-ARROWS.
IT IS NOT A HUNDRED ORCS THAT I FEAR...
"...I FEAR THOUSANDS..."

Art by David Baldeon

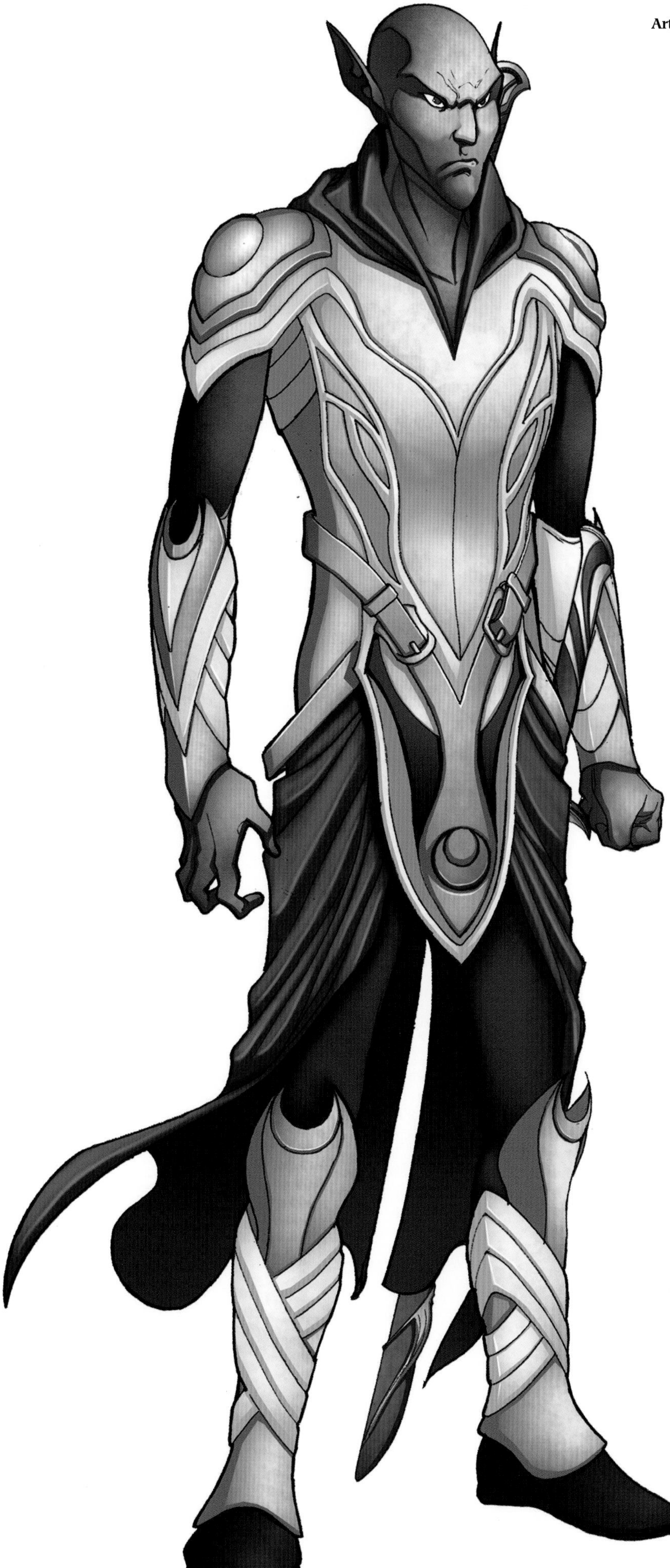

Art by Steve Ellis

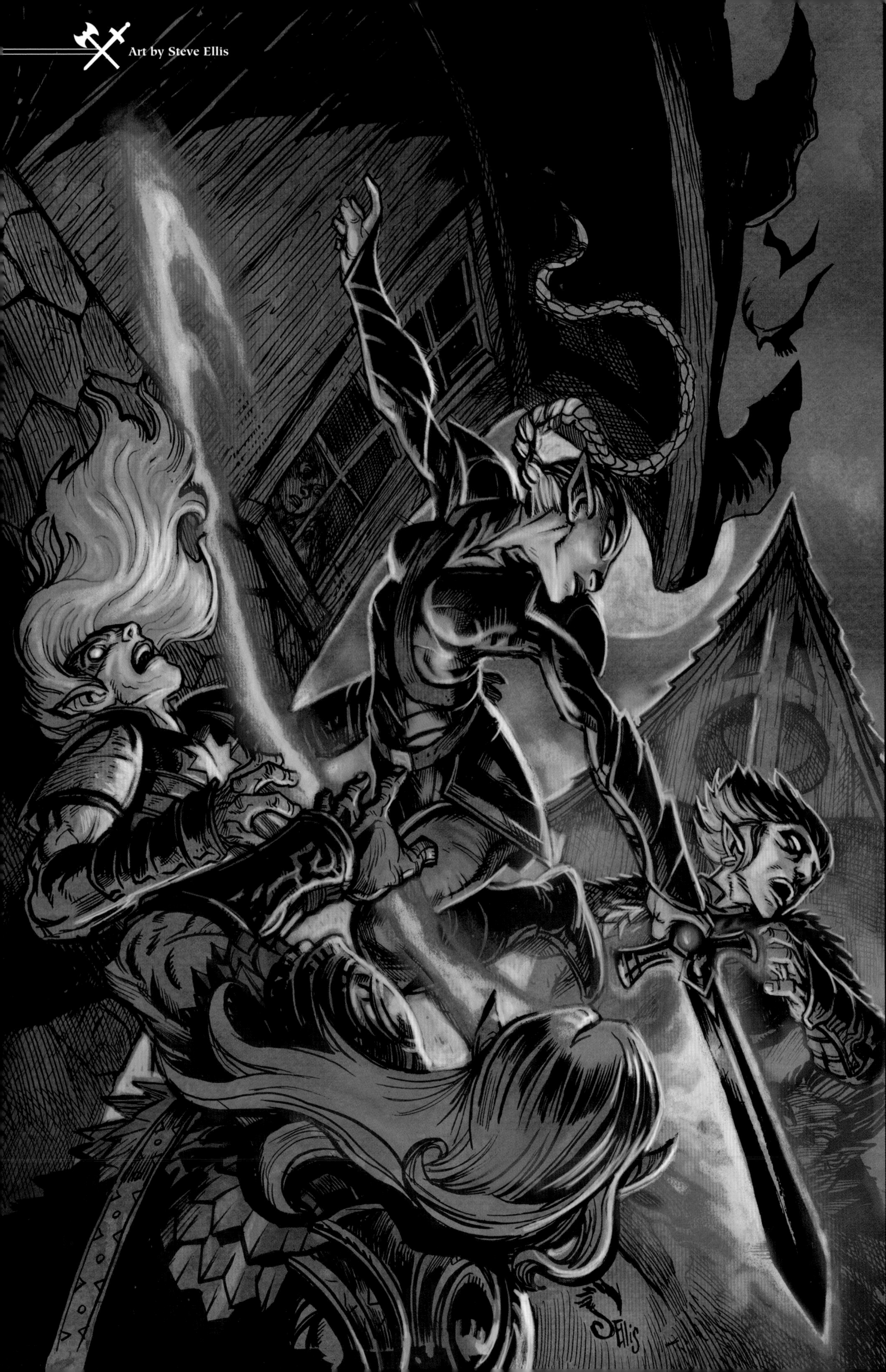
Ellis

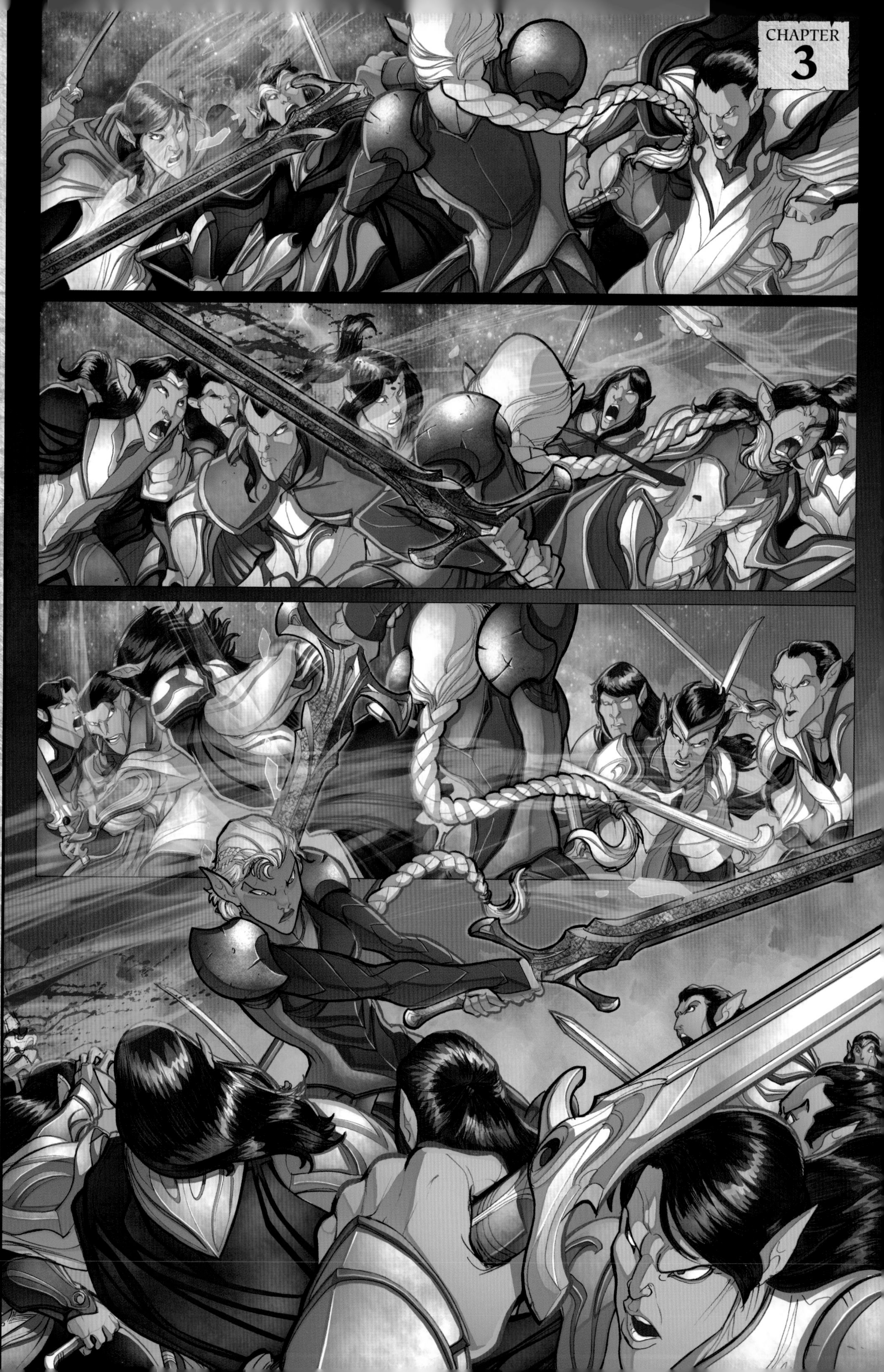
CHAPTER
3

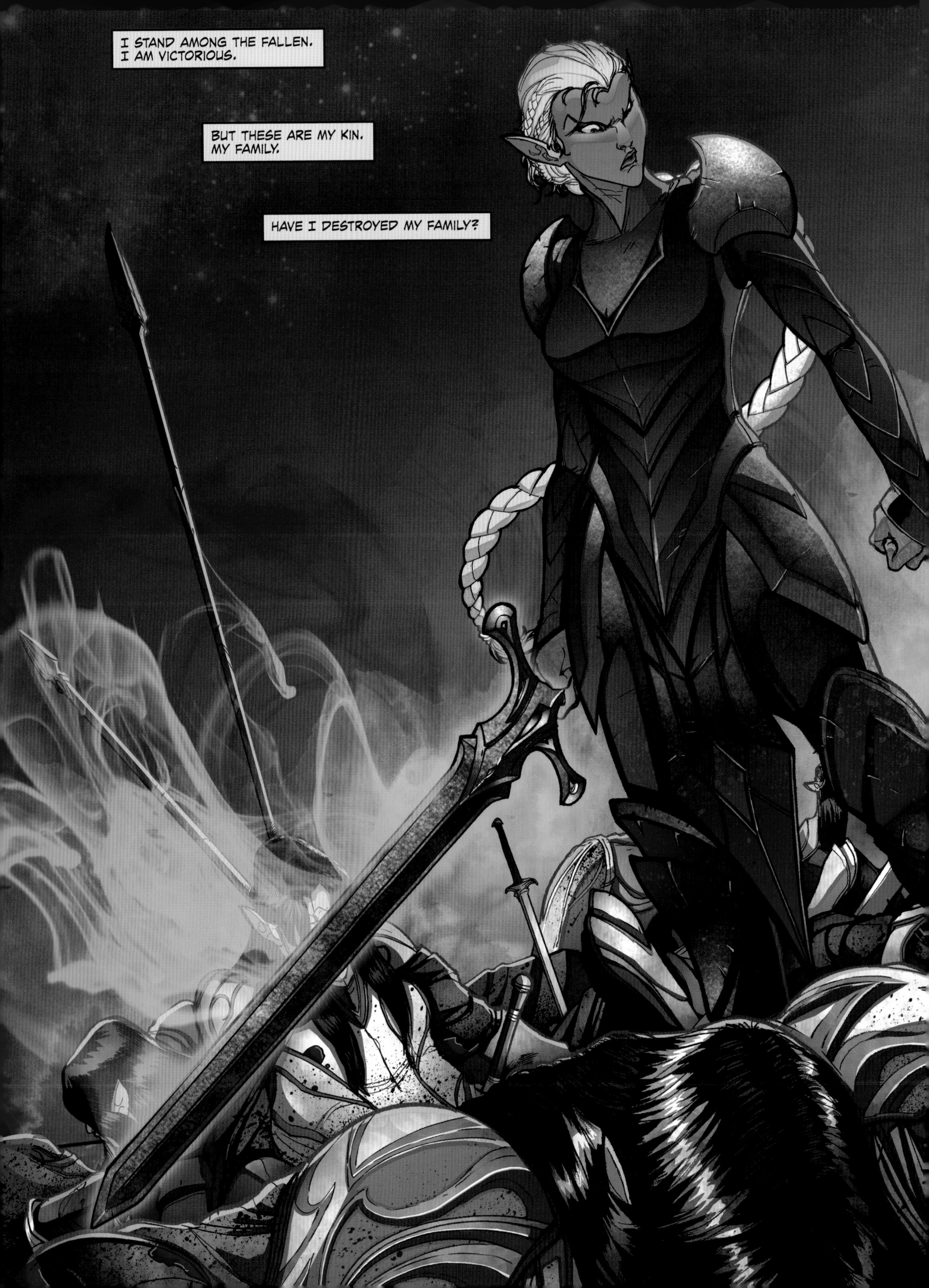
I STAND AMONG THE FALLEN.
I AM VICTORIOUS.
BUT THESE ARE MY KIN.
MY FAMILY.
HAVE I DESTROYED MY FAMILY?

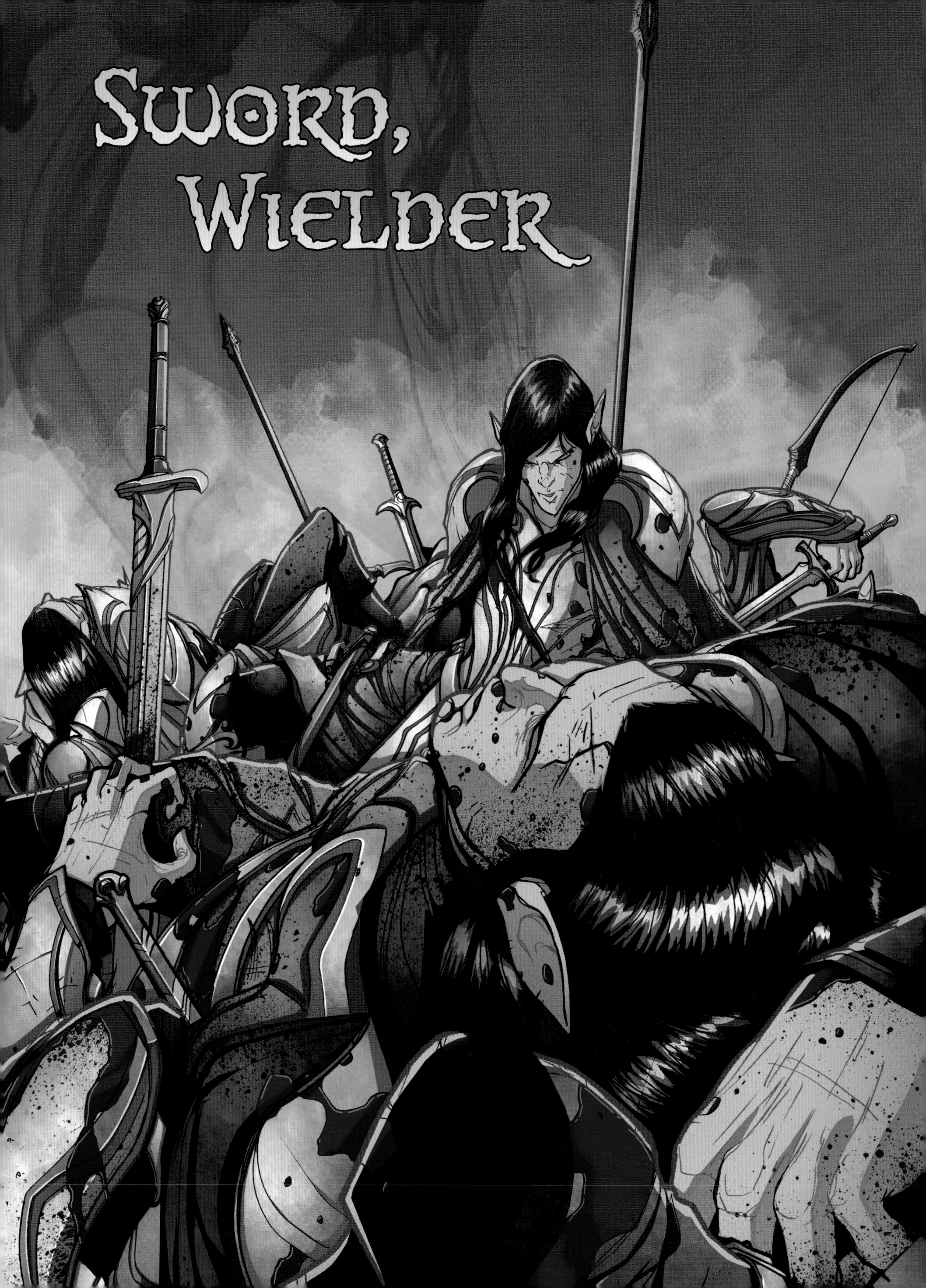
Sword,
Wielder

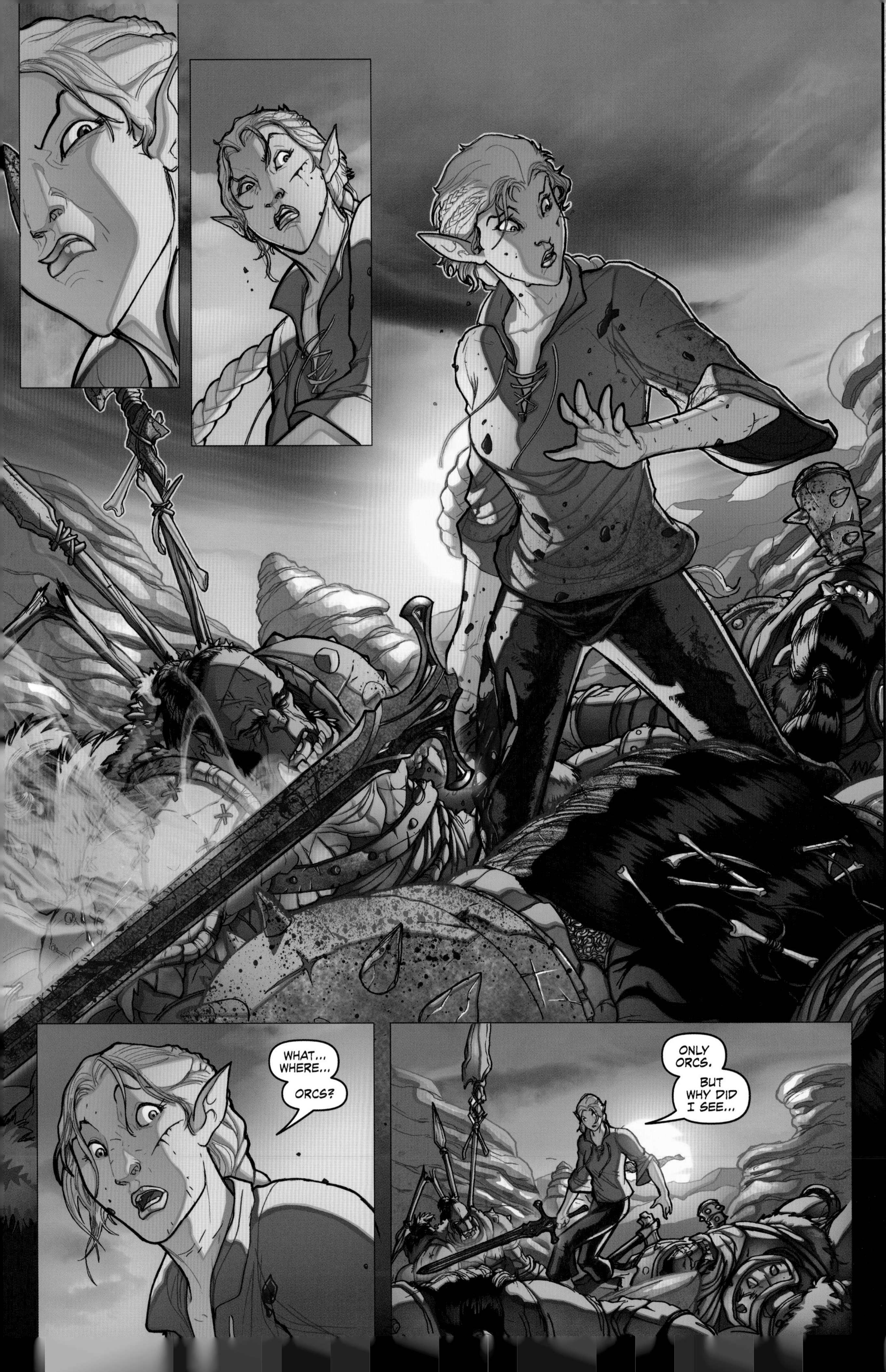
WHAT... WHERE... ORCS?
ONLY ORCS.
BUT WHY DID I SEE...

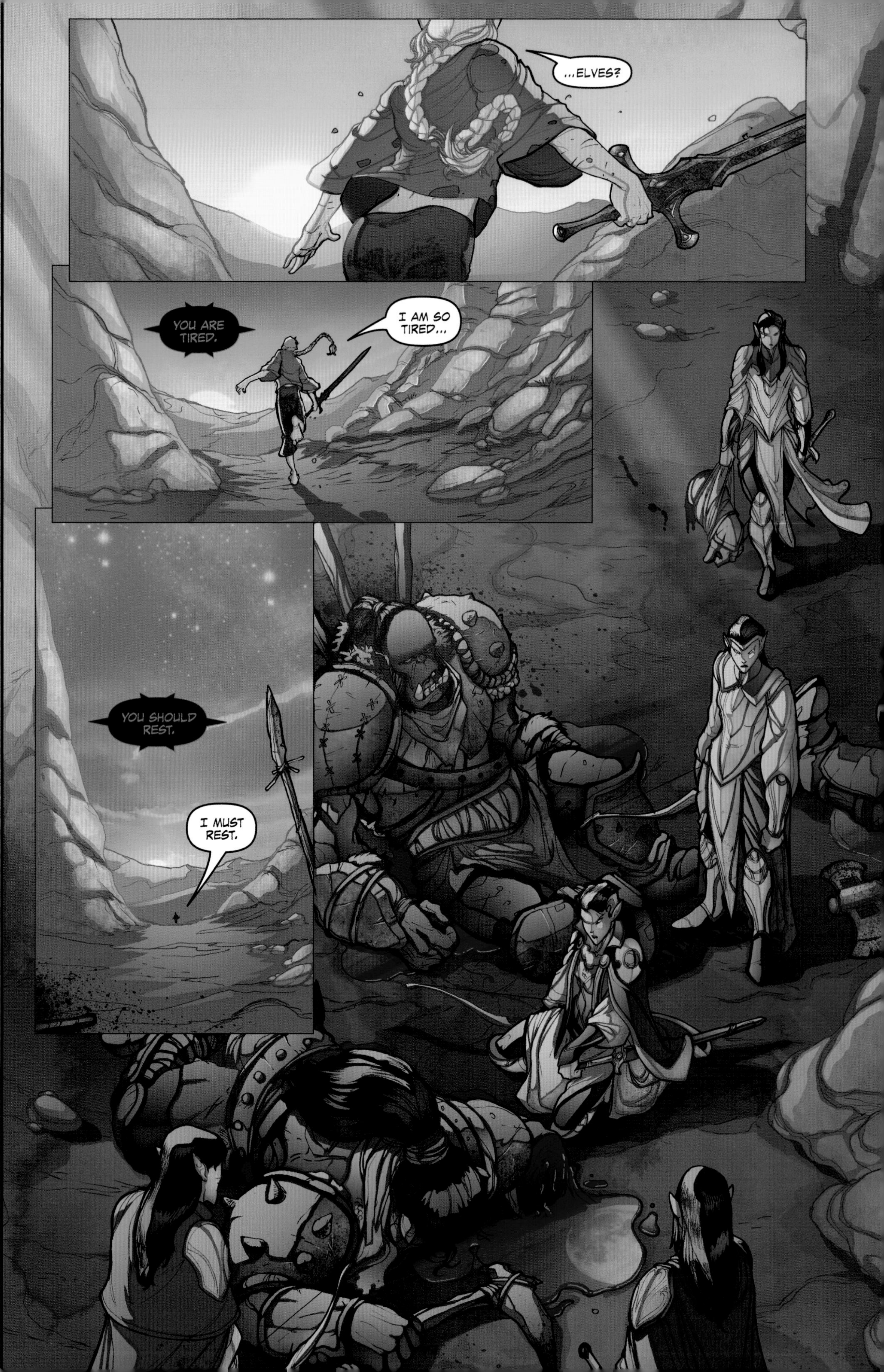
...ELVES?
YOU ARE TIRED.
I AM SO TIRED...
YOU SHOULD REST.
I MUST REST.

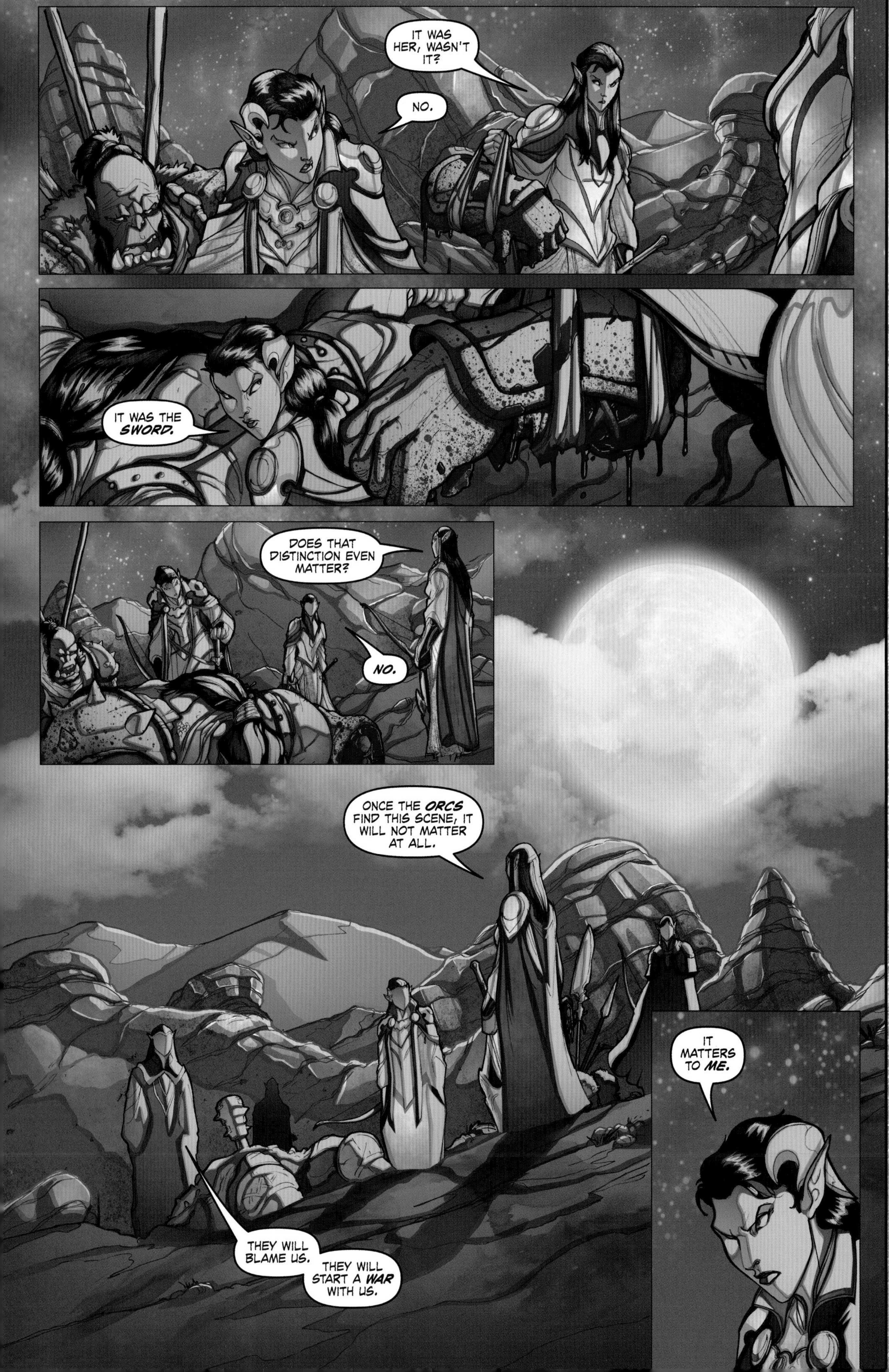

IT WAS HER, WASN'T IT?
NO.
IT WAS THE SWORD.
DOES THAT DISTINCTION EVEN MATTER?
NO.
ONCE THE ORCS FIND THIS SCENE, IT WILL NOT MATTER AT ALL.
THEY WILL BLAME US.
THEY WILL START A WAR WITH US.
IT MATTERS TO ME.

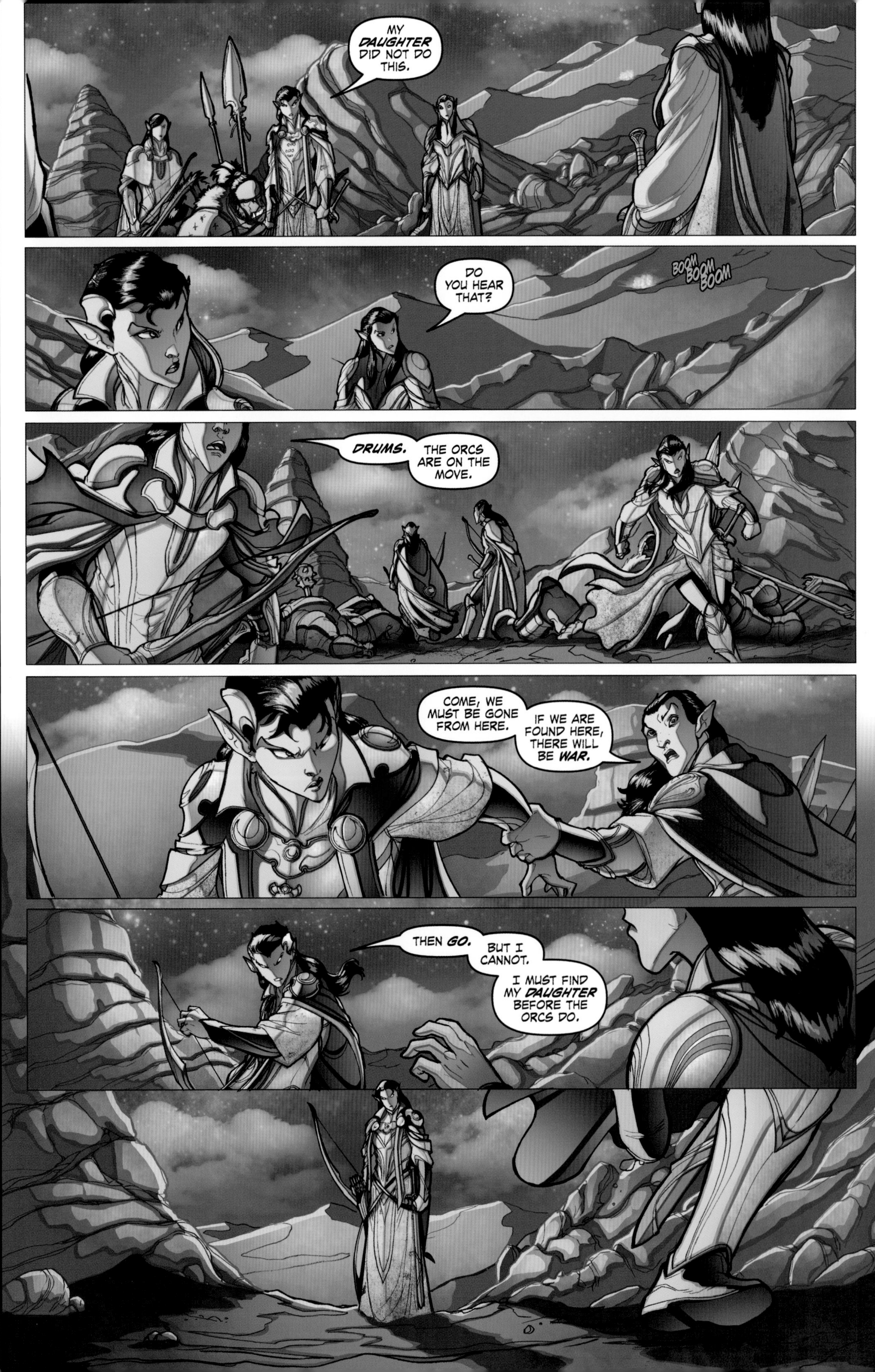
MY DAUGHTER DID NOT DO THIS.
DO YOU HEAR THAT?
BOOM BOOM BOOM
DRUMS.
THE ORCS ARE ON THE MOVE.
COME, WE MUST BE GONE FROM HERE.
IF WE ARE FOUND HERE, THERE WILL BE WAR.
THEN GO.
BUT I CANNOT.
I MUST FIND MY DAUGHTER BEFORE THE ORCS DO.

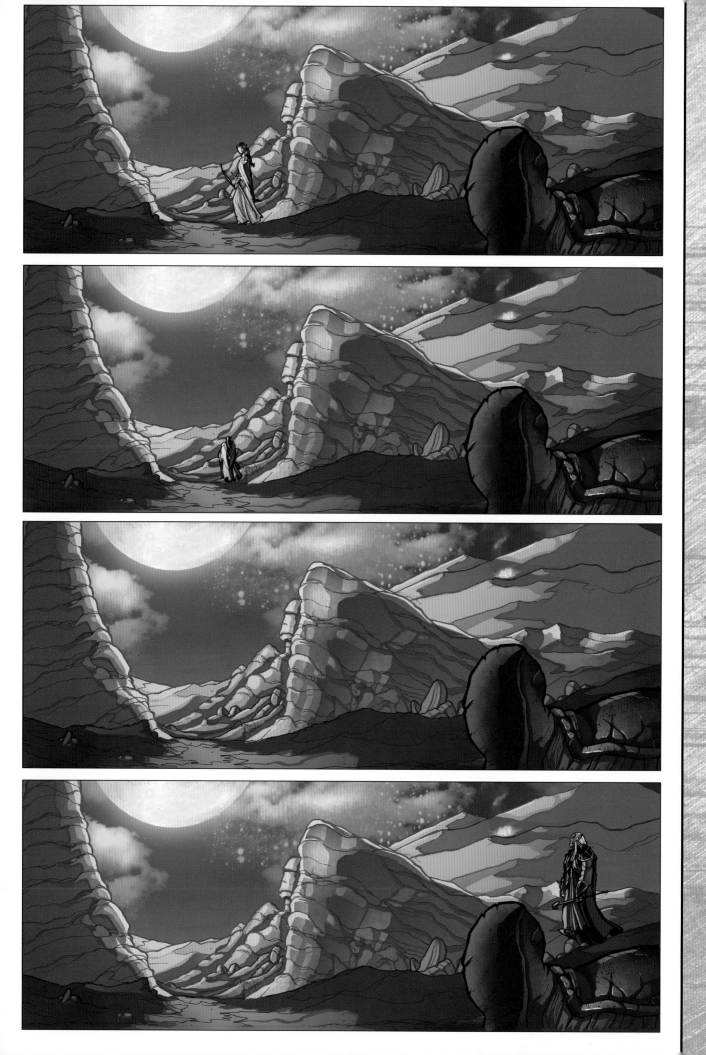

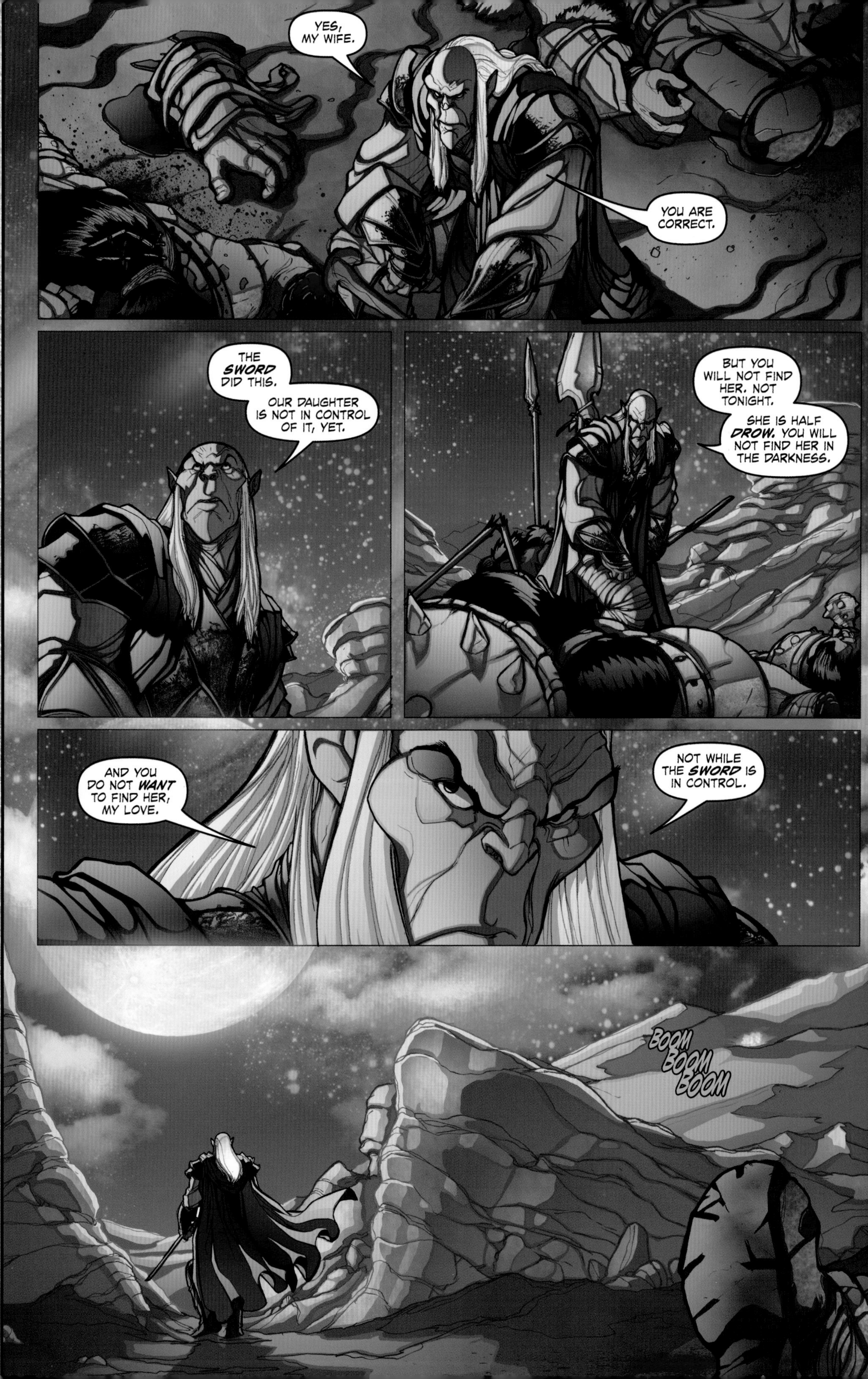
YES, MY WIFE.
YOU ARE CORRECT.
THE SWORD DID THIS.
OUR DAUGHTER IS NOT IN CONTROL OF IT, YET.
BUT YOU WILL NOT FIND HER. NOT TONIGHT.
SHE IS HALF DROW. YOU WILL NOT FIND HER IN THE DARKNESS.
AND YOU DO NOT WANT TO FIND HER, MY LOVE.
NOT WHILE THE SWORD IS IN CONTROL.
BOOM BOOM BOOM

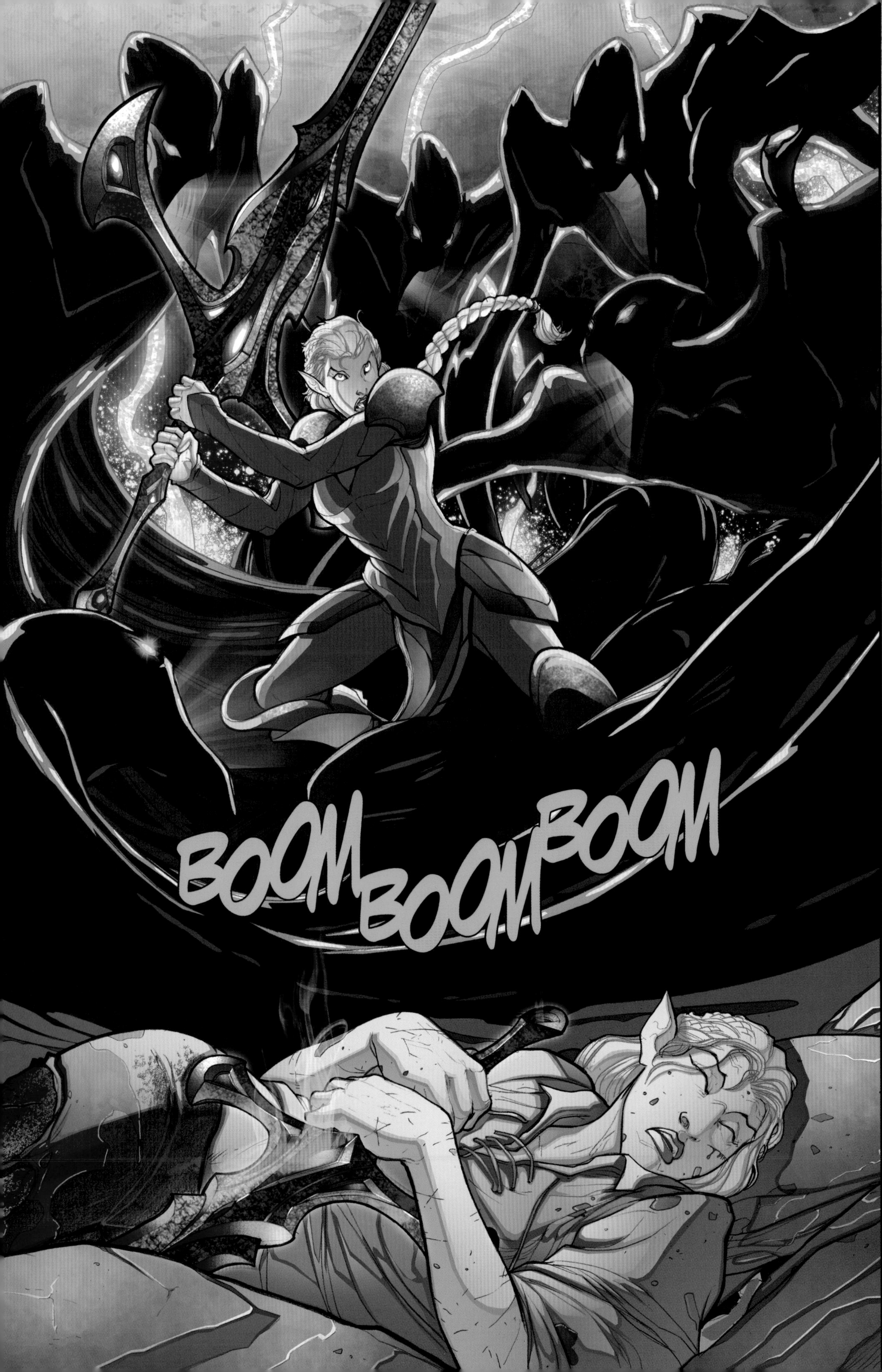
BOOM
BOOM
BOOM

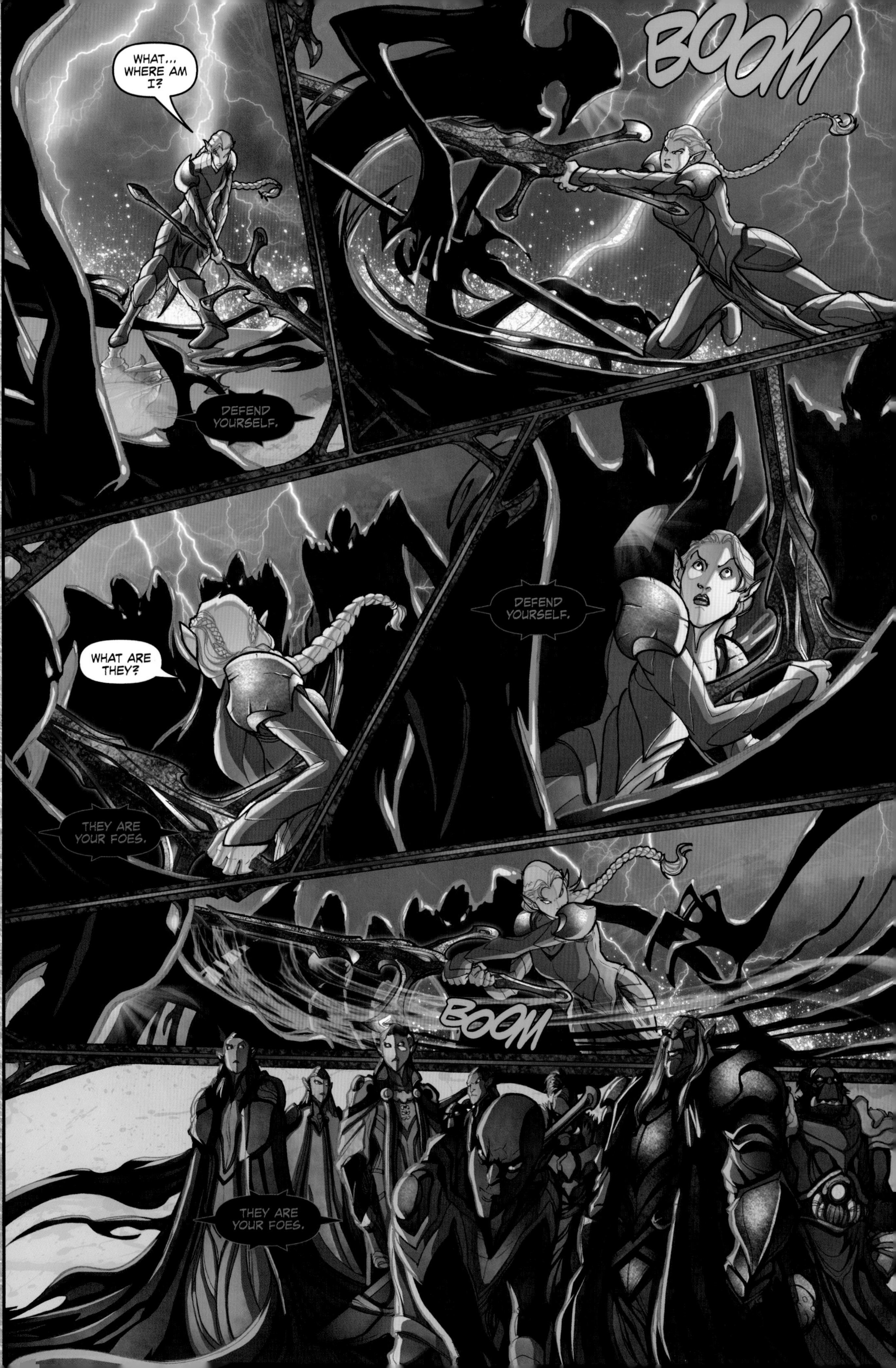
WHAT... WHERE AM I?
BOOM
DEFEND YOURSELF.
DEFEND YOURSELF.
WHAT ARE THEY?
THEY ARE YOUR FOES.
BOOM
THEY ARE YOUR FOES.

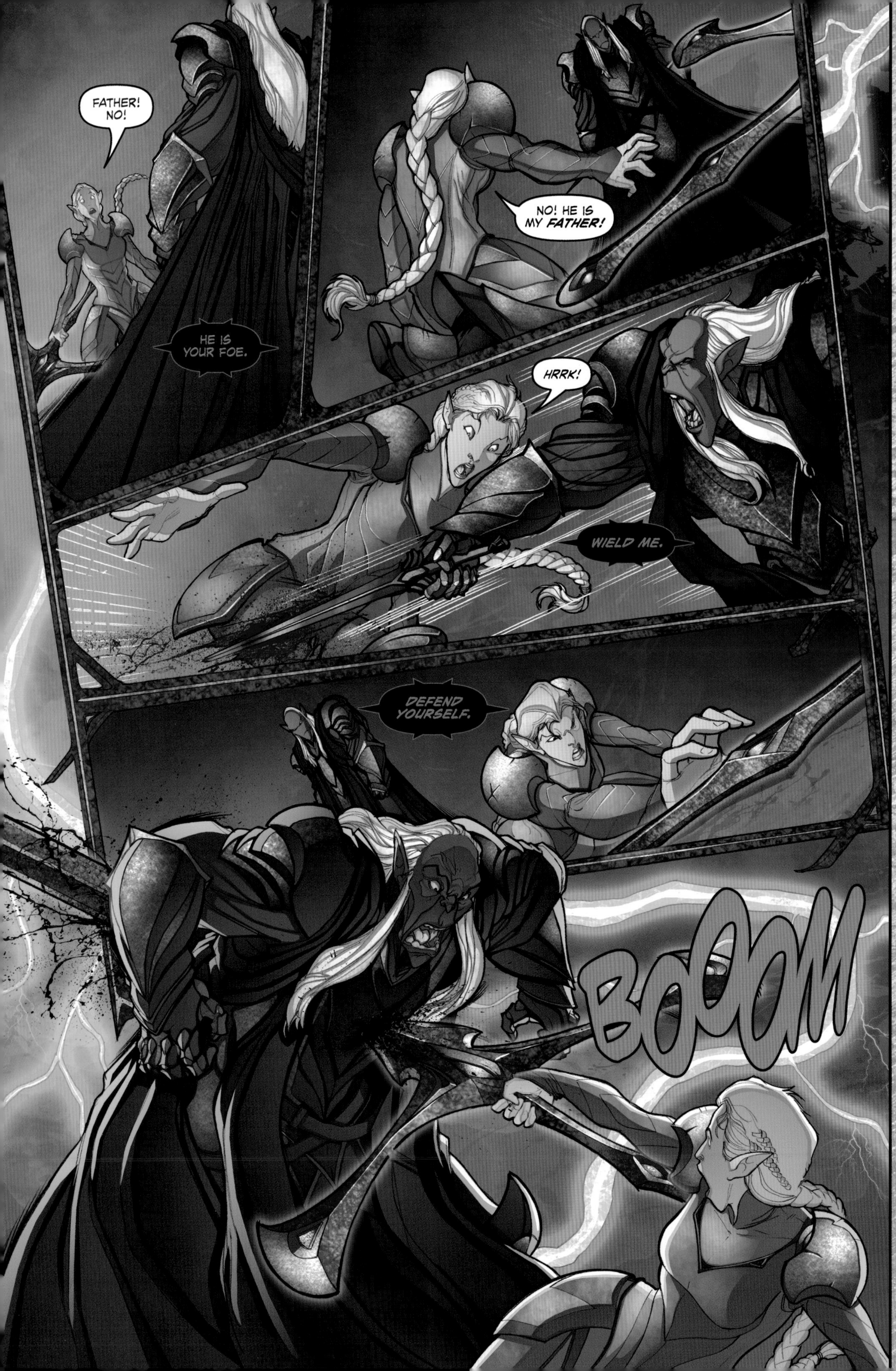
FATHER! NO!
HE IS YOUR FOE.
NO! HE IS MY FATHER!
HRRK!
WIELD ME.
DEFEND YOURSELF.
BOOOM

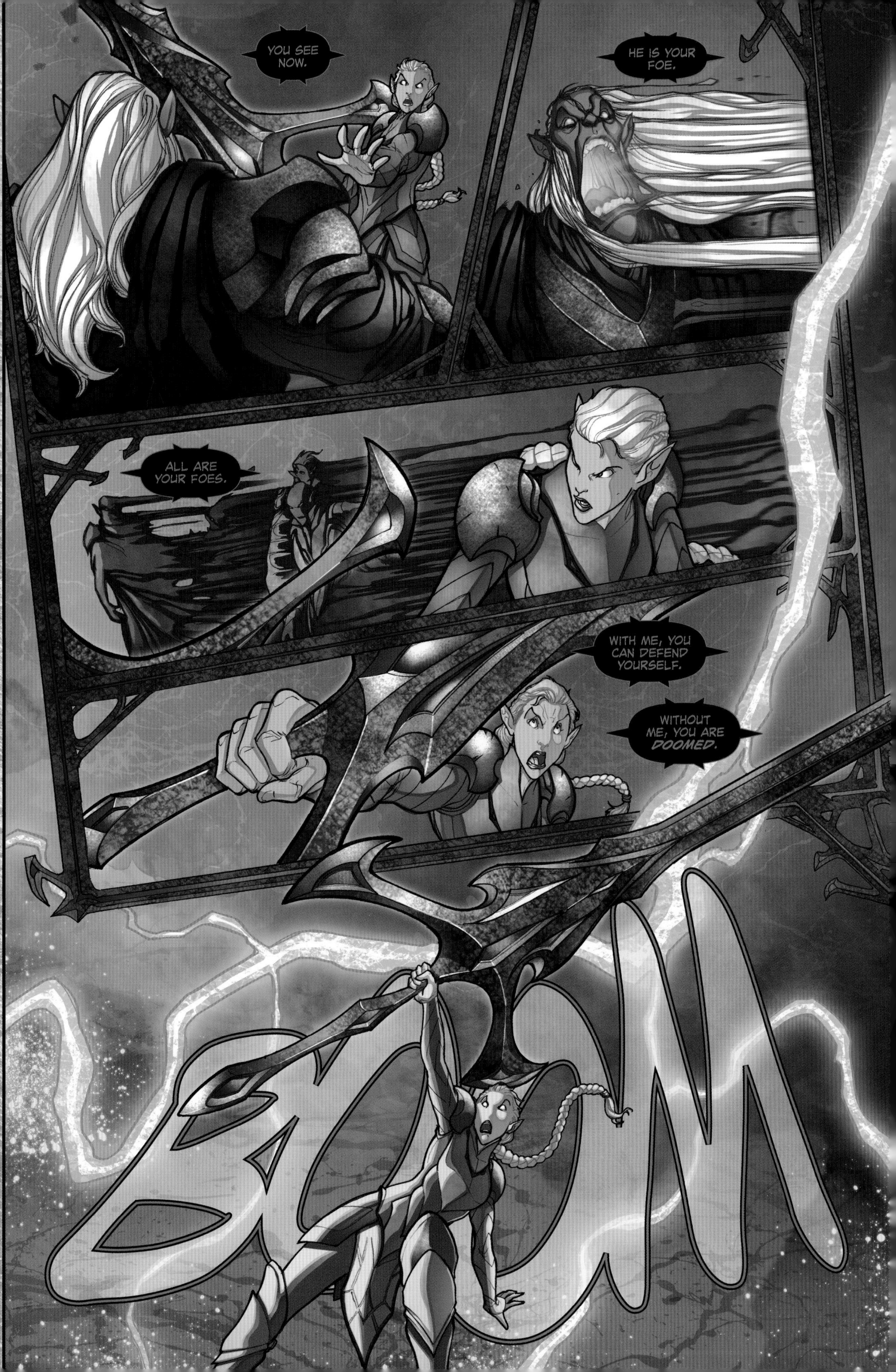
YOU SEE NOW.
HE IS YOUR FOE.
ALL ARE YOUR FOES.
WITH ME, YOU CAN DEFEND YOURSELF.
WITHOUT ME, YOU ARE *DOOMED*.
BOOM

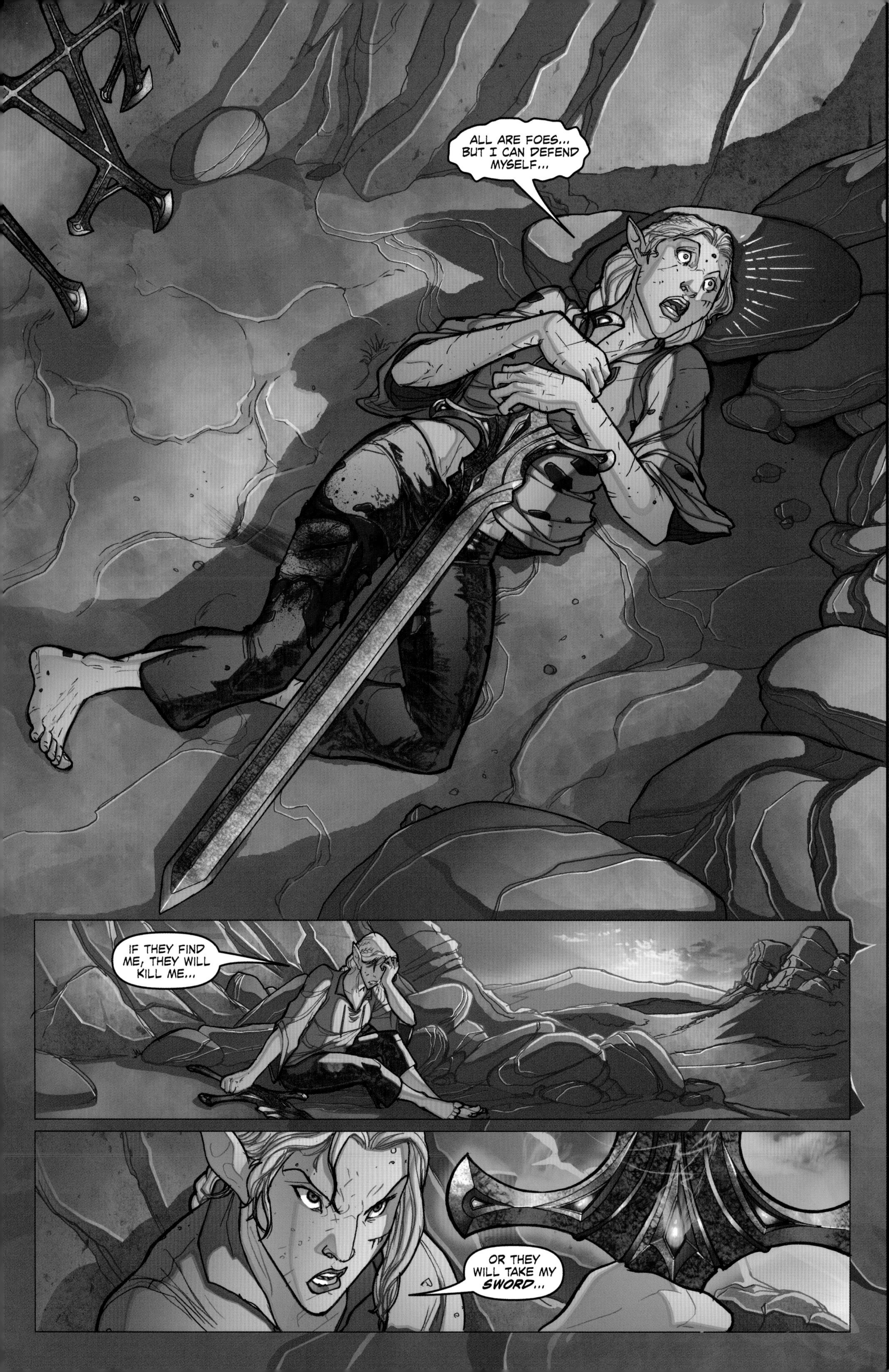
ALL ARE FOES... BUT I CAN DEFEND MYSELF...
IF THEY FIND ME, THEY WILL KILL ME...
OR THEY WILL TAKE MY *SWORD*...

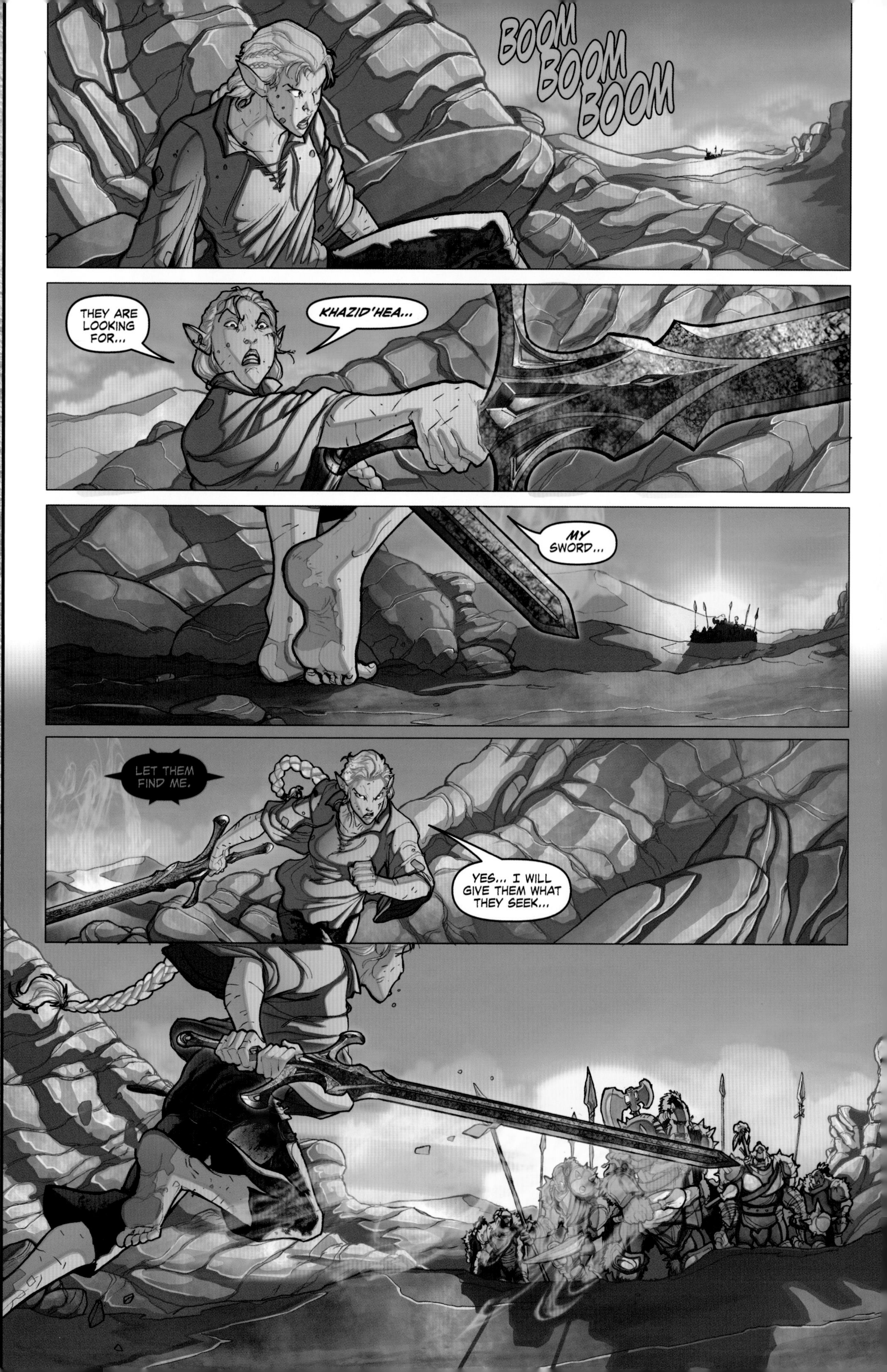
BOOM BOOM BOOM
THEY ARE LOOKING FOR...
KHAZID'HEA...
MY SWORD...
LET THEM FIND ME.
YES... I WILL GIVE THEM WHAT THEY SEEK...

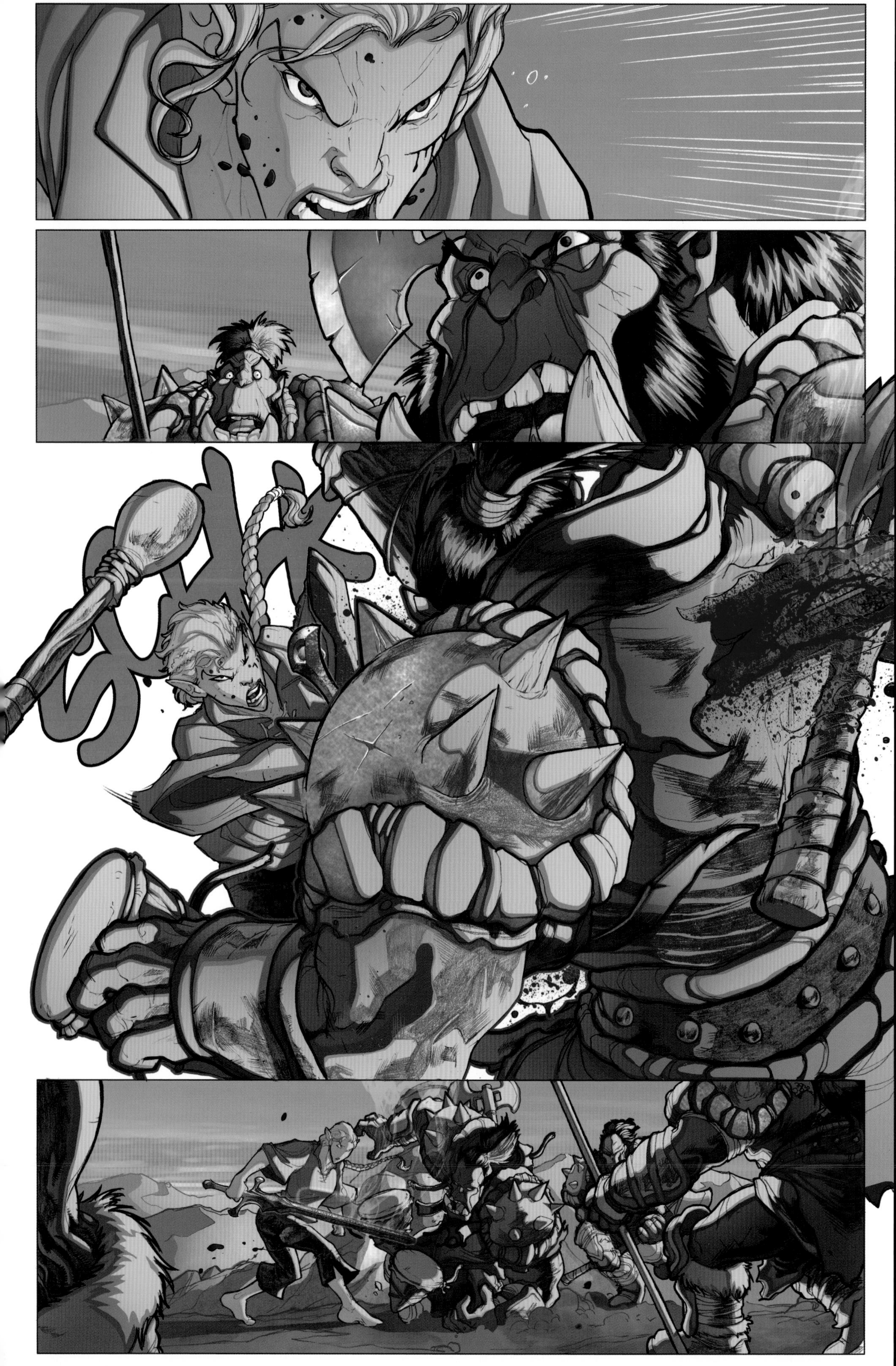

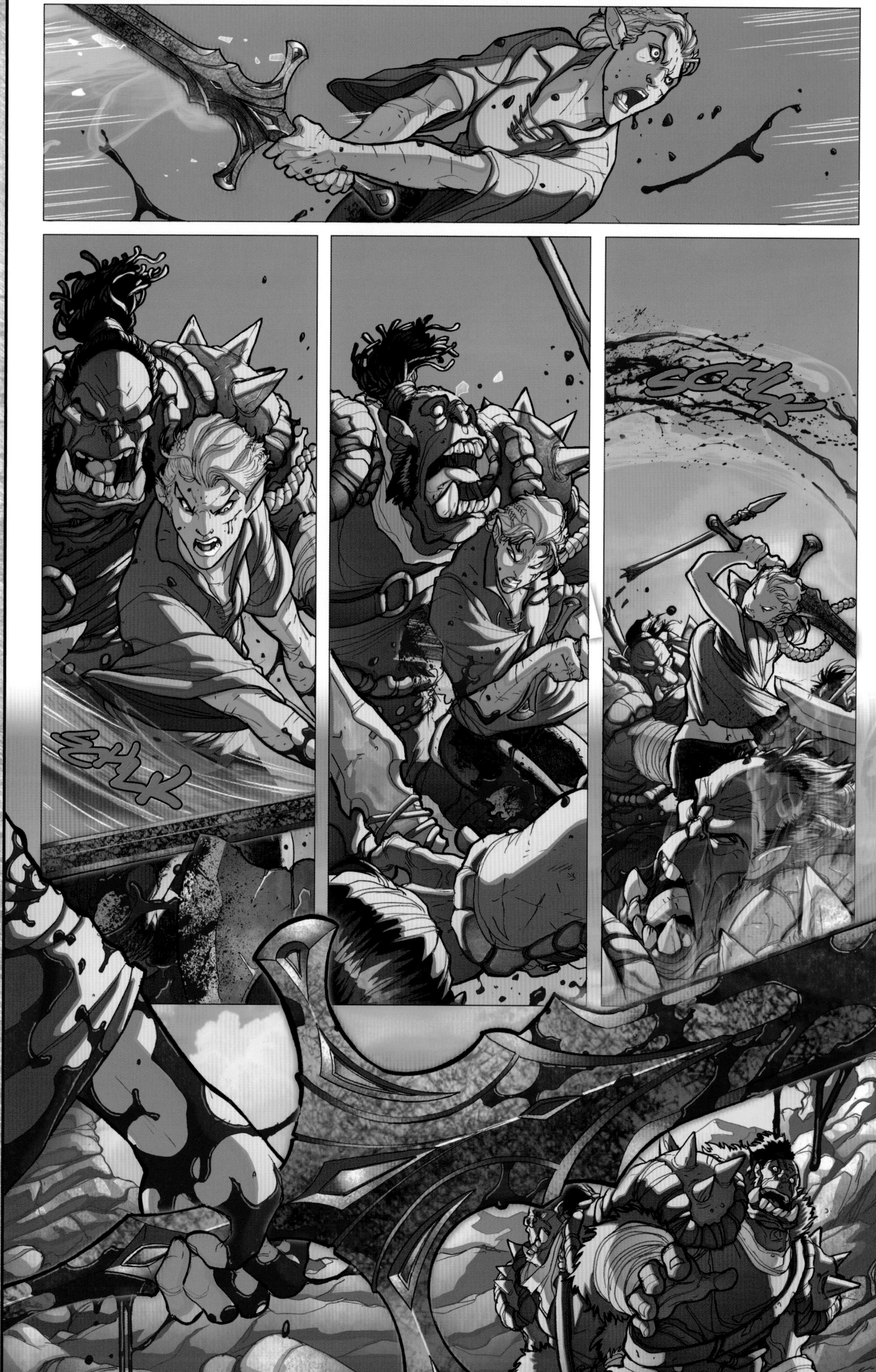
SCHLK
SCHLK

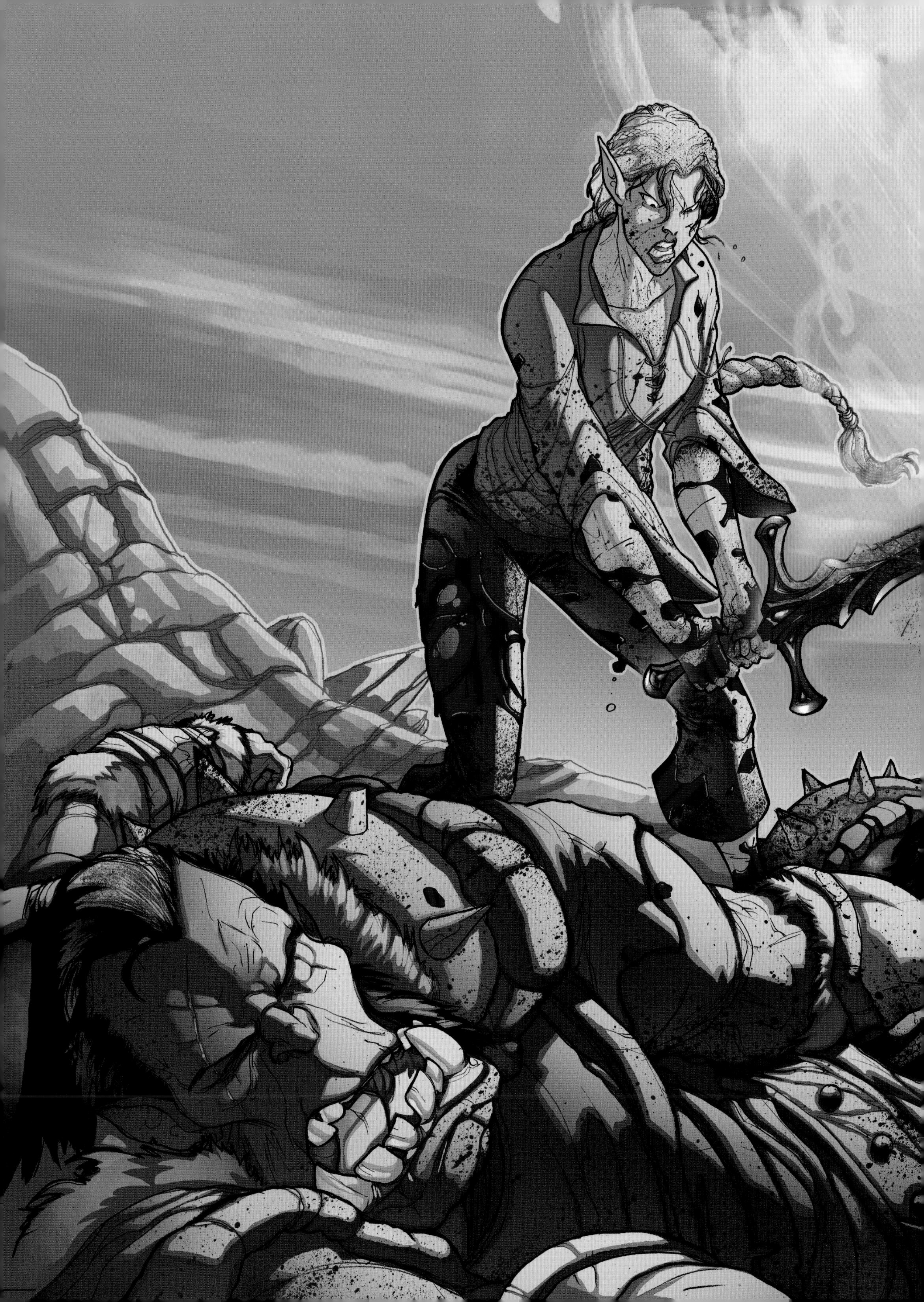

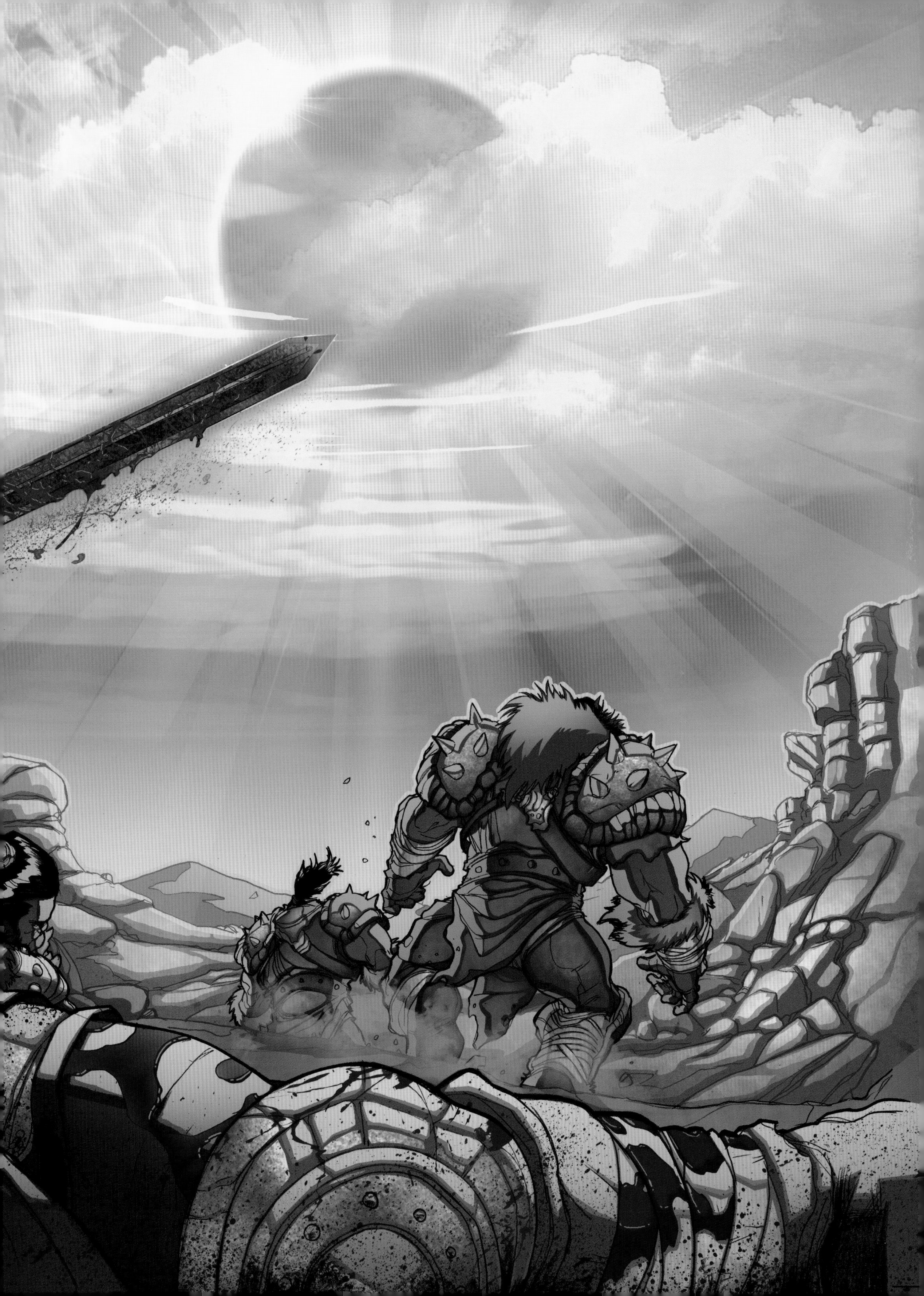

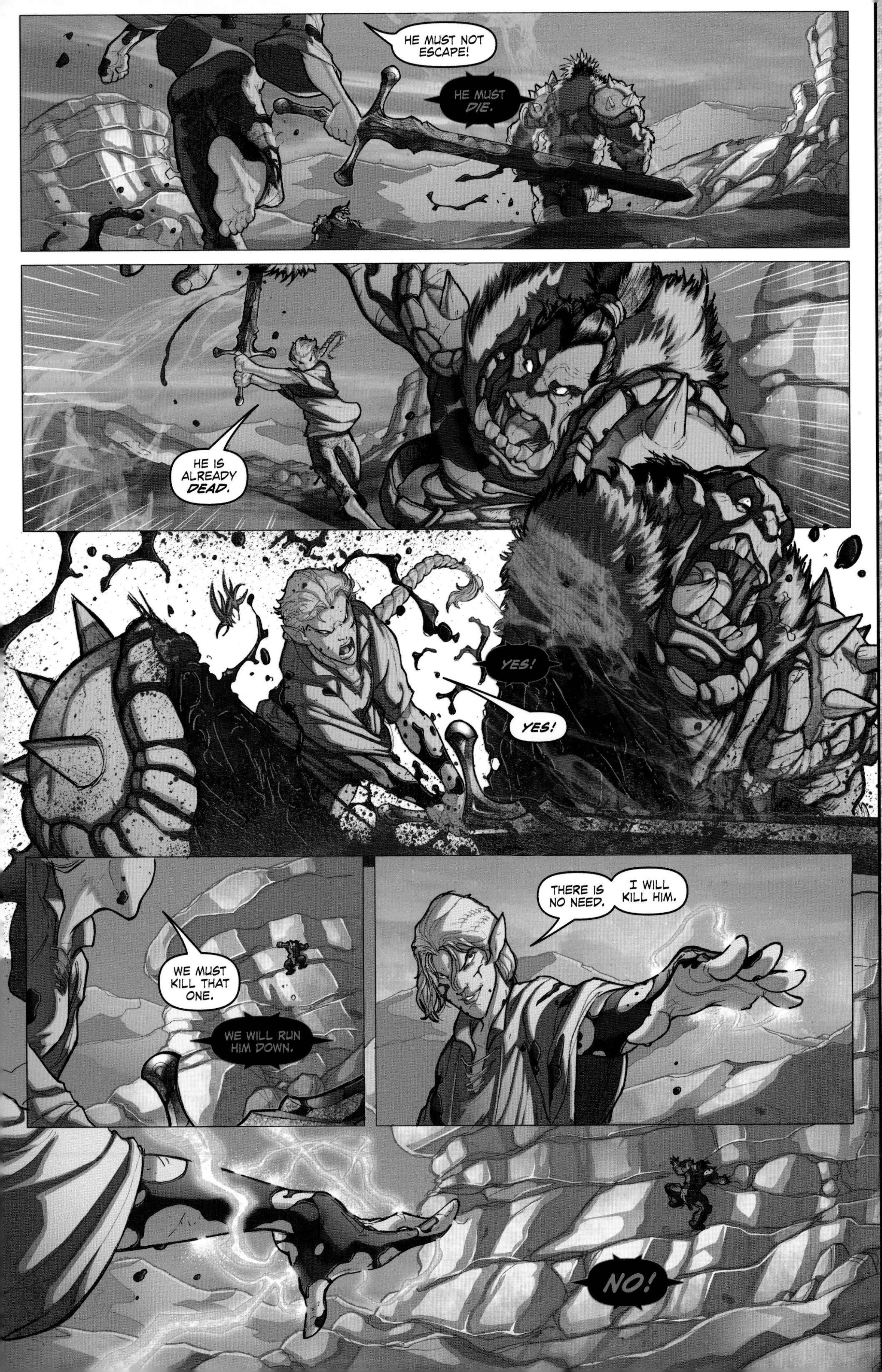
HE MUST NOT ESCAPE!
HE MUST *DIE*.
HE IS ALREADY ***DEAD***.
YES!
YES!
WE MUST KILL THAT ONE.
WE WILL RUN HIM DOWN.
THERE IS NO NEED.
I WILL KILL HIM.
NO!

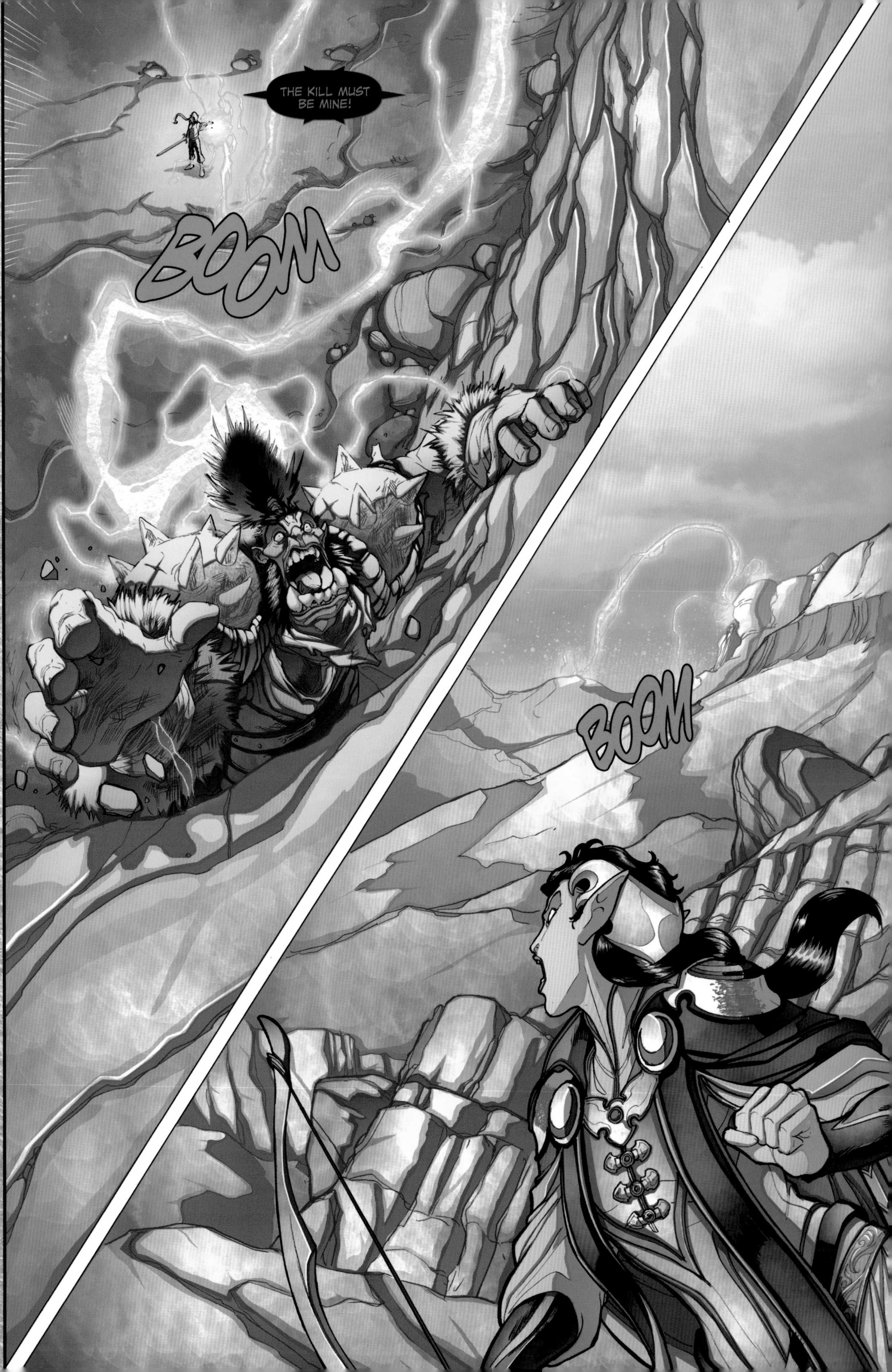
THE KILL MUST BE MINE!
BOOM
BOOM

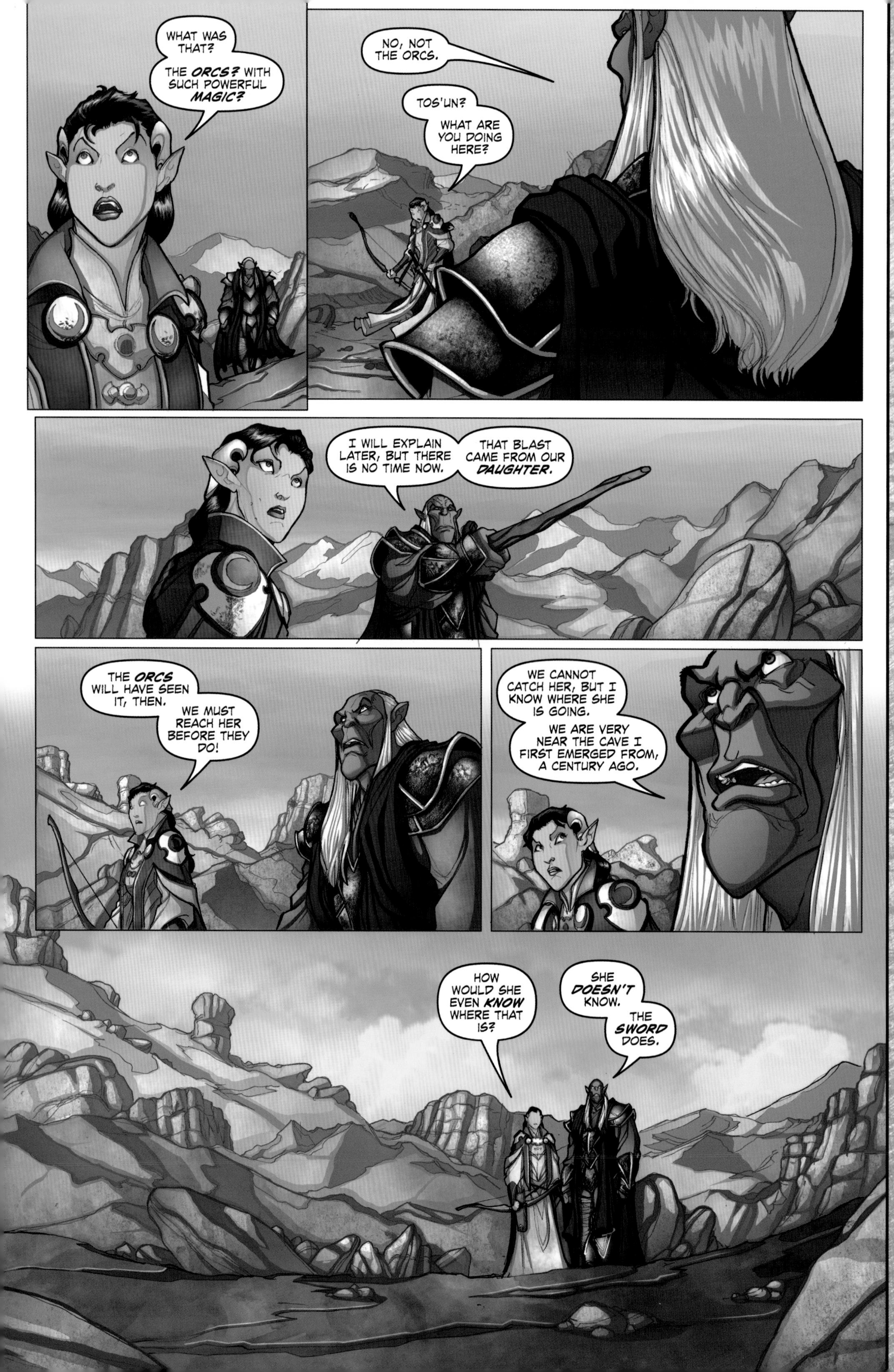
WHAT WAS THAT?
THE ORCS? WITH SUCH POWERFUL MAGIC?
NO, NOT THE ORCS.
TOS'UN?
WHAT ARE YOU DOING HERE?
I WILL EXPLAIN LATER, BUT THERE IS NO TIME NOW.
THAT BLAST CAME FROM OUR DAUGHTER.
THE ORCS WILL HAVE SEEN IT, THEN.
WE MUST REACH HER BEFORE THEY DO!
WE CANNOT CATCH HER, BUT I KNOW WHERE SHE IS GOING.
WE ARE VERY NEAR THE CAVE I FIRST EMERGED FROM, A CENTURY AGO.
HOW WOULD SHE EVEN KNOW WHERE THAT IS?
SHE DOESN'T KNOW.
THE SWORD DOES.

Art by Steve Ellis

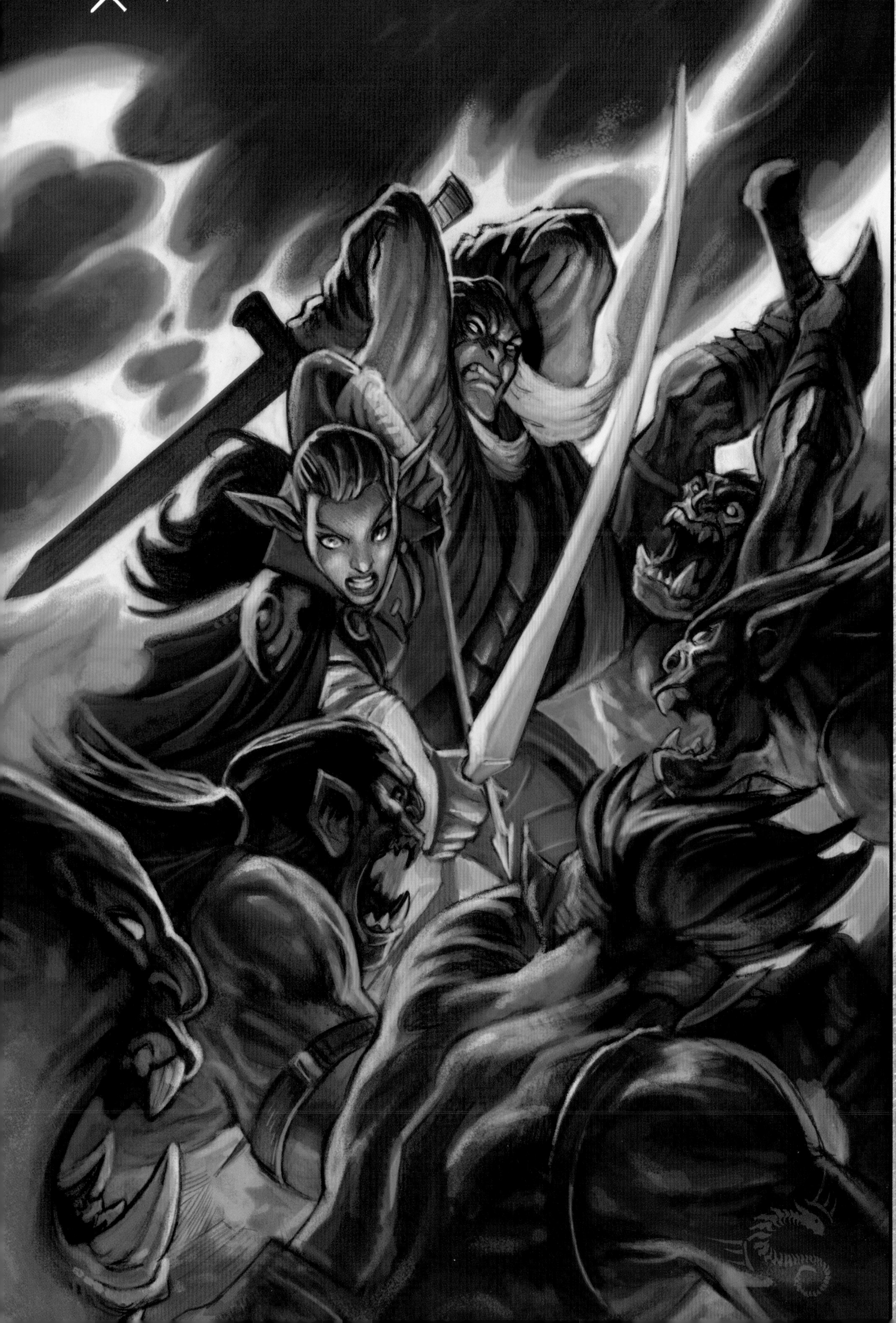

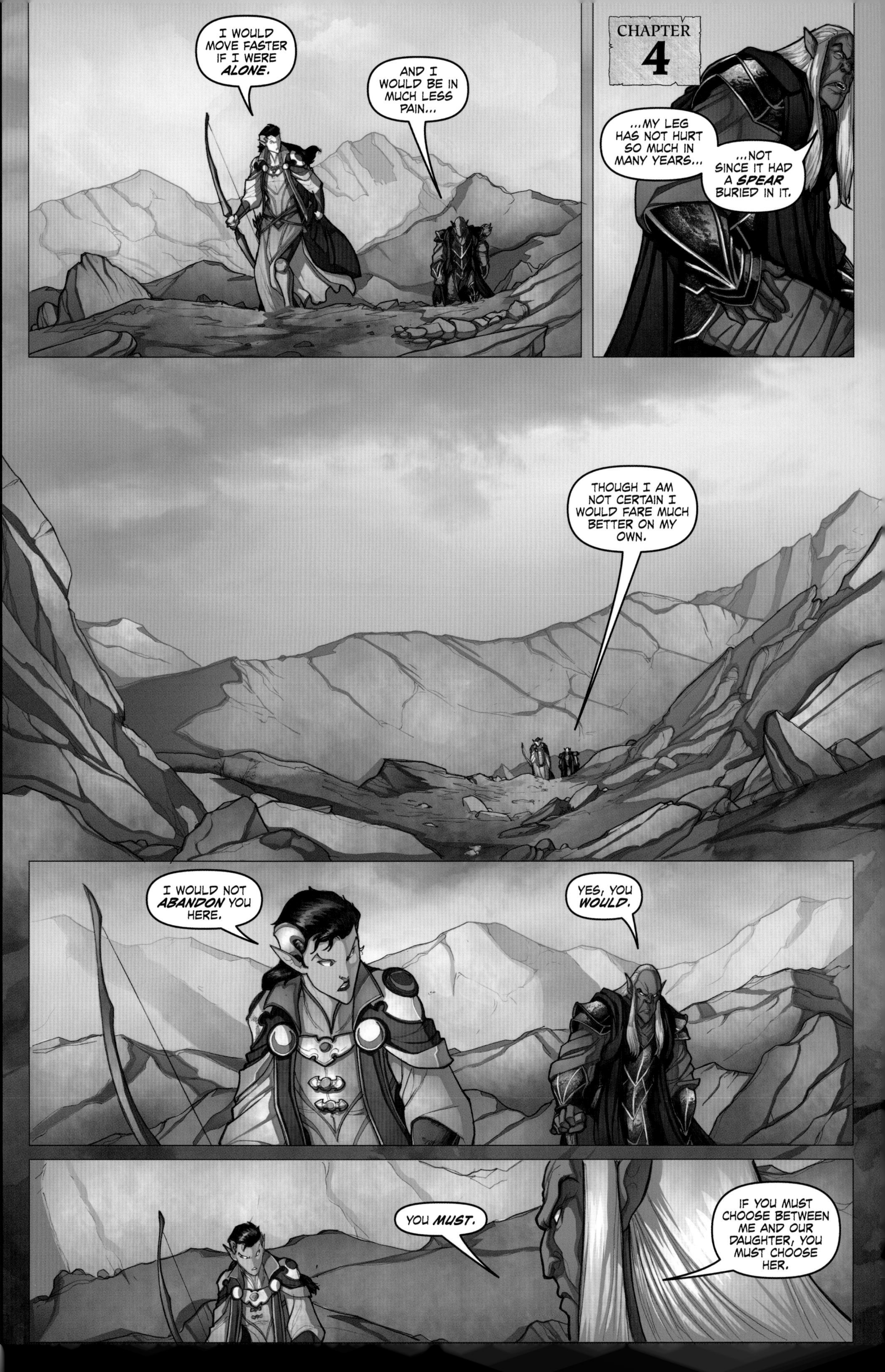
CHAPTER 4
I WOULD MOVE FASTER IF I WERE *ALONE*.
AND I WOULD BE IN MUCH LESS PAIN...
...MY LEG HAS NOT HURT SO MUCH IN MANY YEARS...
...NOT SINCE IT HAD A *SPEAR* BURIED IN IT.
THOUGH I AM NOT CERTAIN I WOULD FARE MUCH BETTER ON MY OWN.
I WOULD NOT *ABANDON* YOU HERE.
YES, YOU *WOULD*.
YOU *MUST*.
IF YOU MUST CHOOSE BETWEEN ME AND OUR DAUGHTER, YOU MUST CHOOSE HER.

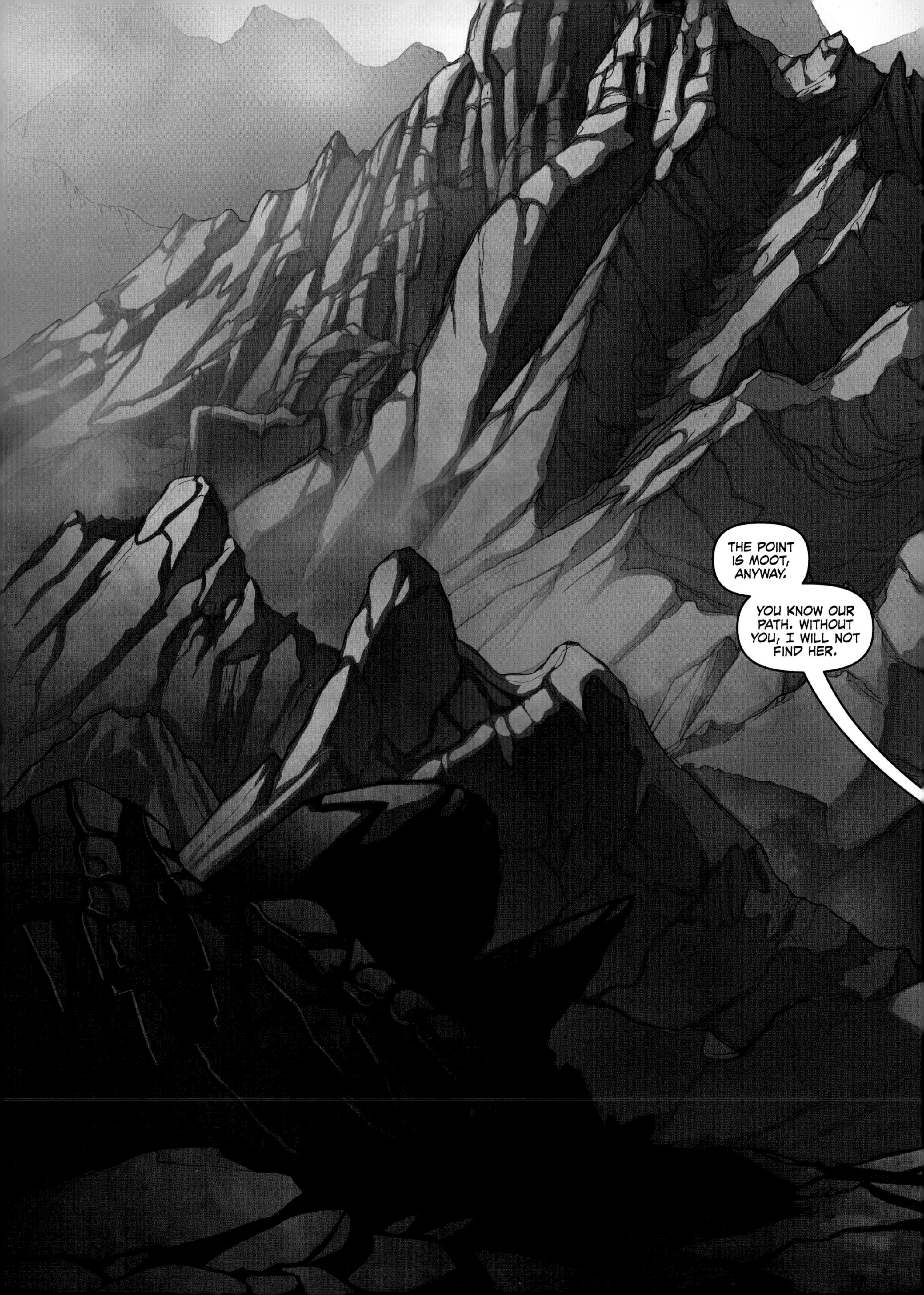
THE POINT IS MOOT, ANYWAY.
YOU KNOW OUR PATH. WITHOUT YOU, I WILL NOT FIND HER.

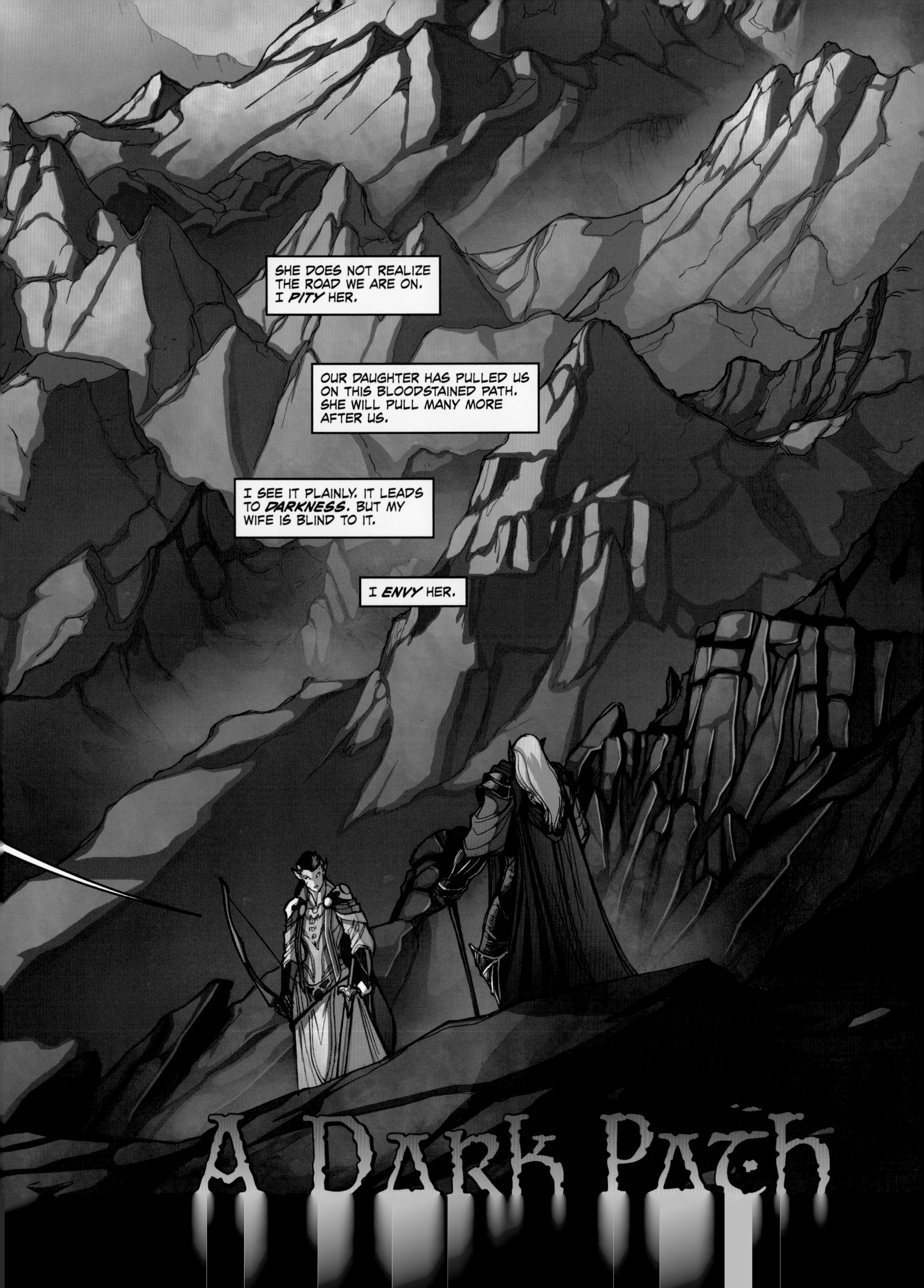
SHE DOES NOT REALIZE THE ROAD WE ARE ON. I PITY HER.
OUR DAUGHTER HAS PULLED US ON THIS BLOODSTAINED PATH. SHE WILL PULL MANY MORE AFTER US.
I SEE IT PLAINLY. IT LEADS TO DARKNESS. BUT MY WIFE IS BLIND TO IT.
I ENVY HER.
A DARK PATH

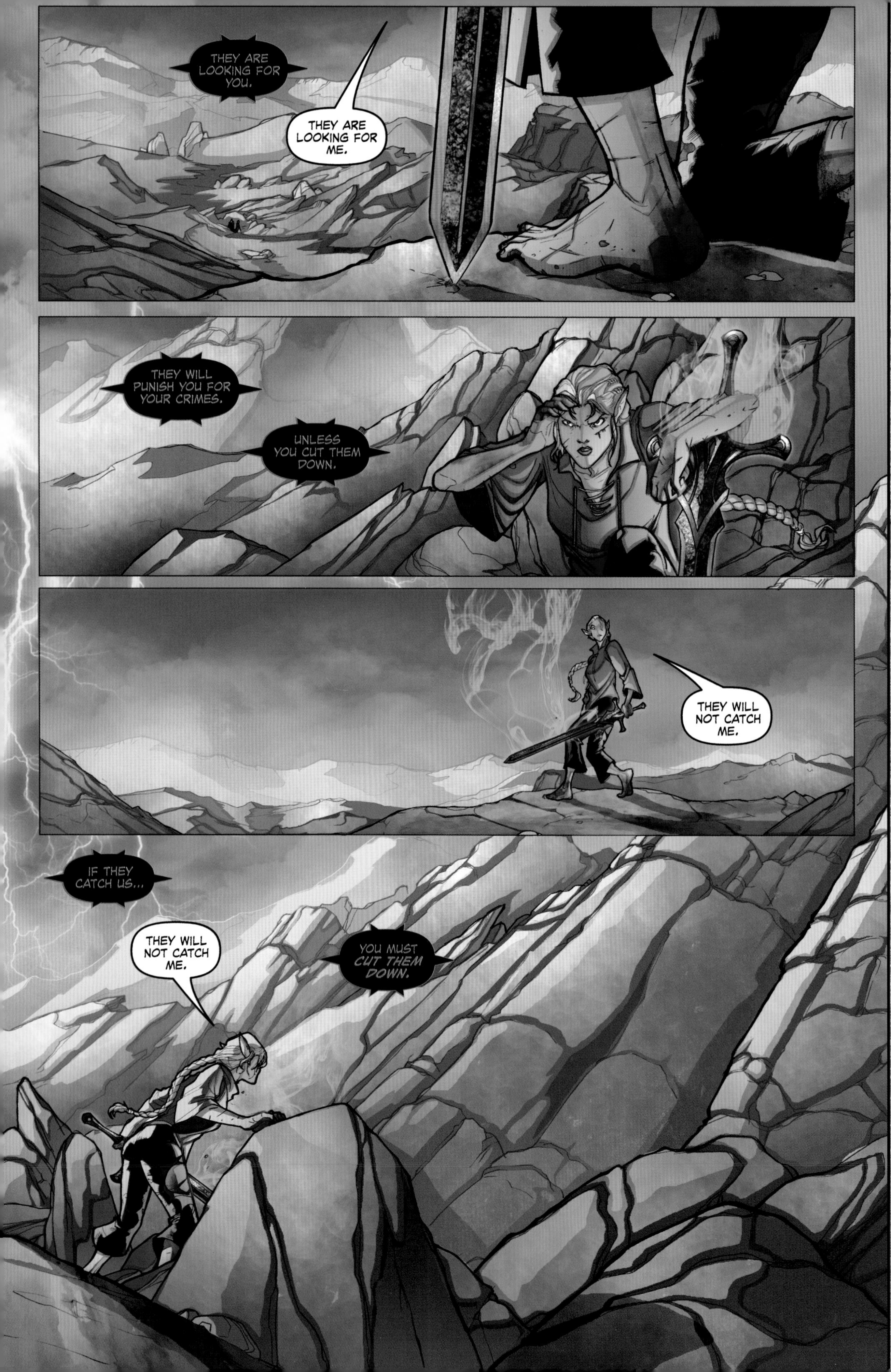
THEY ARE LOOKING FOR YOU.
THEY ARE LOOKING FOR ME.
THEY WILL PUNISH YOU FOR YOUR CRIMES.
UNLESS YOU CUT THEM DOWN.
THEY WILL NOT CATCH ME.
IF THEY CATCH US...
THEY WILL NOT CATCH ME.
YOU MUST *CUT THEM DOWN.*

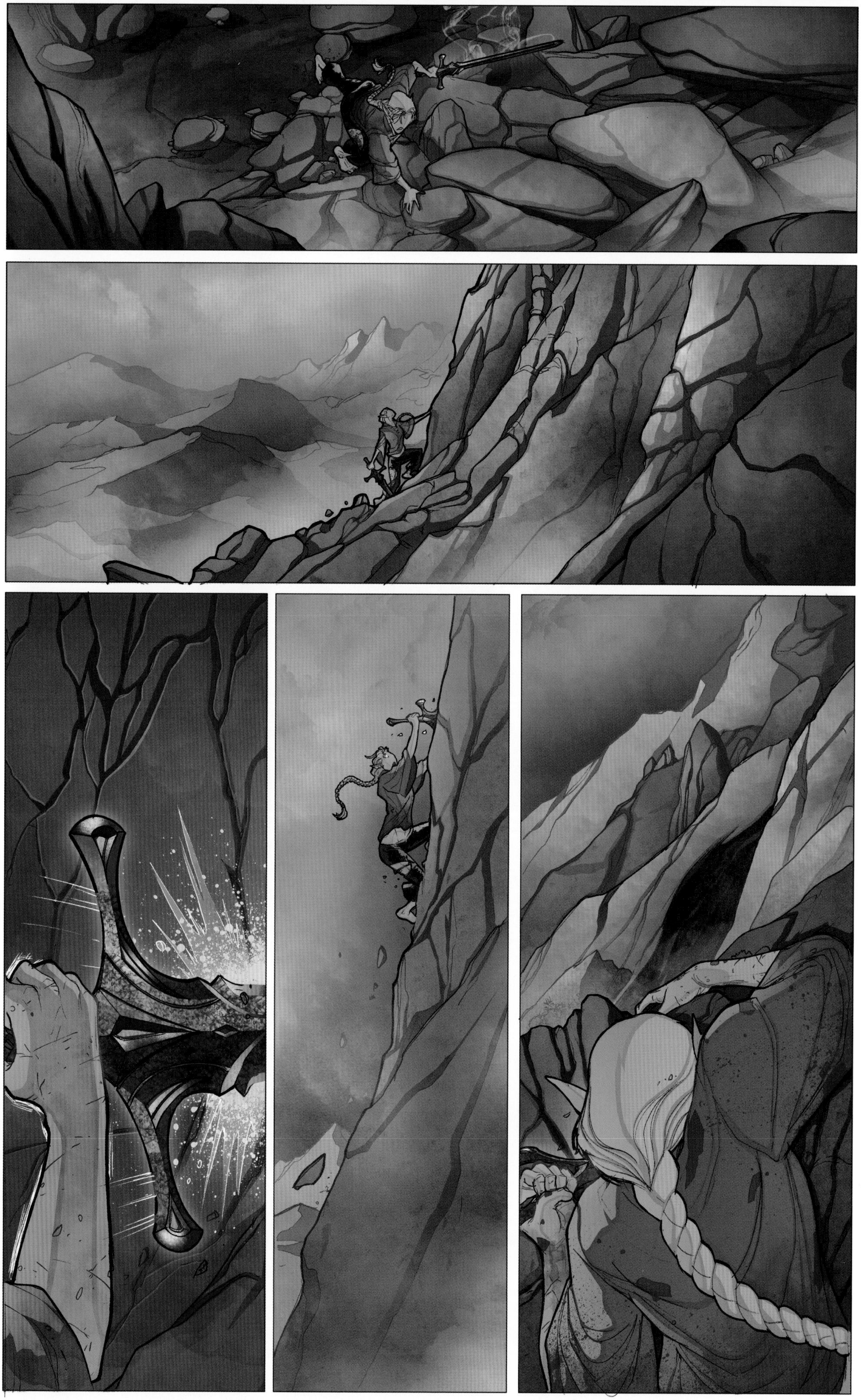

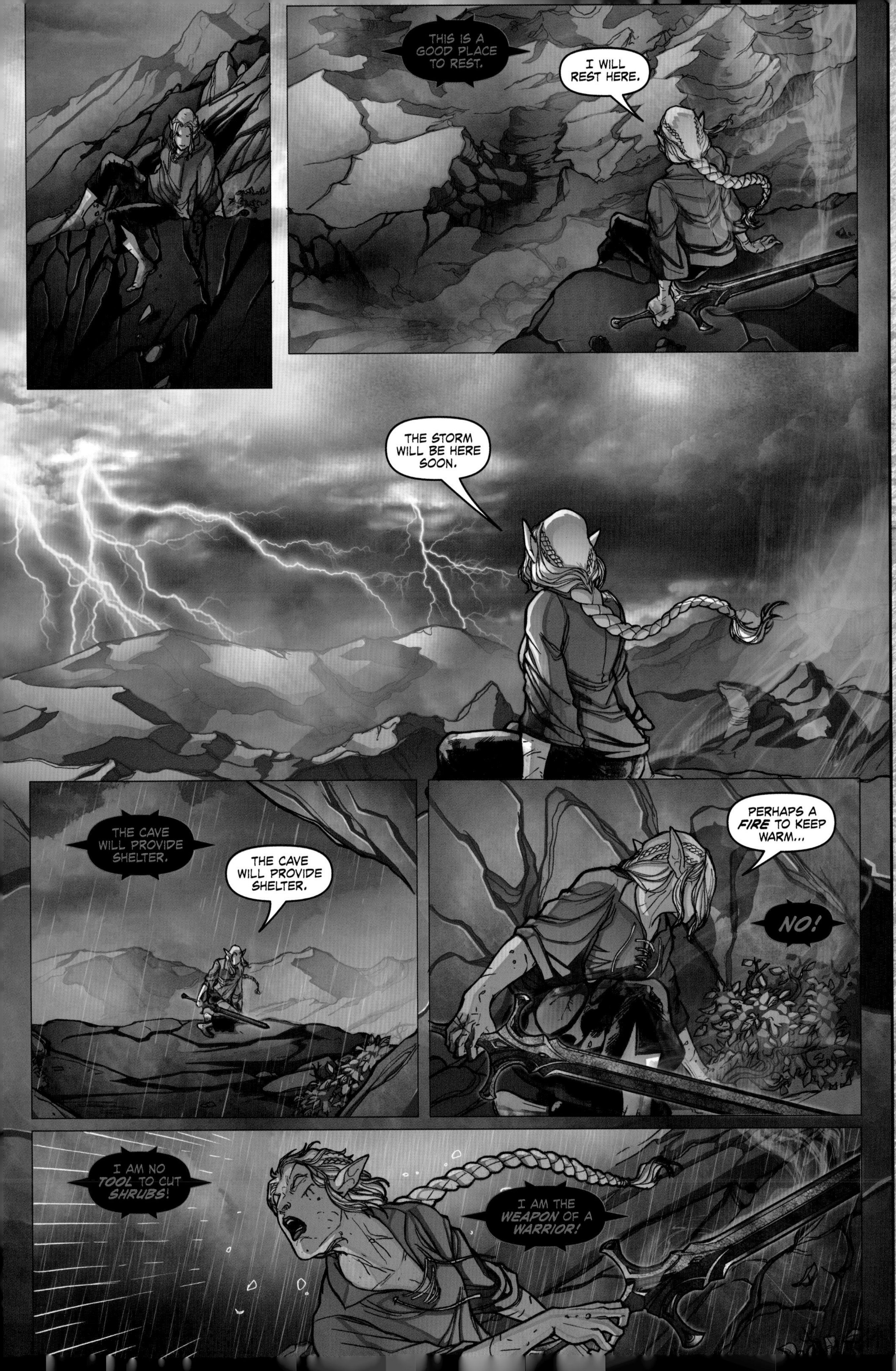
THIS IS A GOOD PLACE TO REST.
I WILL REST HERE.
THE STORM WILL BE HERE SOON.
THE CAVE WILL PROVIDE SHELTER.
THE CAVE WILL PROVIDE SHELTER.
PERHAPS A FIRE TO KEEP WARM...
NO!
I AM NO TOOL TO CUT SHRUBS!
I AM THE WEAPON OF A WARRIOR!

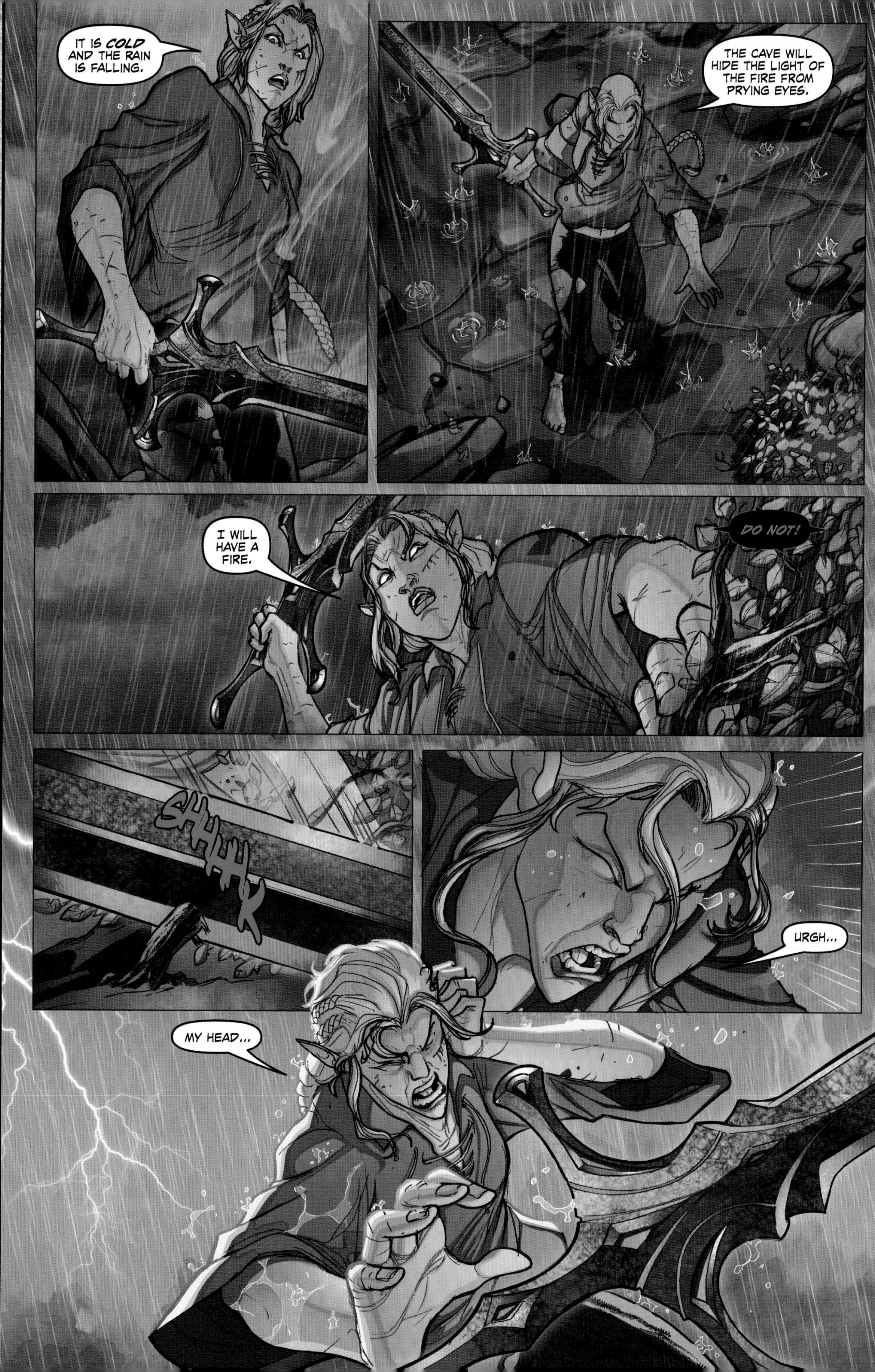
IT IS COLD AND THE RAIN IS FALLING.
THE CAVE WILL HIDE THE LIGHT OF THE FIRE FROM PRYING EYES.
I WILL HAVE A FIRE.
DO NOT!
SHHHK
URGH...
MY HEAD...

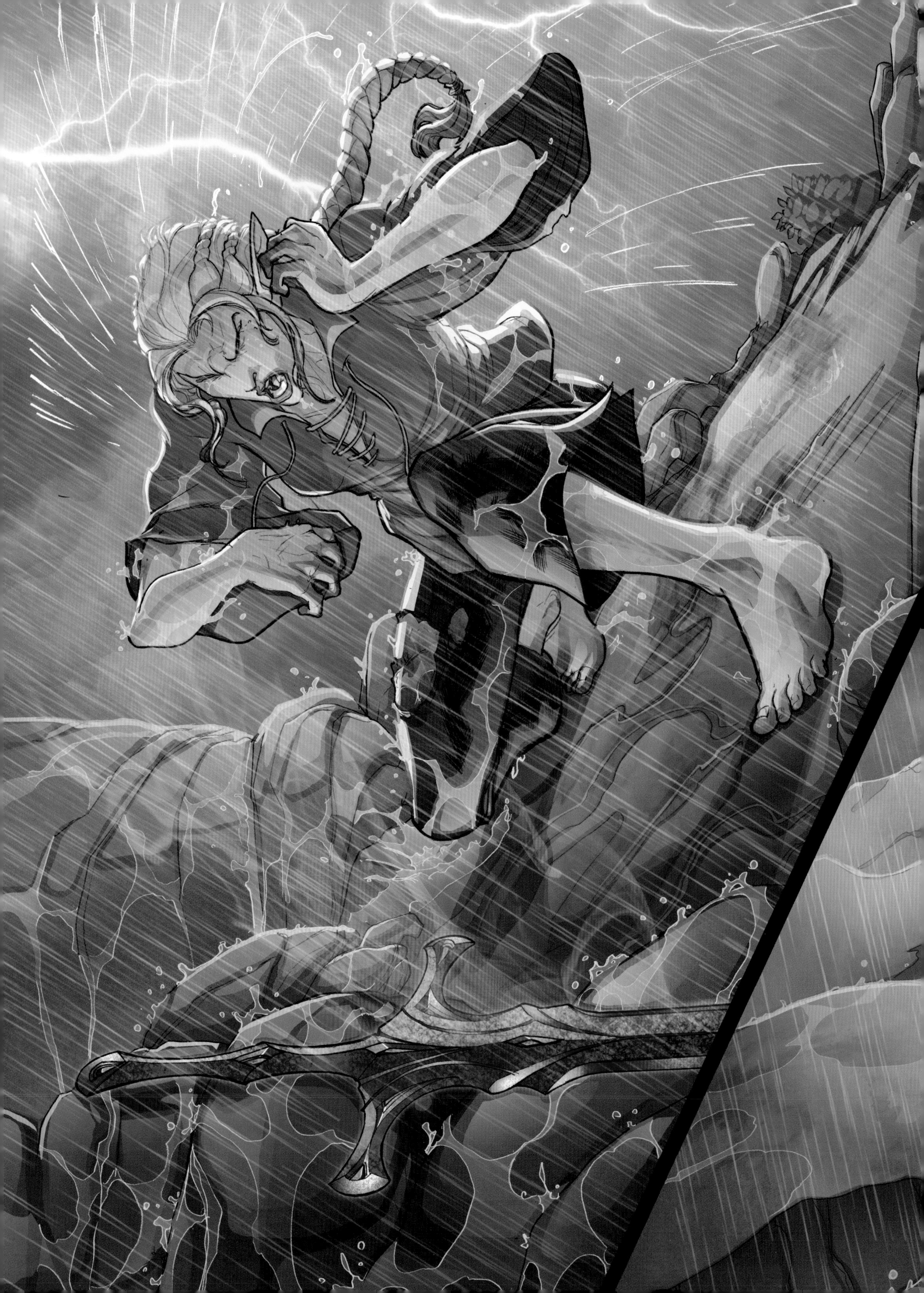

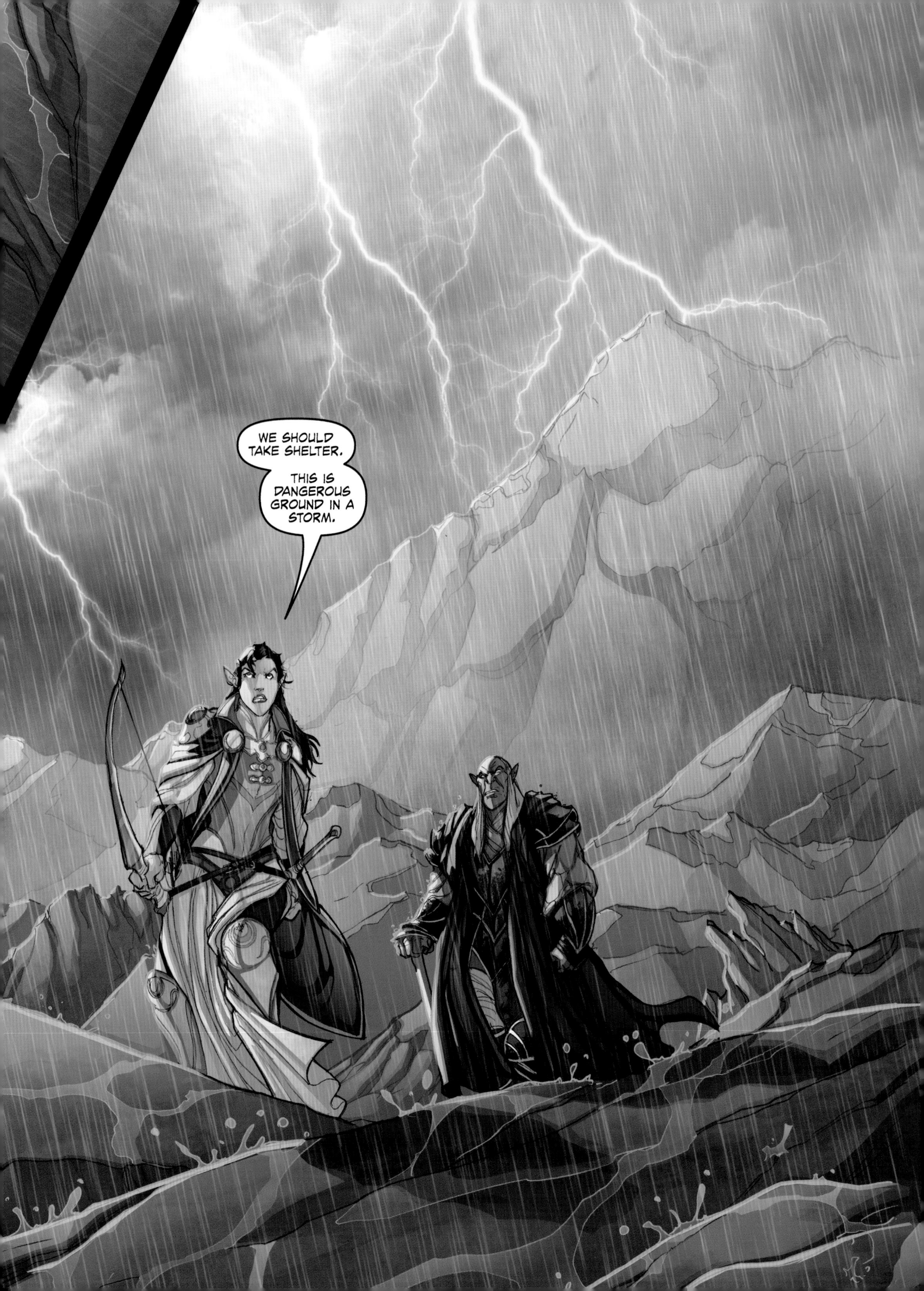
WE SHOULD TAKE SHELTER.
THIS IS DANGEROUS GROUND IN A STORM.

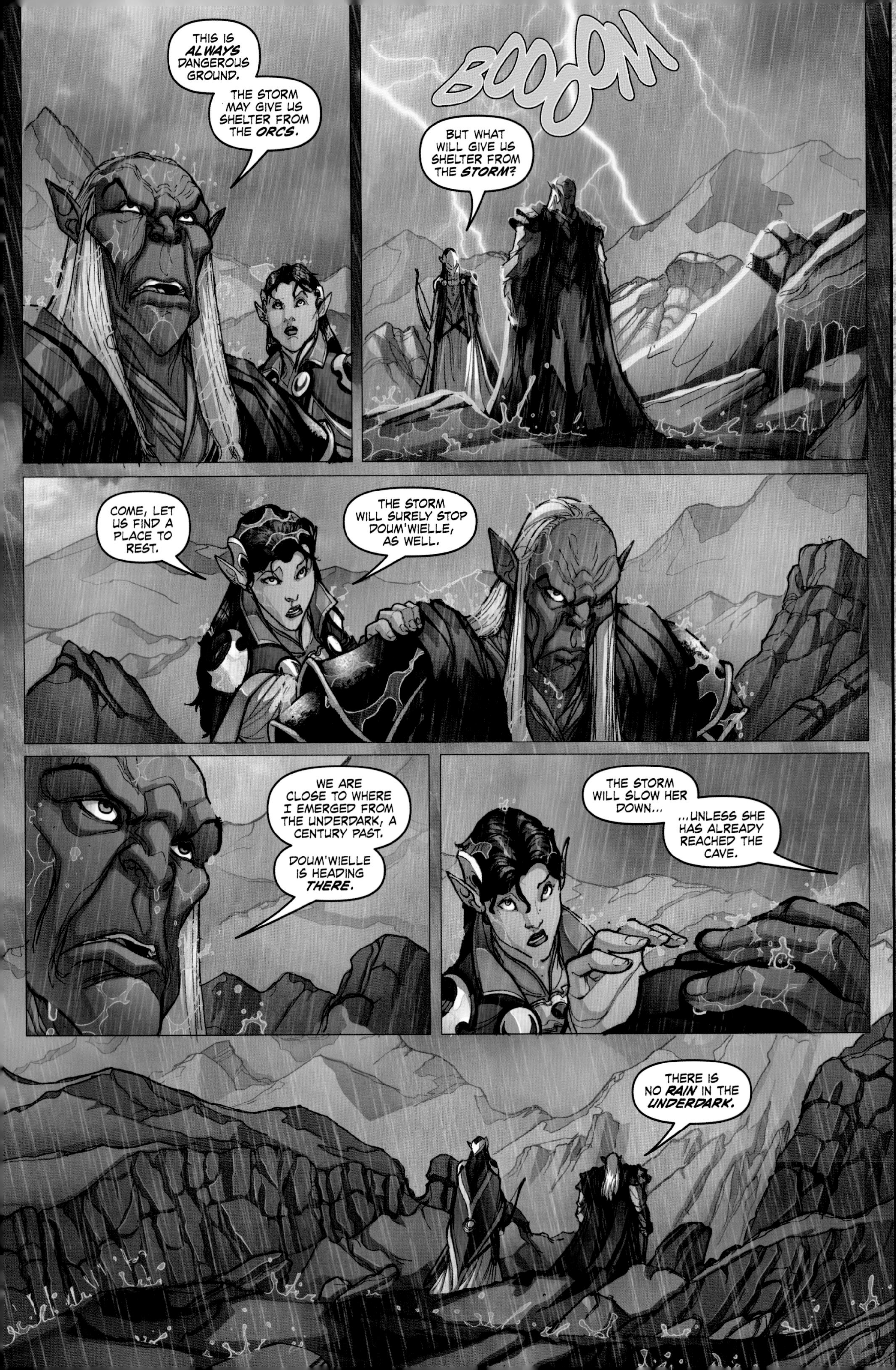
THIS IS ALWAYS DANGEROUS GROUND.
THE STORM MAY GIVE US SHELTER FROM THE ORCS.
BOOOOM
BUT WHAT WILL GIVE US SHELTER FROM THE STORM?
COME, LET US FIND A PLACE TO REST.
THE STORM WILL SURELY STOP DOUM'WIELLE, AS WELL.
WE ARE CLOSE TO WHERE I EMERGED FROM THE UNDERDARK, A CENTURY PAST.
DOUM'WIELLE IS HEADING THERE.
THE STORM WILL SLOW HER DOWN...
...UNLESS SHE HAS ALREADY REACHED THE CAVE.
THERE IS NO RAIN IN THE UNDERDARK.

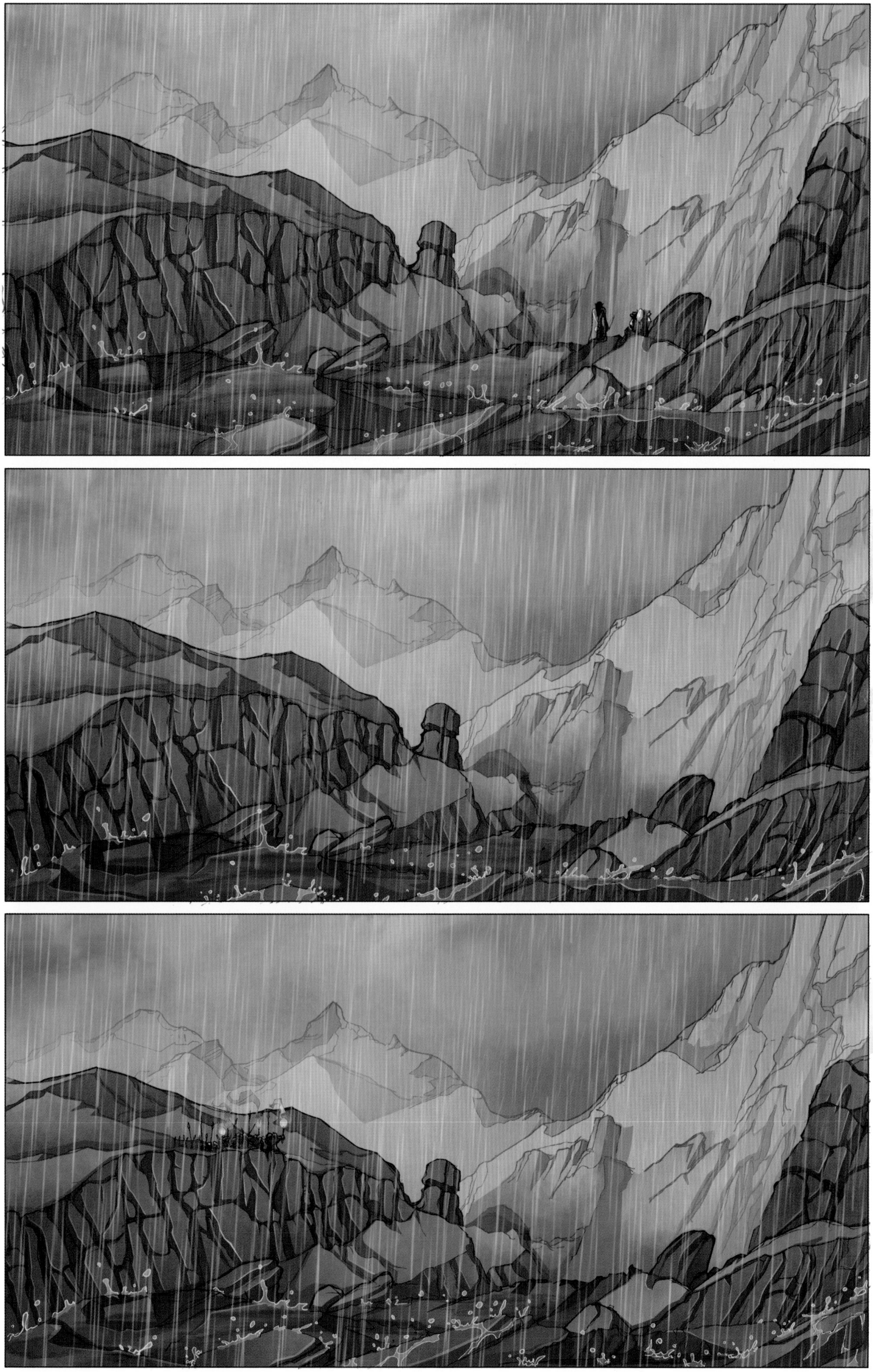

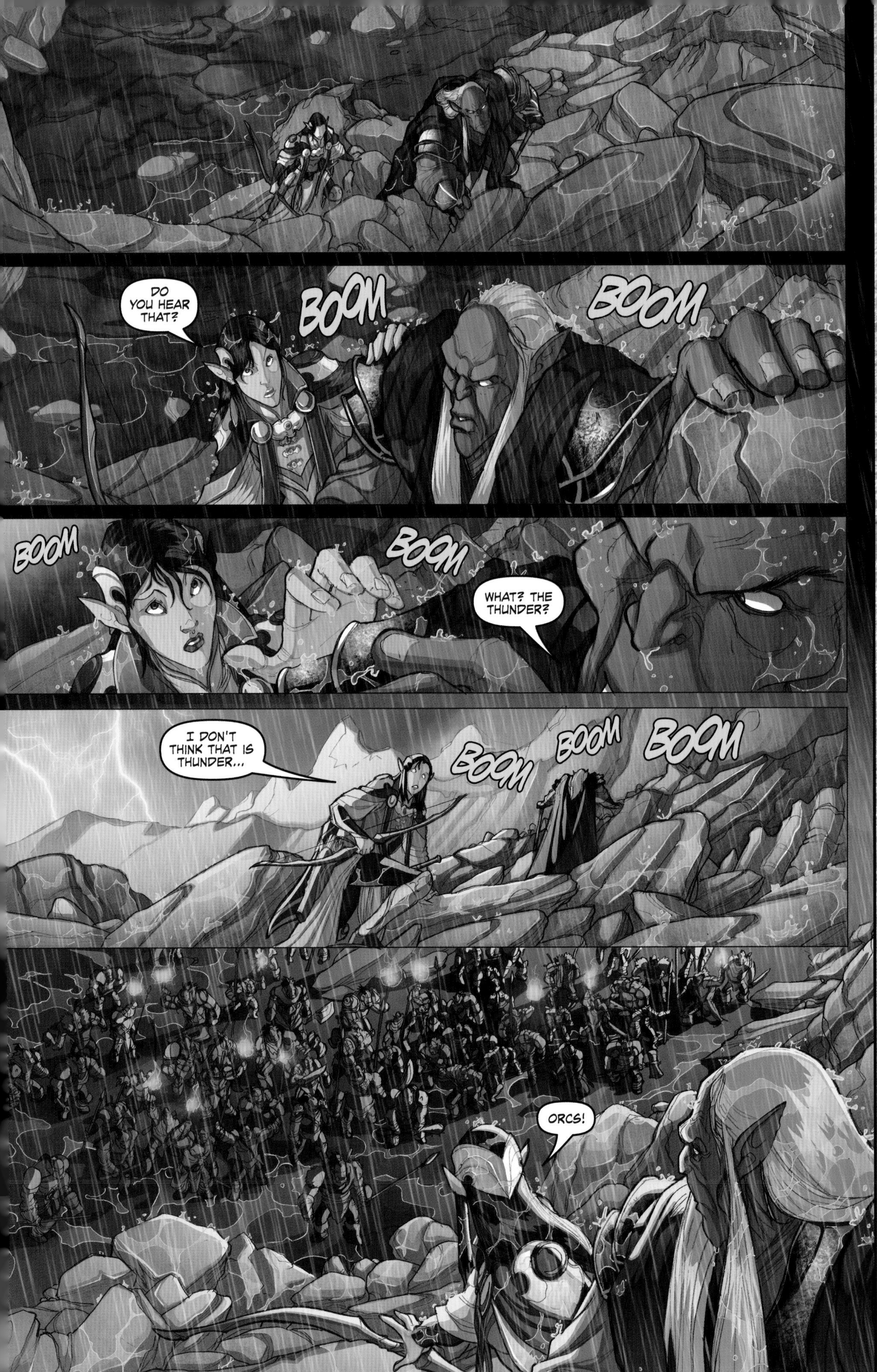
DO YOU HEAR THAT?
BOOM
BOOM
BOOM
BOOM
WHAT? THE THUNDER?
I DON'T THINK THAT IS THUNDER...
BOOM
BOOM
BOOM
ORCS!

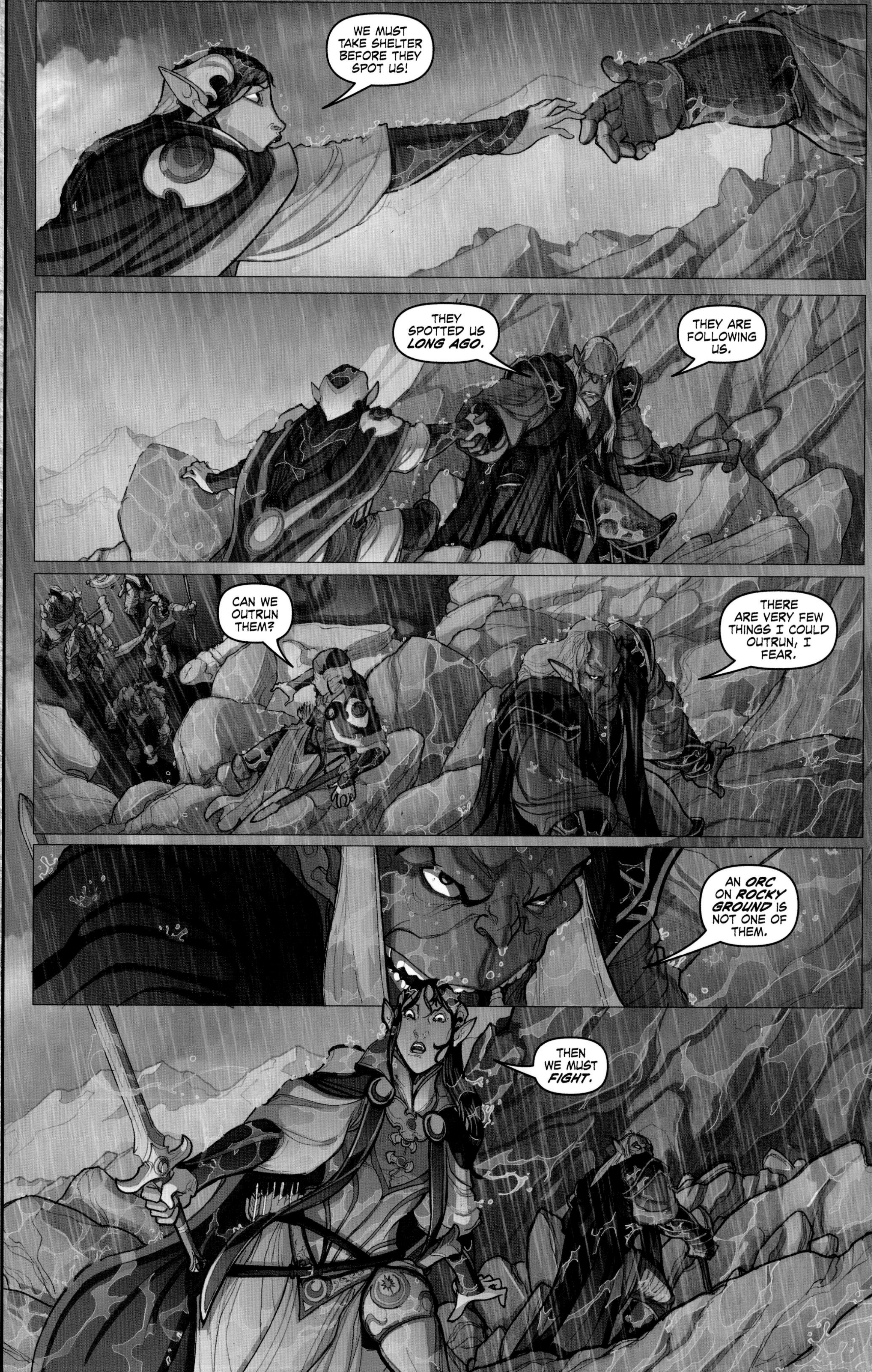
WE MUST TAKE SHELTER BEFORE THEY SPOT US!
THEY SPOTTED US *LONG AGO.*
THEY ARE FOLLOWING US.
CAN WE OUTRUN THEM?
THERE ARE VERY FEW THINGS I COULD OUTRUN, I FEAR.
AN *ORC* ON *ROCKY GROUND* IS NOT ONE OF THEM.
THEN WE MUST *FIGHT.*

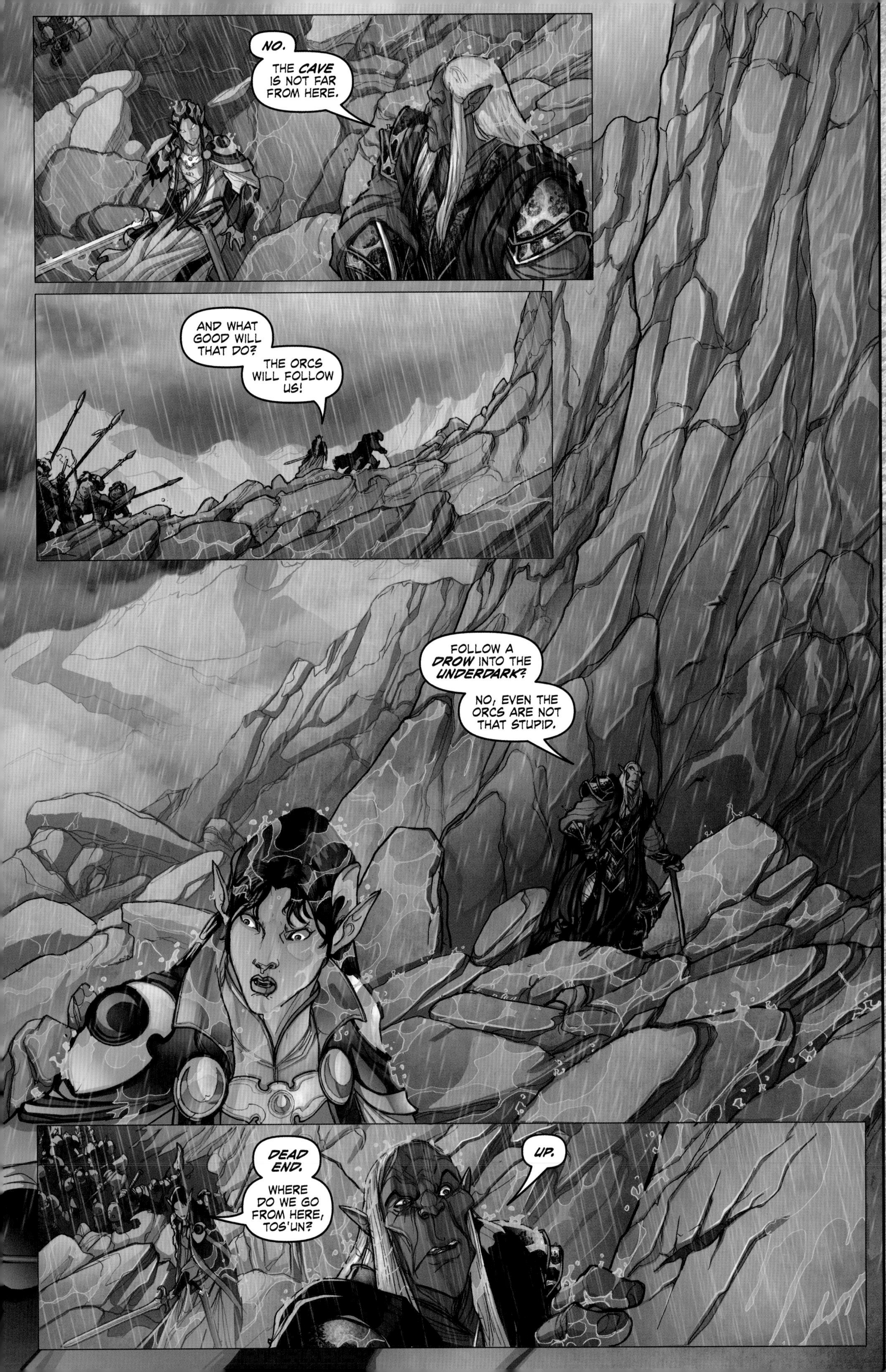
NO.
THE CAVE IS NOT FAR FROM HERE.
AND WHAT GOOD WILL THAT DO?
THE ORCS WILL FOLLOW US!
FOLLOW A DROW INTO THE UNDERDARK?
NO, EVEN THE ORCS ARE NOT THAT STUPID.
DEAD END.
WHERE DO WE GO FROM HERE, TOS'UN?
UP.

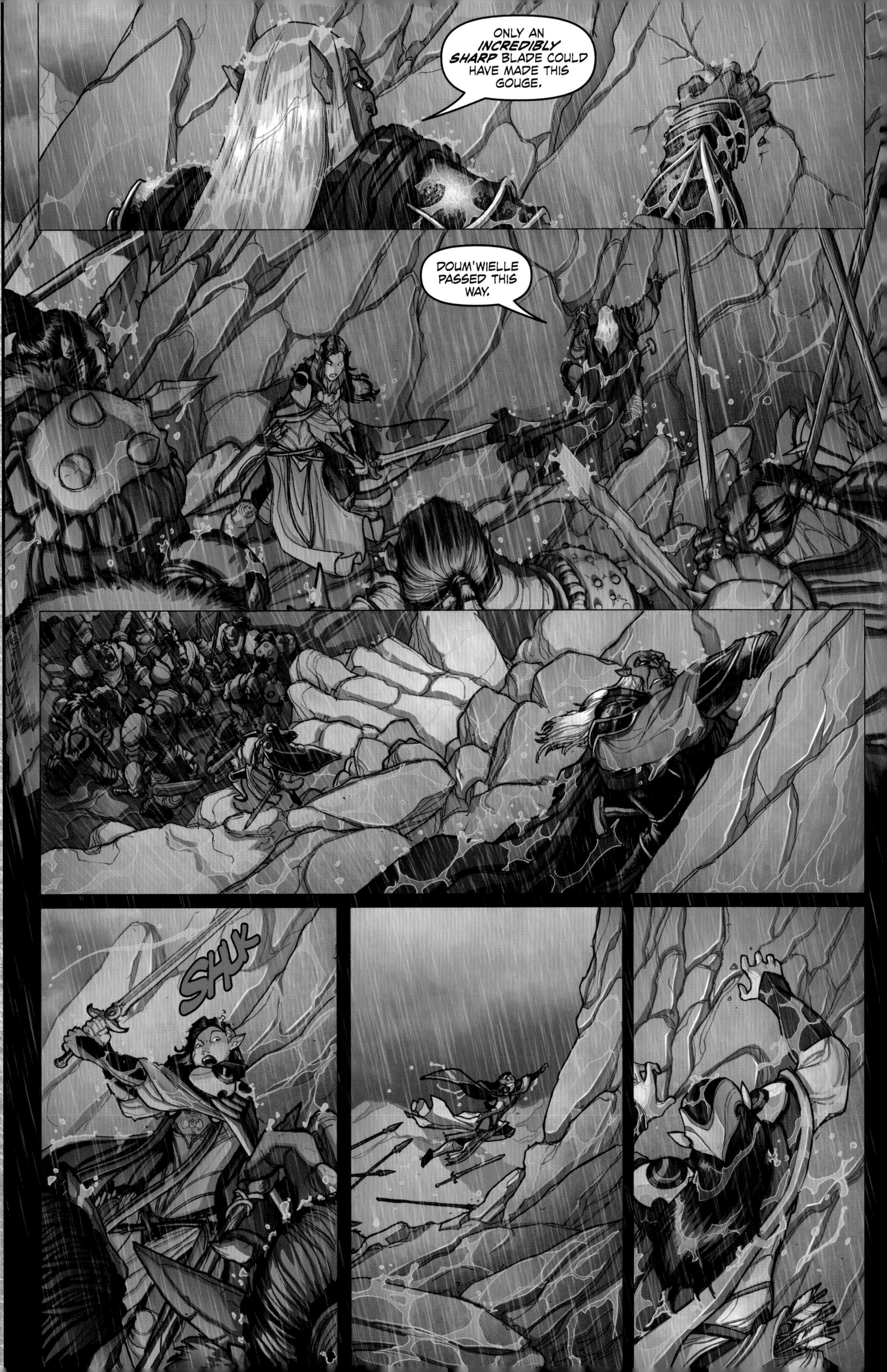
ONLY AN *INCREDIBLY SHARP* BLADE COULD HAVE MADE THIS GOUGE.
DOUM'WIELLE PASSED THIS WAY.
SHUK

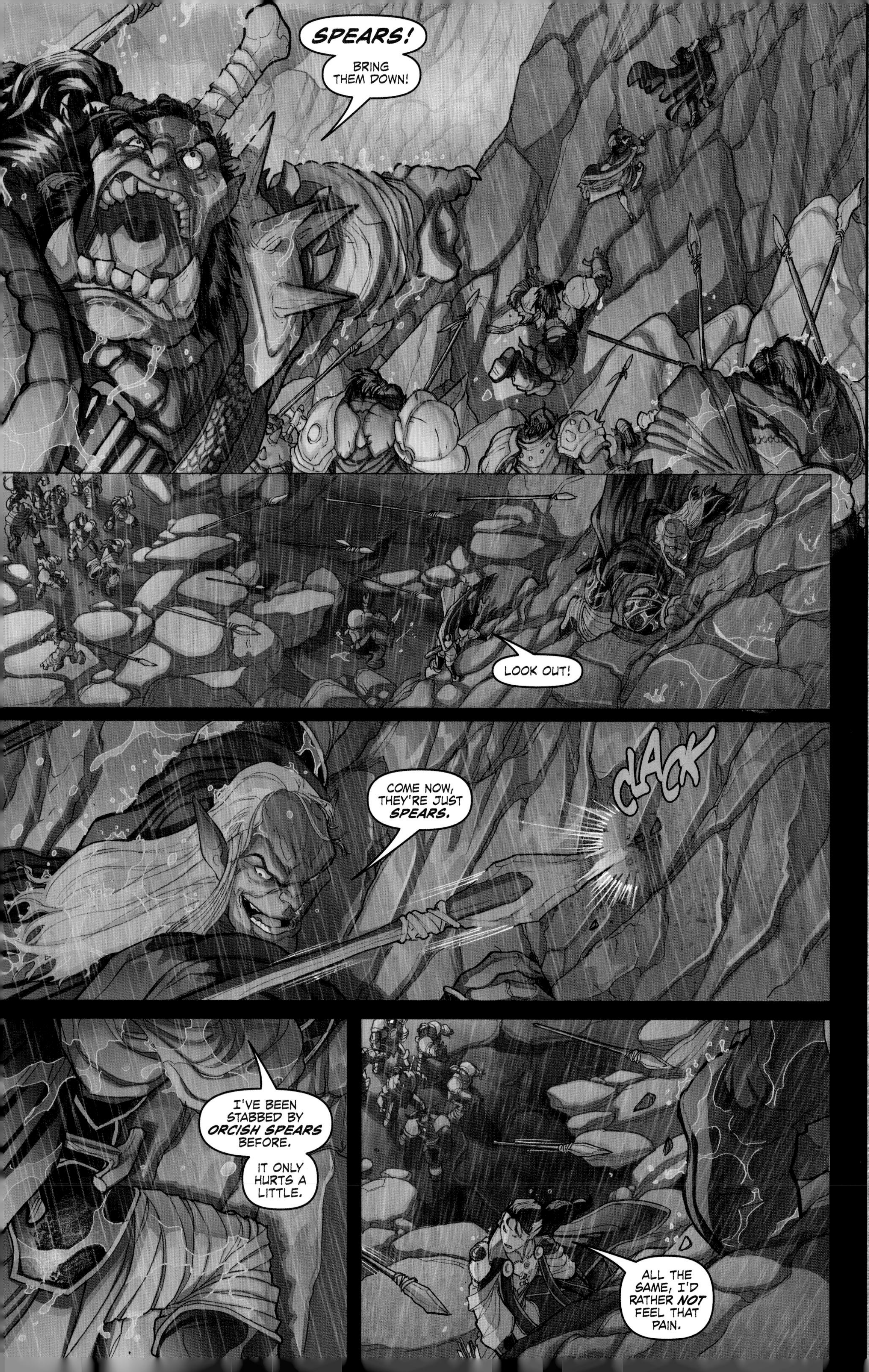
SPEARS! BRING THEM DOWN!
LOOK OUT!
COME NOW, THEY'RE JUST SPEARS.
CLACK
I'VE BEEN STABBED BY ORCISH SPEARS BEFORE.
IT ONLY HURTS A LITTLE.
ALL THE SAME, I'D RATHER NOT FEEL THAT PAIN.

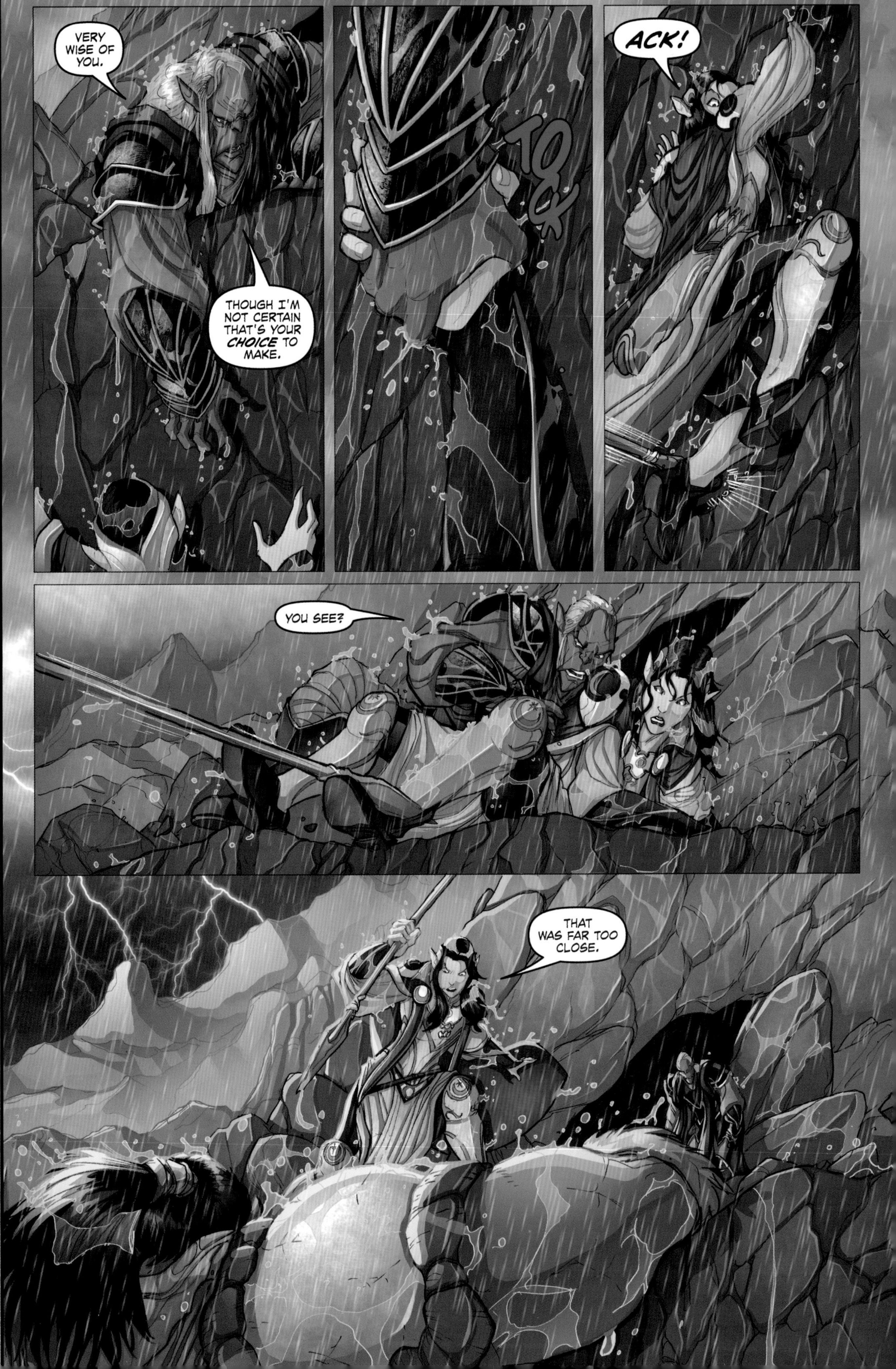
VERY WISE OF YOU.
THOUGH I'M NOT CERTAIN THAT'S YOUR CHOICE TO MAKE.
TOK
ACK!
YOU SEE?
THAT WAS FAR TOO CLOSE.

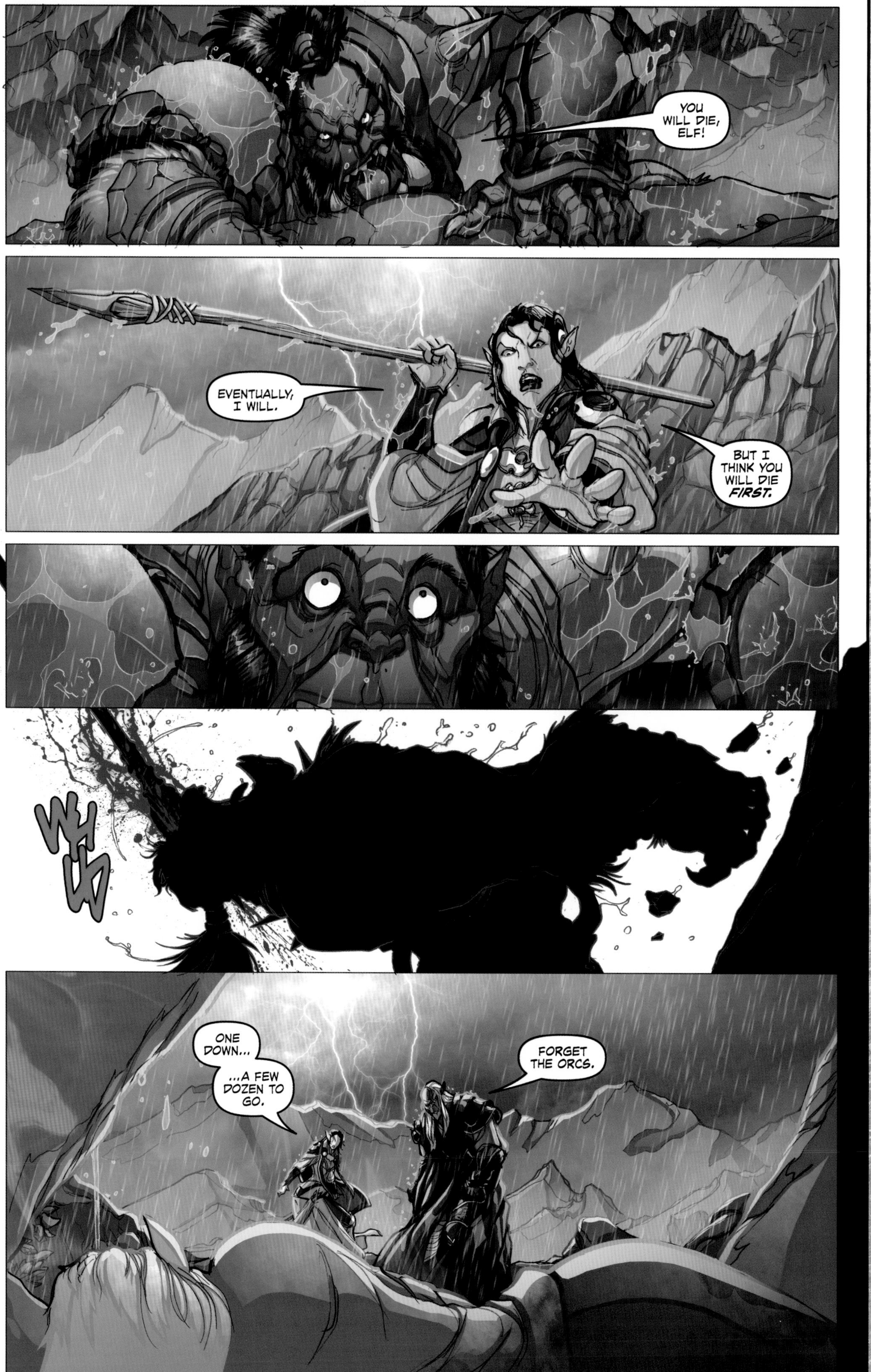
YOU WILL DIE, ELF!
EVENTUALLY, I WILL.
BUT I THINK YOU WILL DIE *FIRST.*
WHUD
ONE DOWN...
...A FEW DOZEN TO GO.
FORGET THE ORCS.

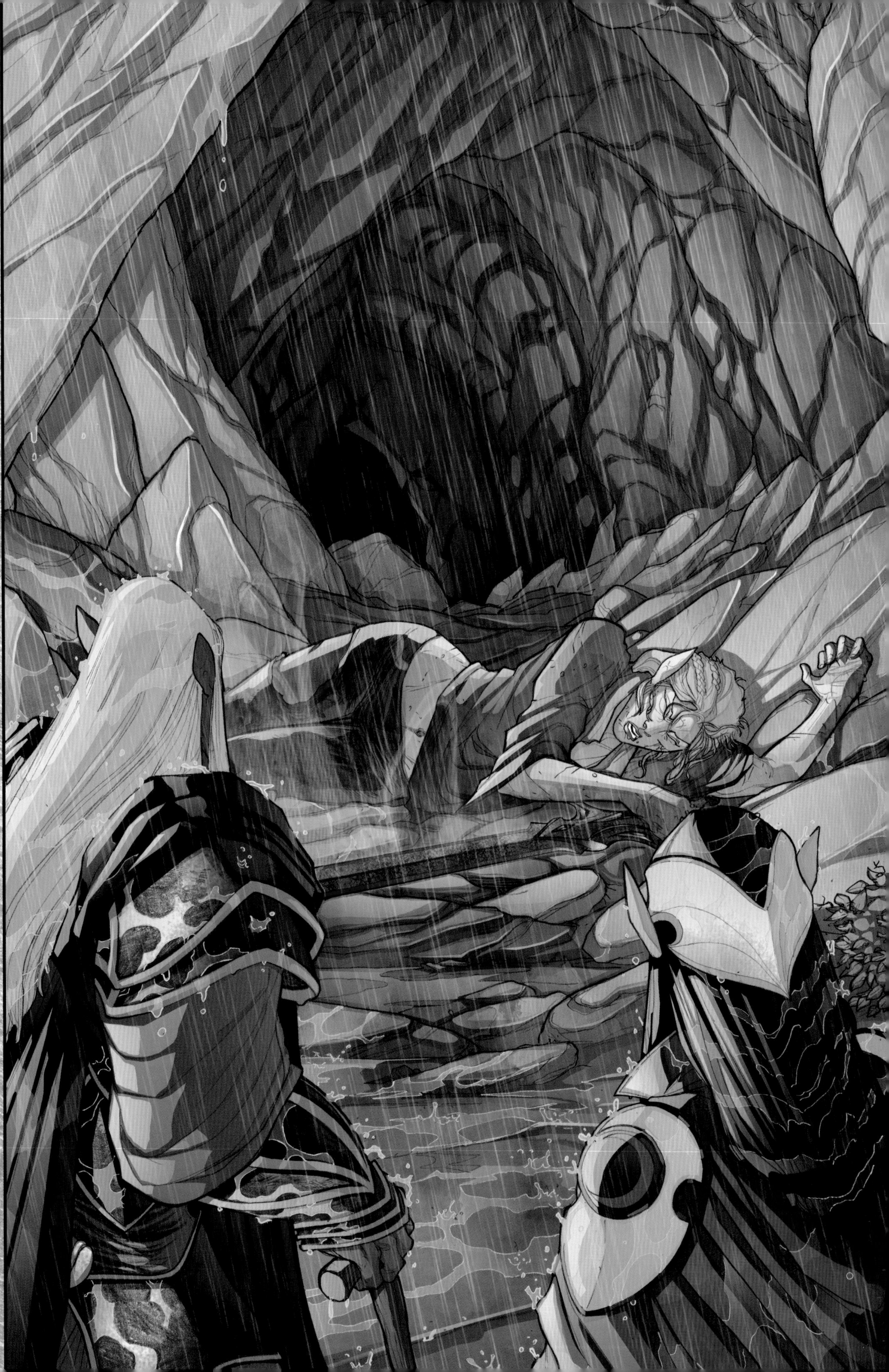

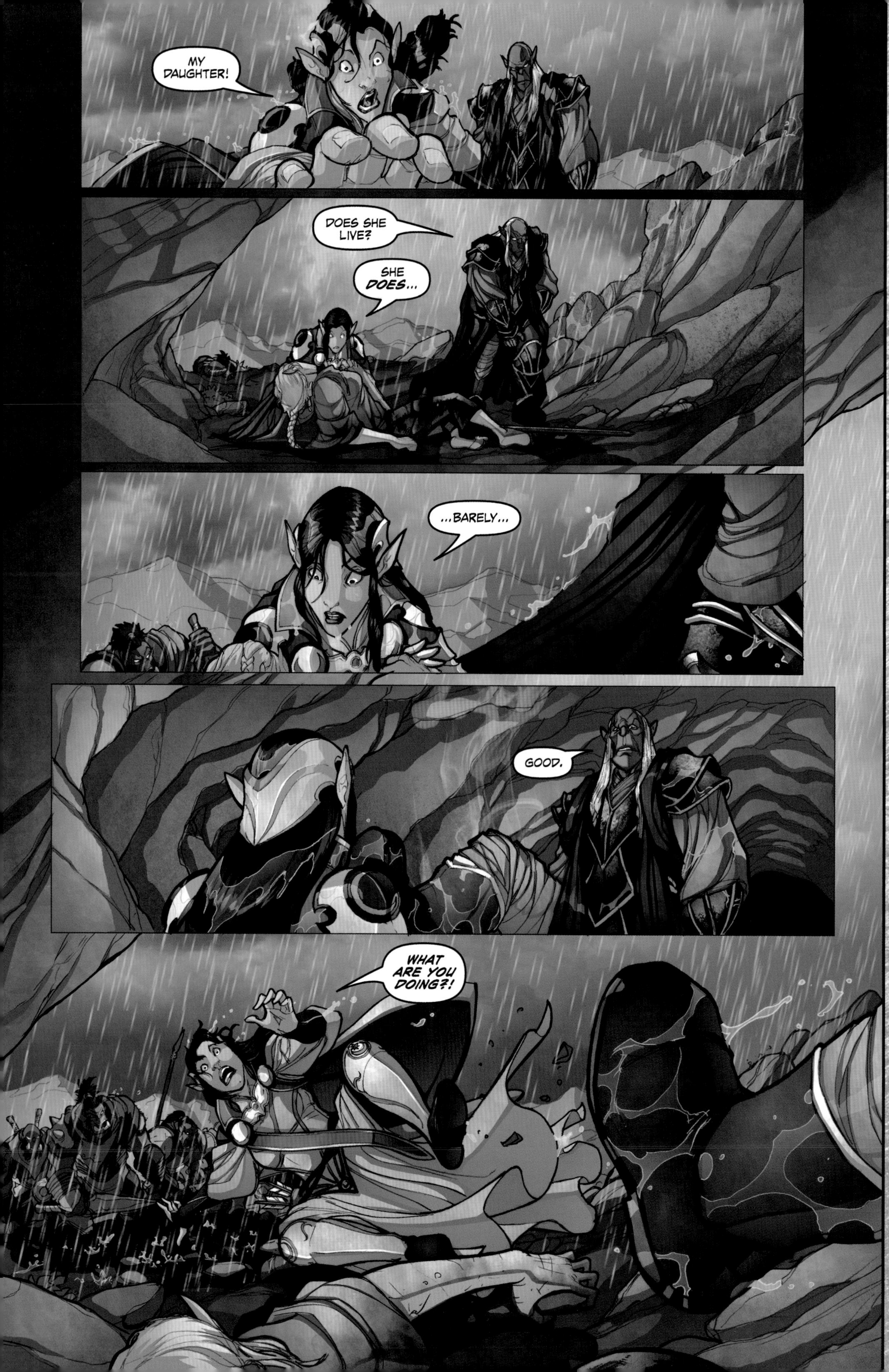
MY DAUGHTER!
DOES SHE LIVE?
SHE *DOES*...
...BARELY...
GOOD.
WHAT ARE YOU DOING?!

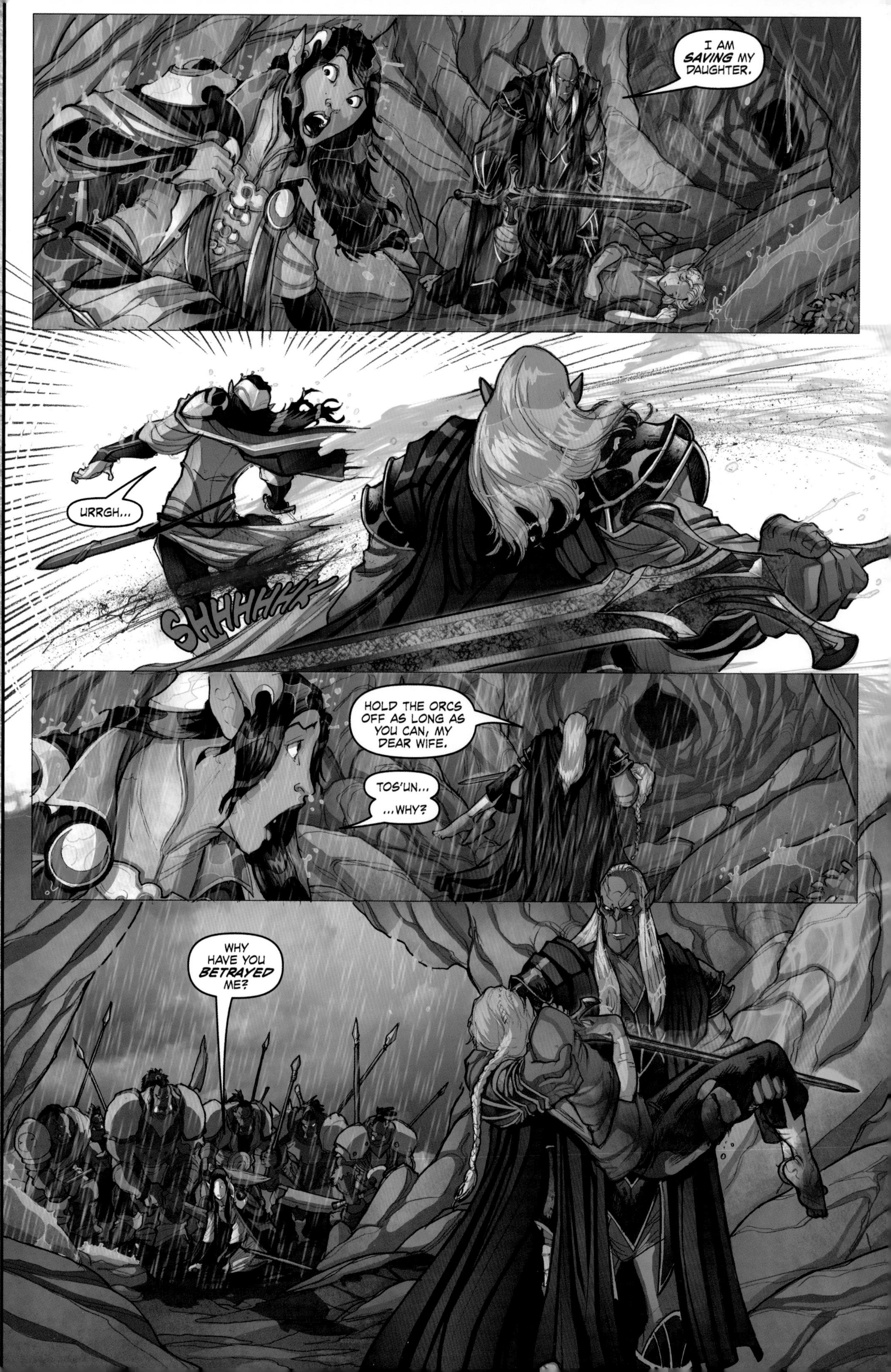
I AM SAVING MY DAUGHTER.
URRGH...
SHHHHKK
HOLD THE ORCS OFF AS LONG AS YOU CAN, MY DEAR WIFE.
TOS'UN...
...WHY?
WHY HAVE YOU BETRAYED ME?

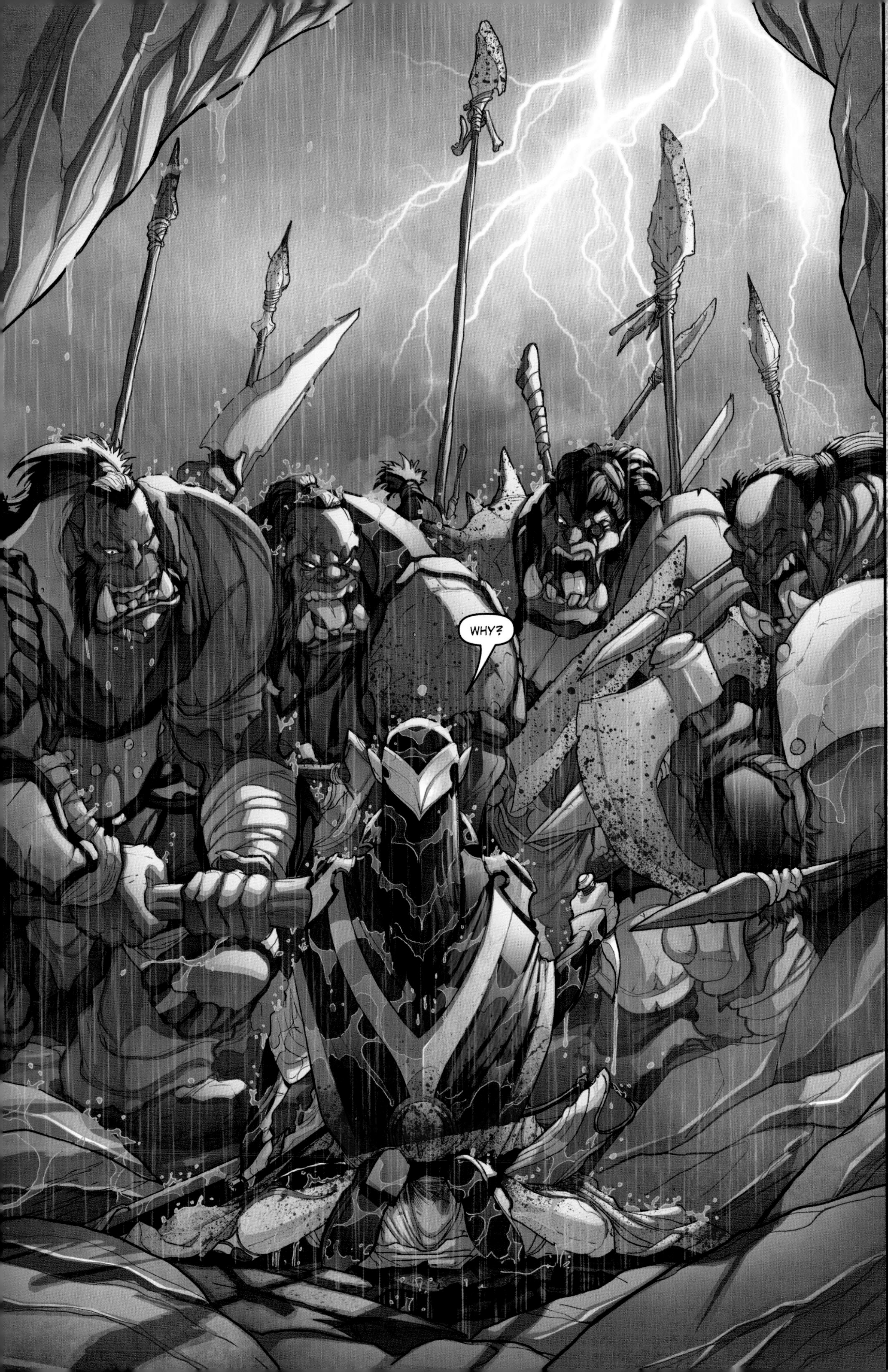
WHY?

Art by David Baldeon
Colors by David Garcia Cruz

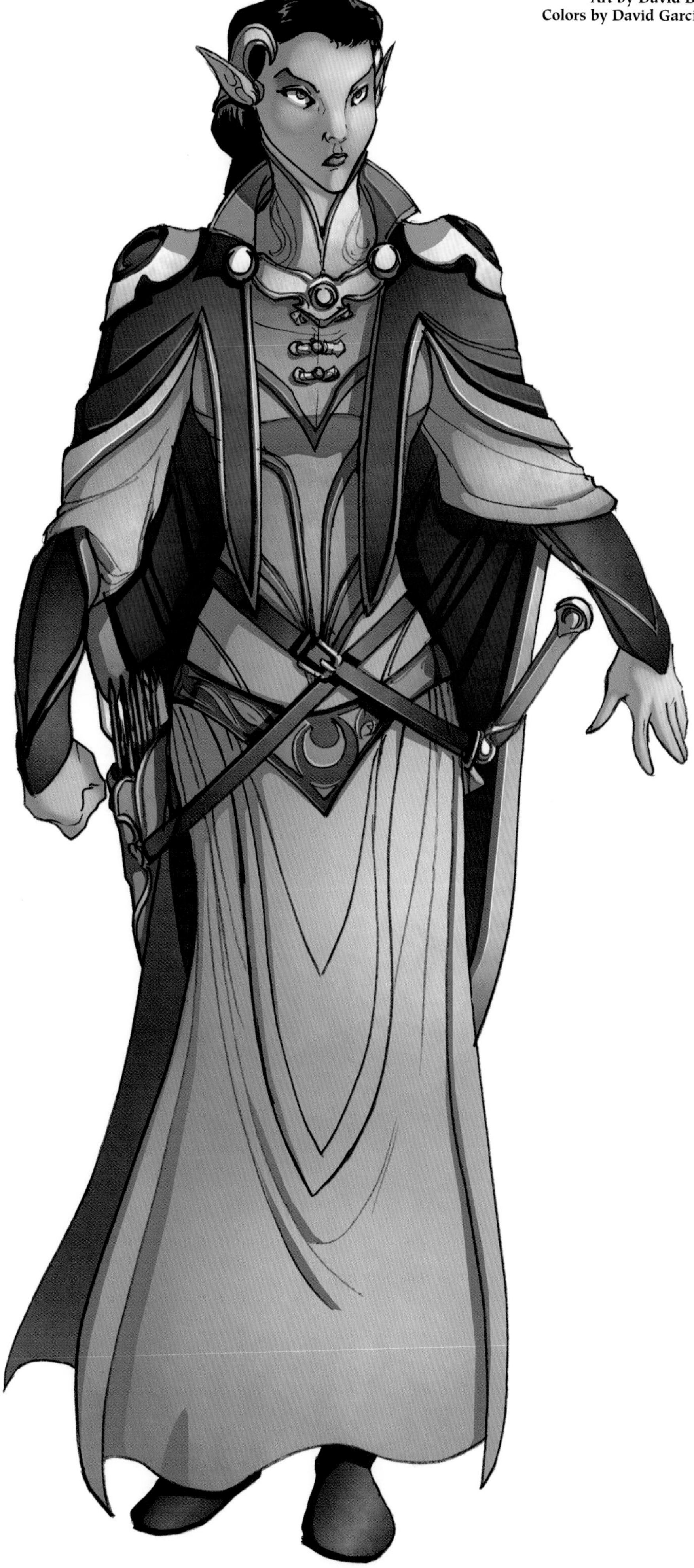

Art by Steve Ellis

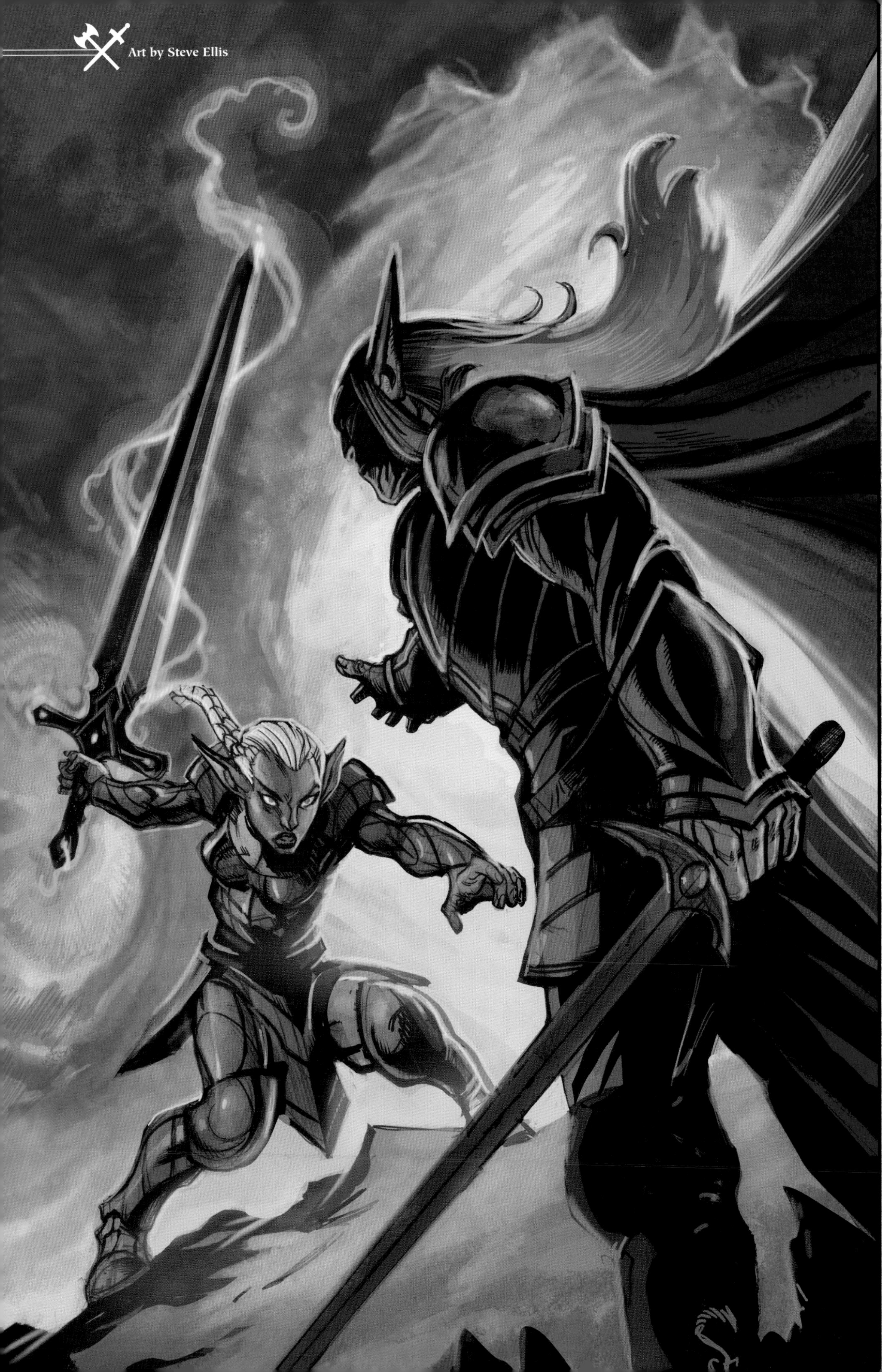

CHAPTER 5

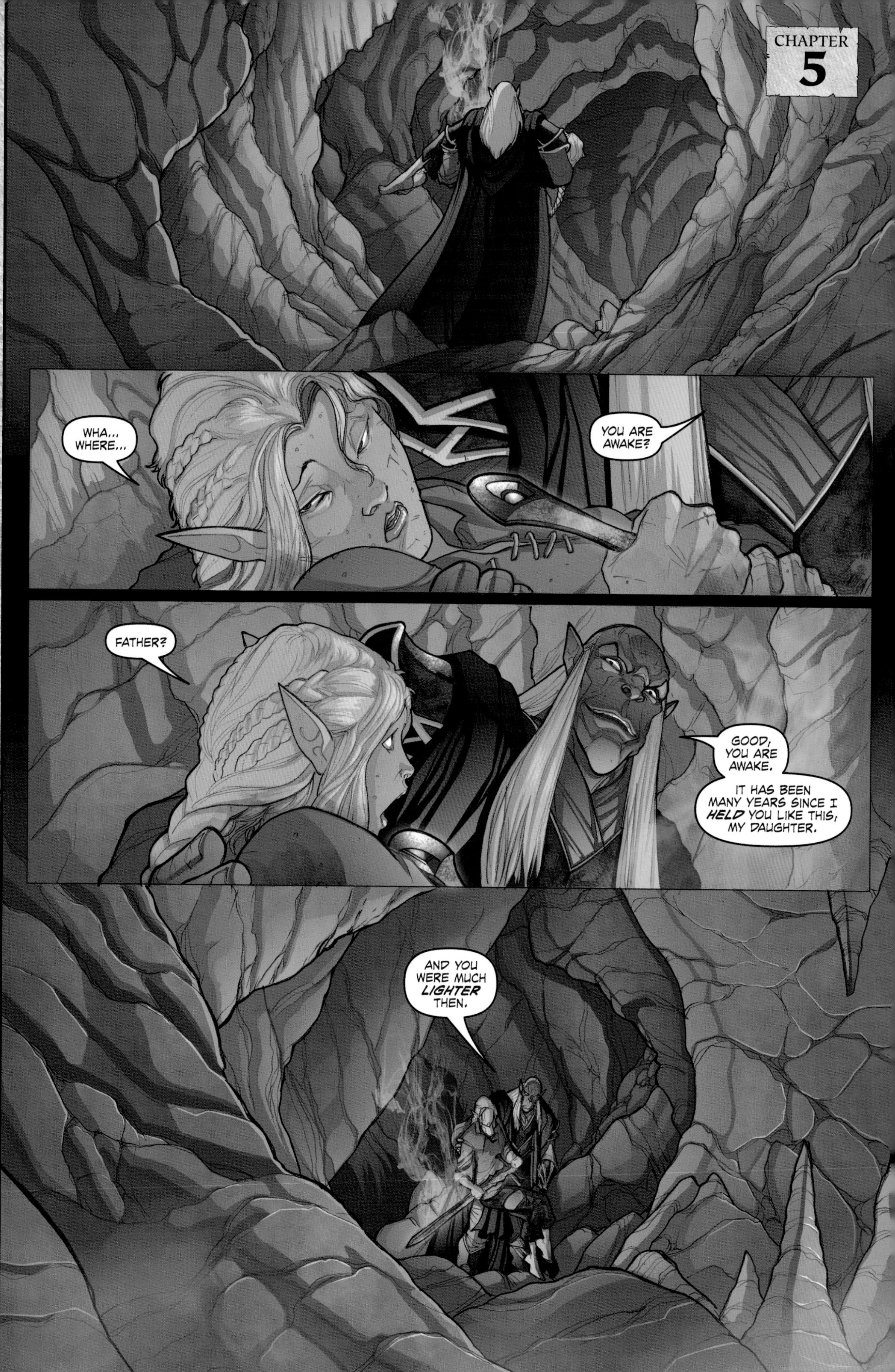
WHA... WHERE...
YOU ARE AWAKE?
FATHER?
GOOD, YOU ARE AWAKE.
IT HAS BEEN MANY YEARS SINCE I HELD YOU LIKE THIS, MY DAUGHTER.
AND YOU WERE MUCH LIGHTER THEN.

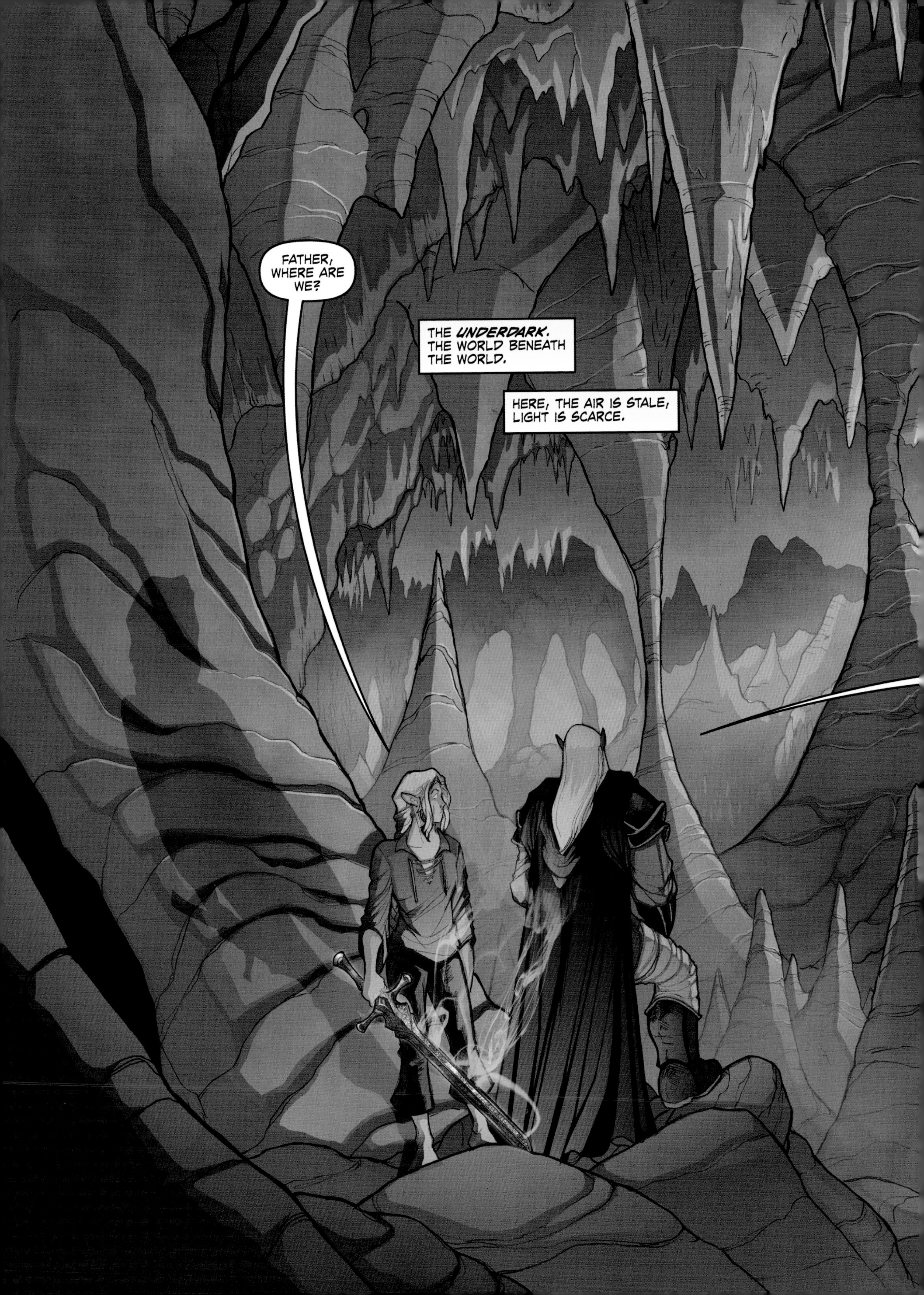
FATHER, WHERE ARE WE?
THE UNDERDARK. THE WORLD BENEATH THE WORLD.
HERE, THE AIR IS STALE, LIGHT IS SCARCE.

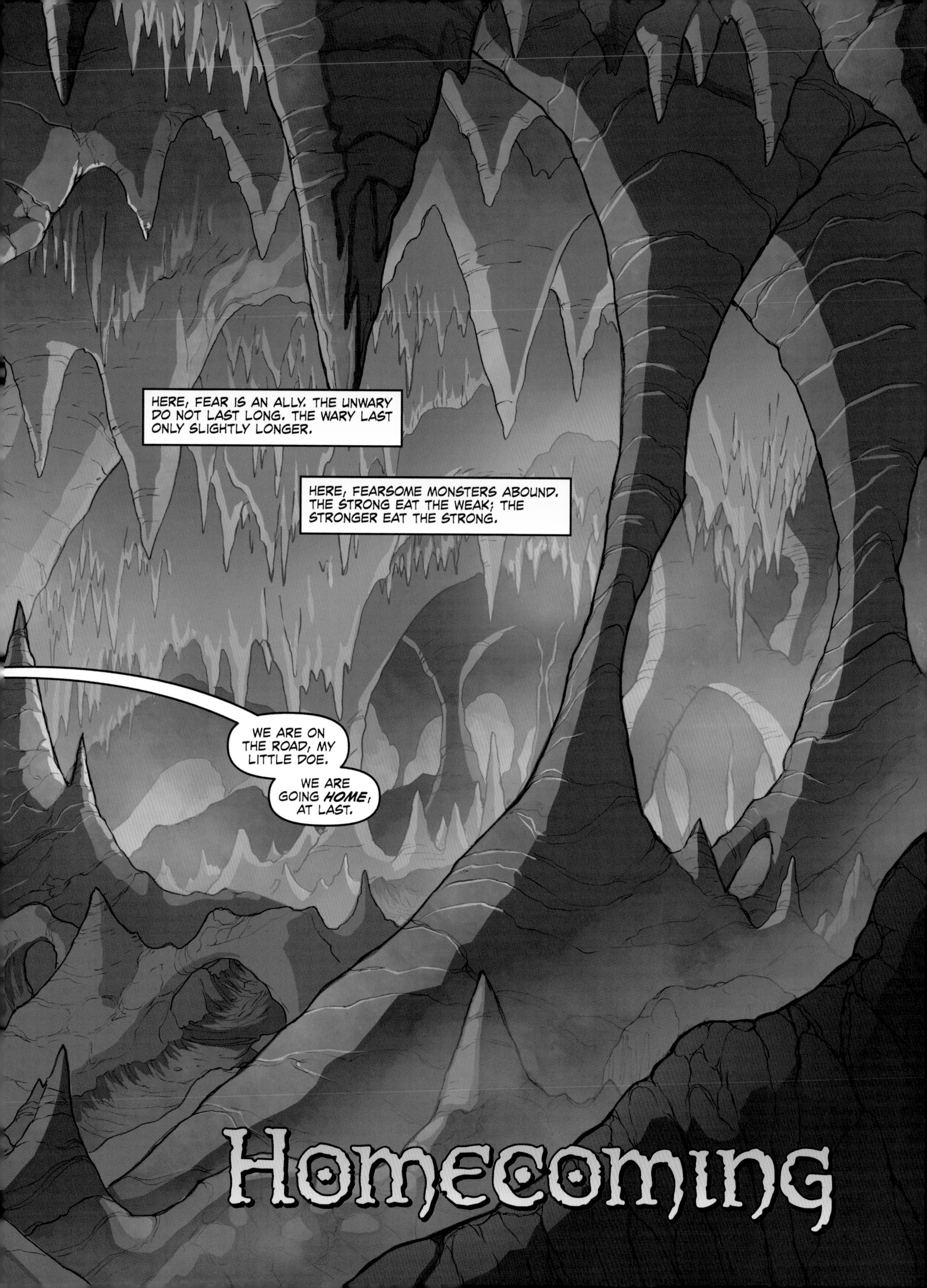
HERE, FEAR IS AN ALLY. THE UNWARY DO NOT LAST LONG. THE WARY LAST ONLY SLIGHTLY LONGER.
HERE, FEARSOME MONSTERS ABOUND. THE STRONG EAT THE WEAK; THE STRONGER EAT THE STRONG.
WE ARE ON THE ROAD, MY LITTLE DOE.
WE ARE GOING *HOME*, AT LAST.
Homecoming

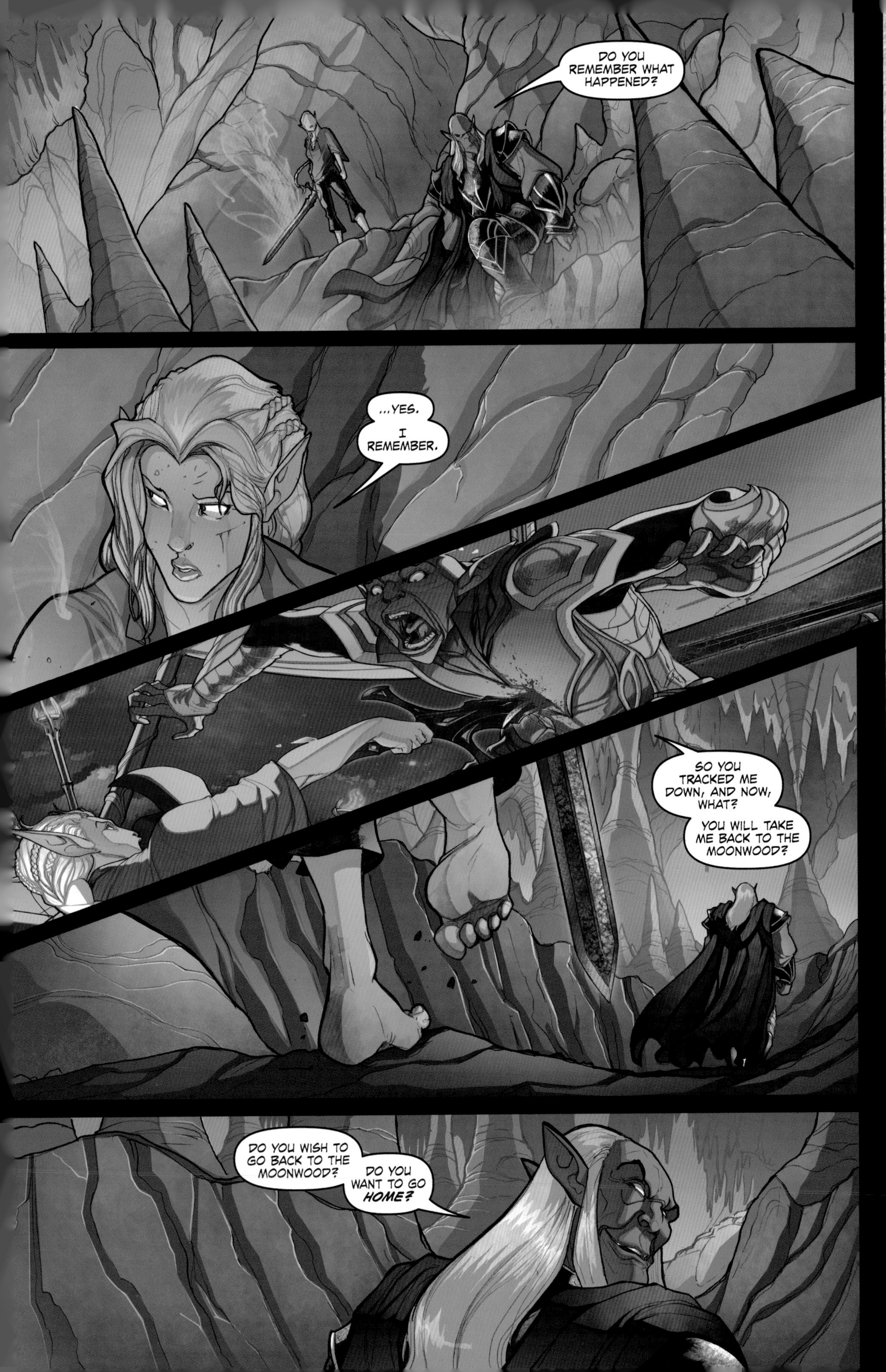
DO YOU REMEMBER WHAT HAPPENED?
...YES.
I REMEMBER.
SO YOU TRACKED ME DOWN, AND NOW, WHAT?
YOU WILL TAKE ME BACK TO THE MOONWOOD?
DO YOU WISH TO GO BACK TO THE MOONWOOD?
DO YOU WANT TO GO *HOME?*

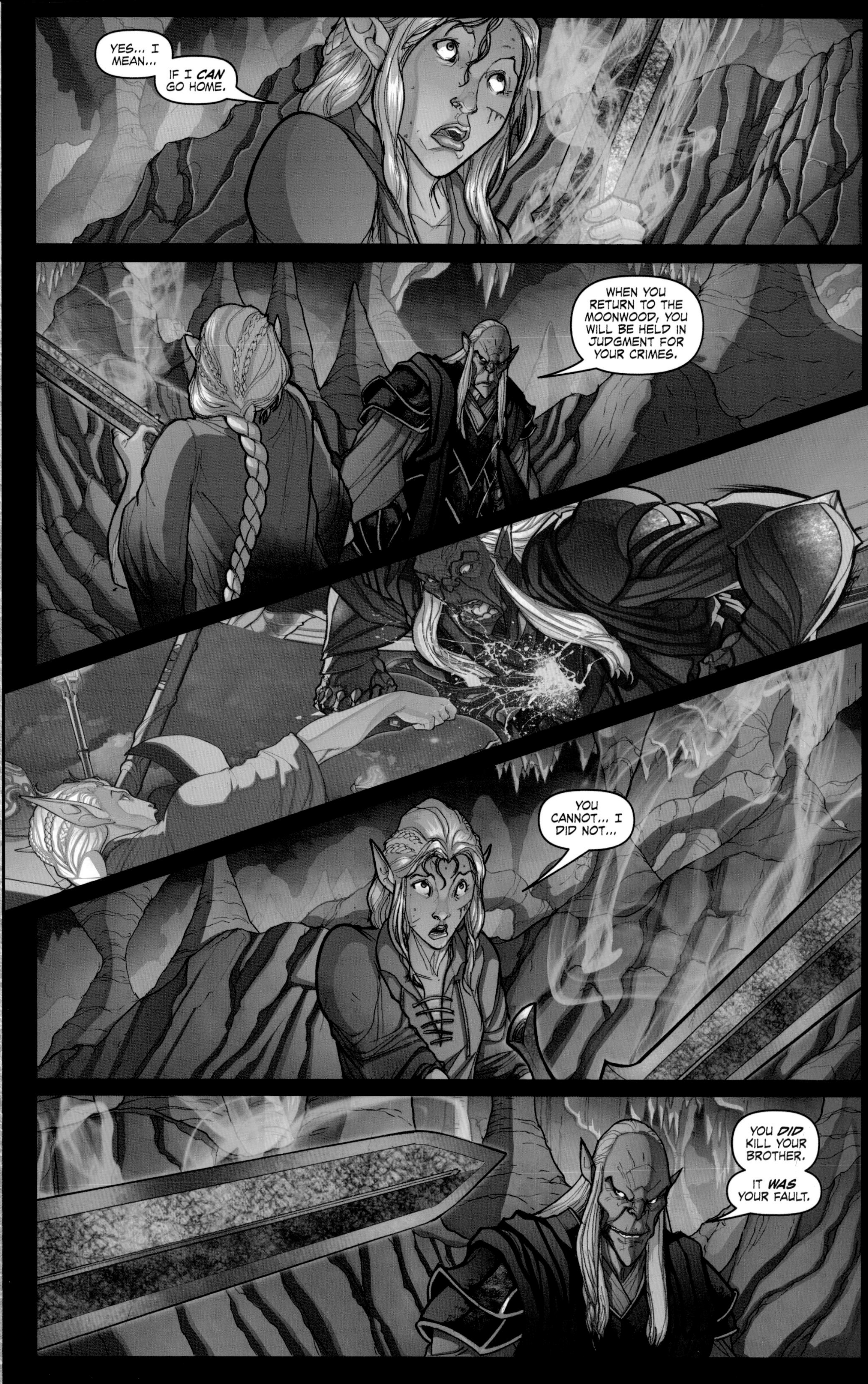
YES... I MEAN...
IF I CAN GO HOME.
WHEN YOU RETURN TO THE MOONWOOD, YOU WILL BE HELD IN JUDGMENT FOR YOUR CRIMES.
YOU CANNOT... I DID NOT...
YOU DID KILL YOUR BROTHER.
IT WAS YOUR FAULT.

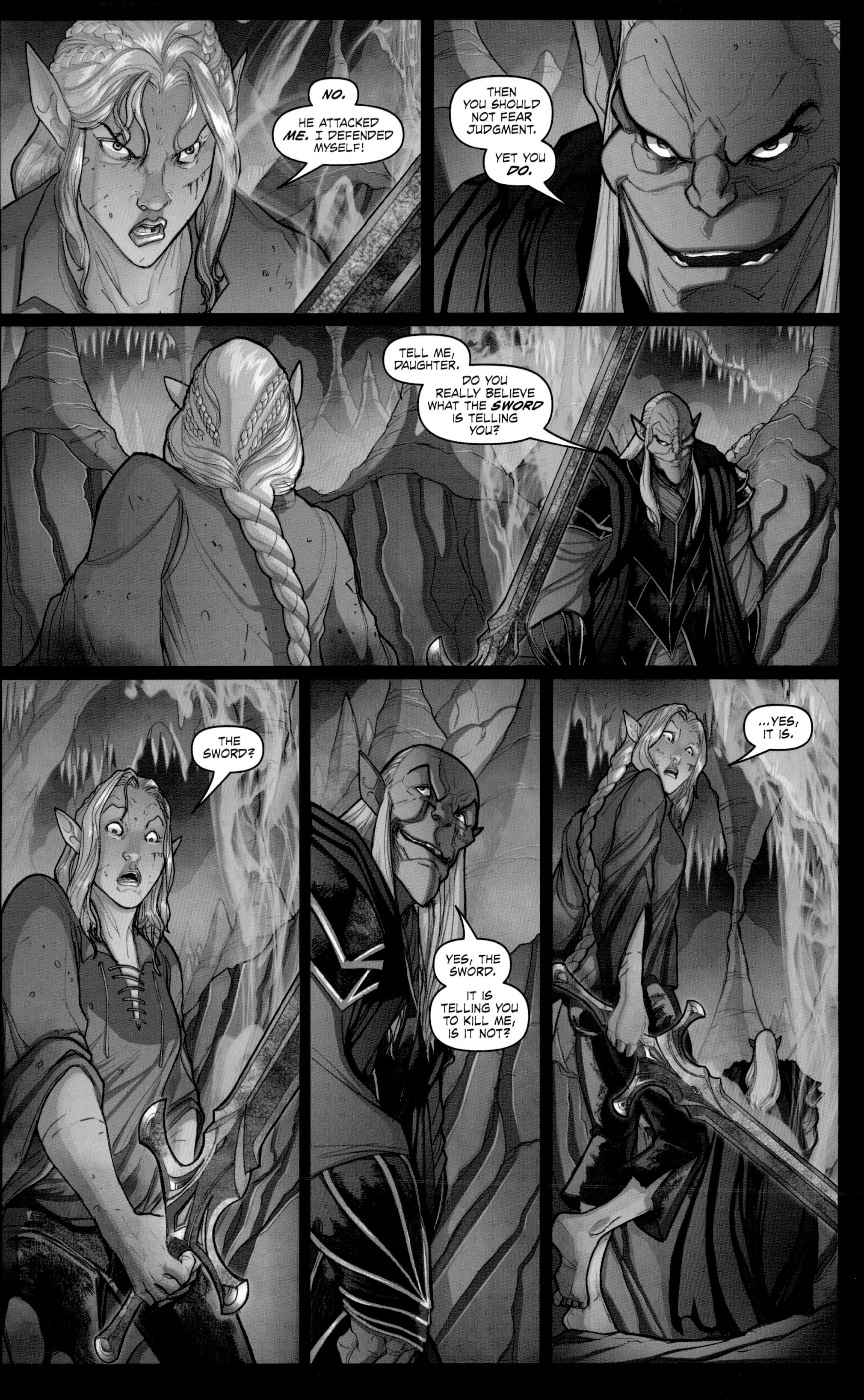

NO.
HE ATTACKED ME. I DEFENDED MYSELF!
THEN YOU SHOULD NOT FEAR JUDGMENT.
YET YOU DO.
TELL ME, DAUGHTER.
DO YOU REALLY BELIEVE WHAT THE SWORD IS TELLING YOU?
THE SWORD?
YES, THE SWORD.
IT IS TELLING YOU TO KILL ME, IS IT NOT?
...YES, IT IS.

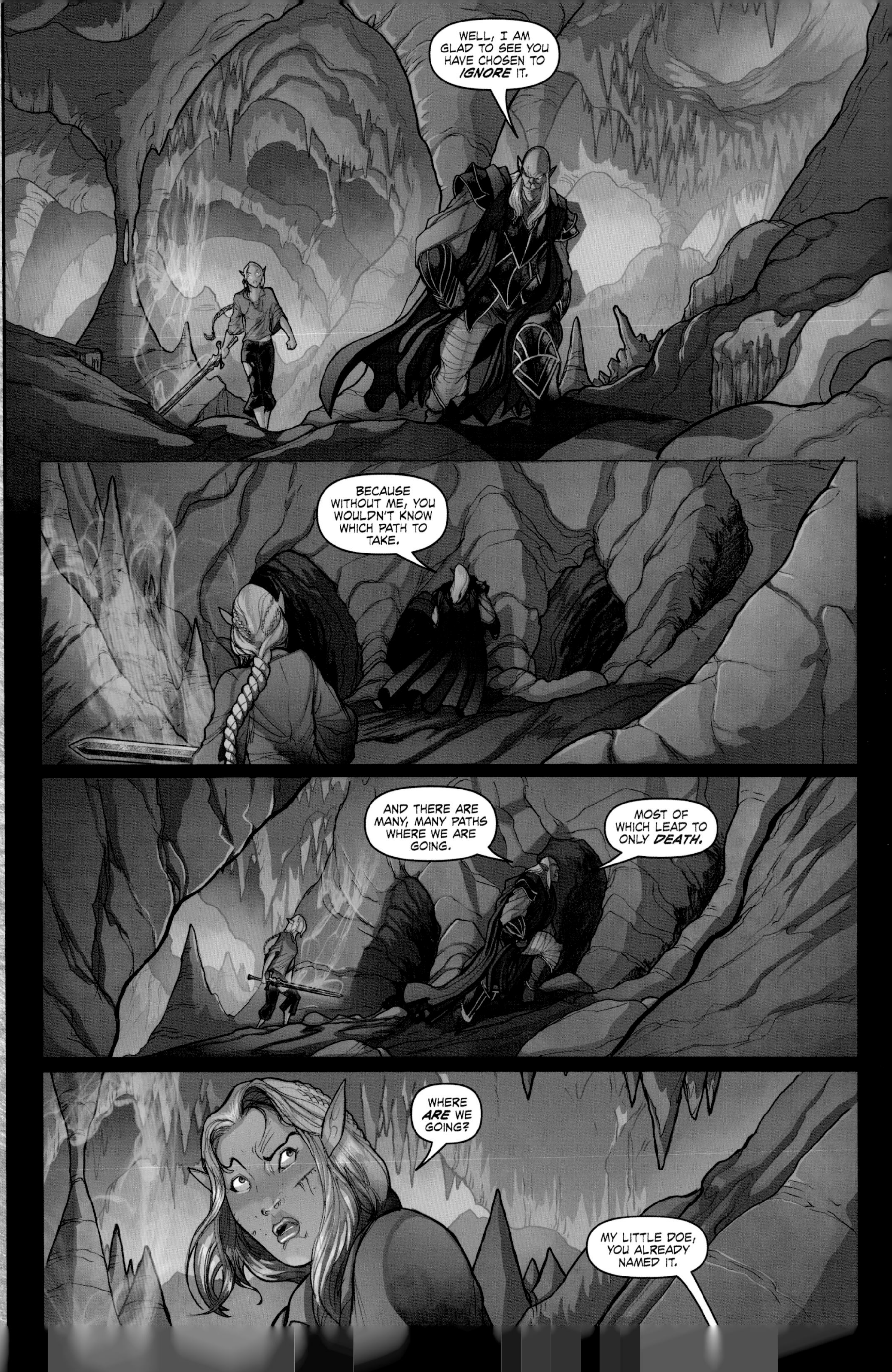
WELL, I AM GLAD TO SEE YOU HAVE CHOSEN TO IGNORE IT.
BECAUSE WITHOUT ME, YOU WOULDN'T KNOW WHICH PATH TO TAKE.
AND THERE ARE MANY, MANY PATHS WHERE WE ARE GOING.
MOST OF WHICH LEAD TO ONLY DEATH.
WHERE ARE WE GOING?
MY LITTLE DOE, YOU ALREADY NAMED IT.

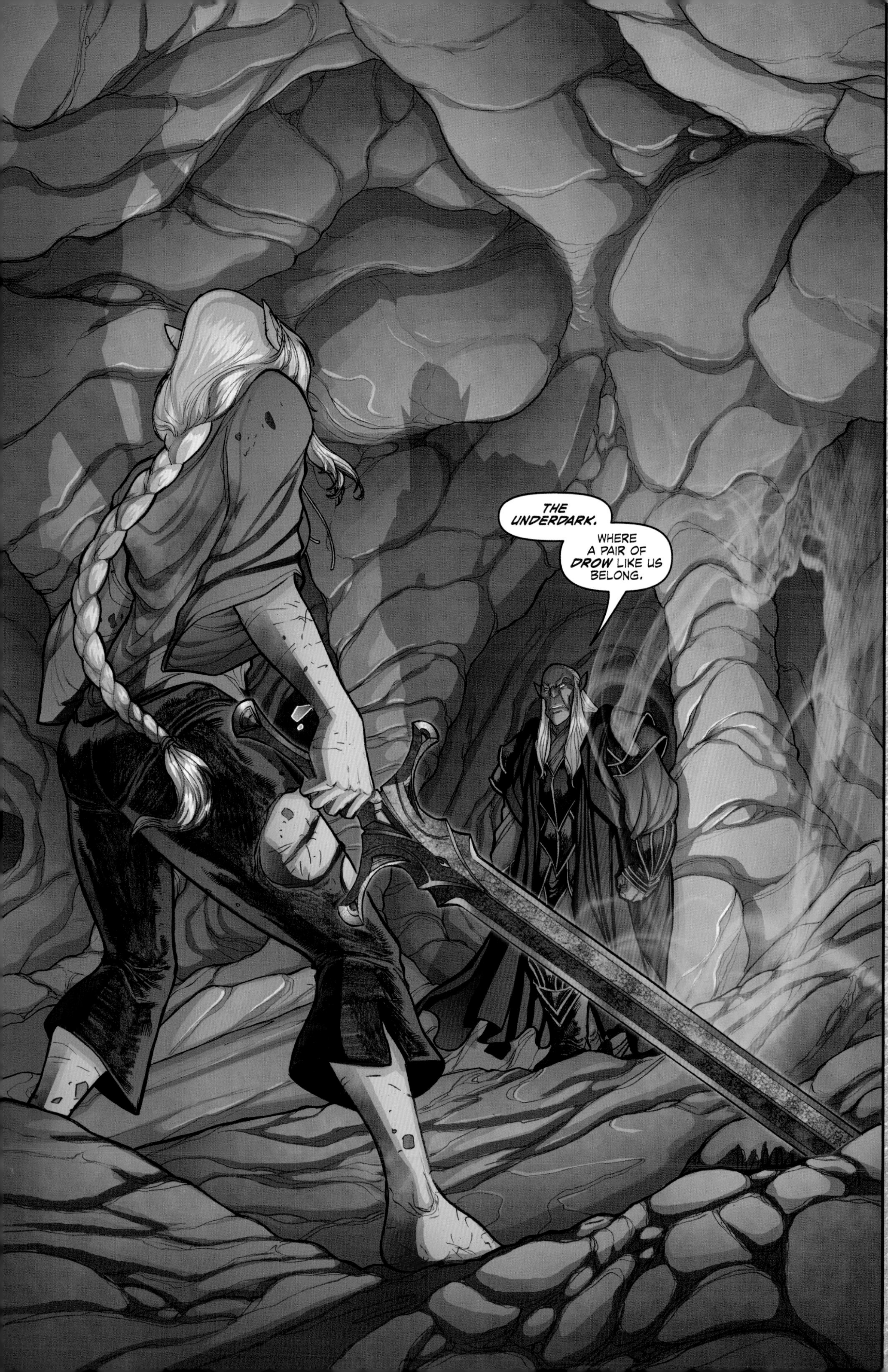
THE UNDERDARK.
WHERE A PAIR OF DROW LIKE US BELONG.

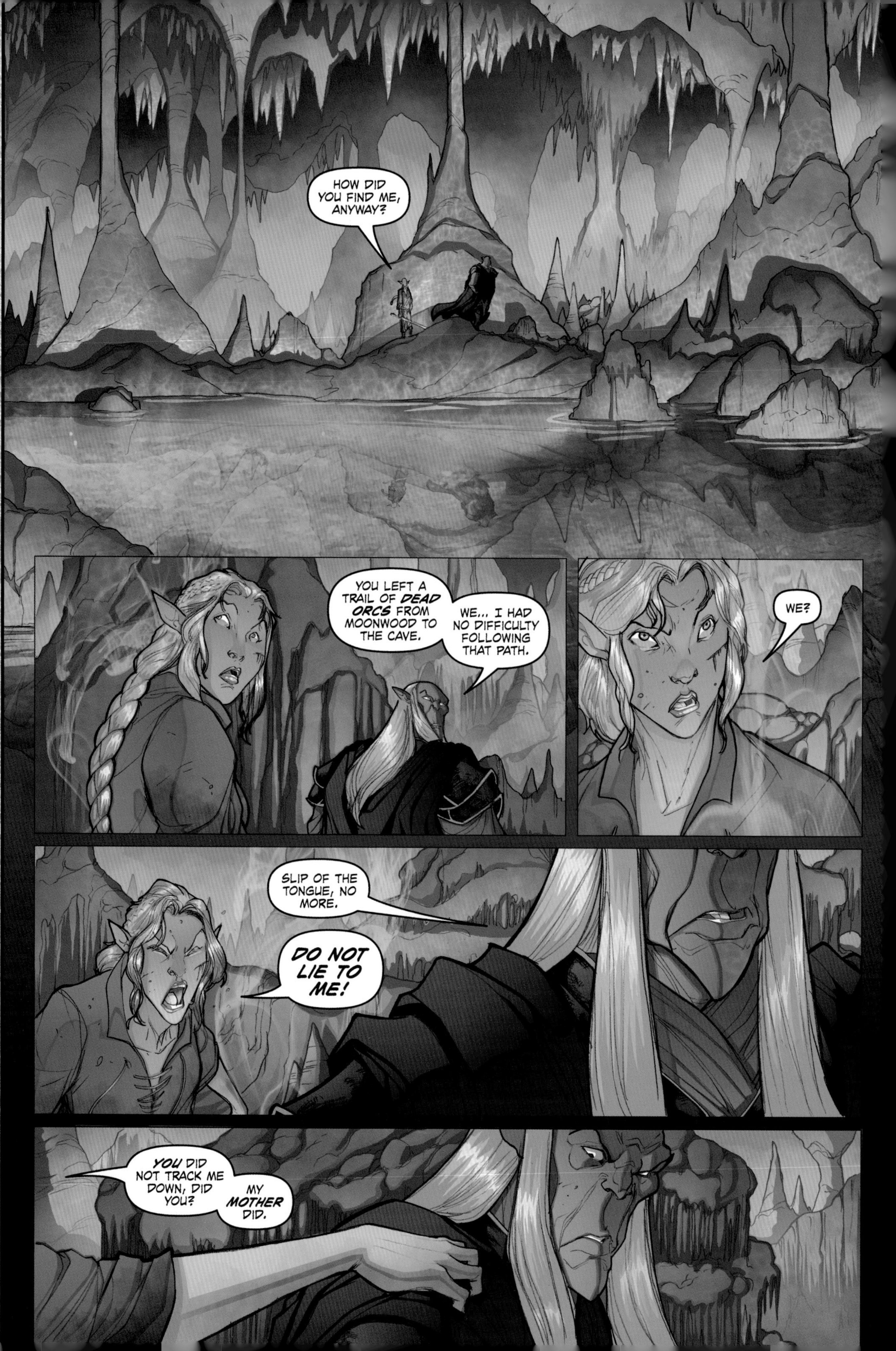
HOW DID YOU FIND ME, ANYWAY?
YOU LEFT A TRAIL OF DEAD ORCS FROM MOONWOOD TO THE CAVE.
WE... I HAD NO DIFFICULTY FOLLOWING THAT PATH.
WE?
SLIP OF THE TONGUE, NO MORE.
DO NOT LIE TO ME!
YOU DID NOT TRACK ME DOWN, DID YOU?
MY MOTHER DID.

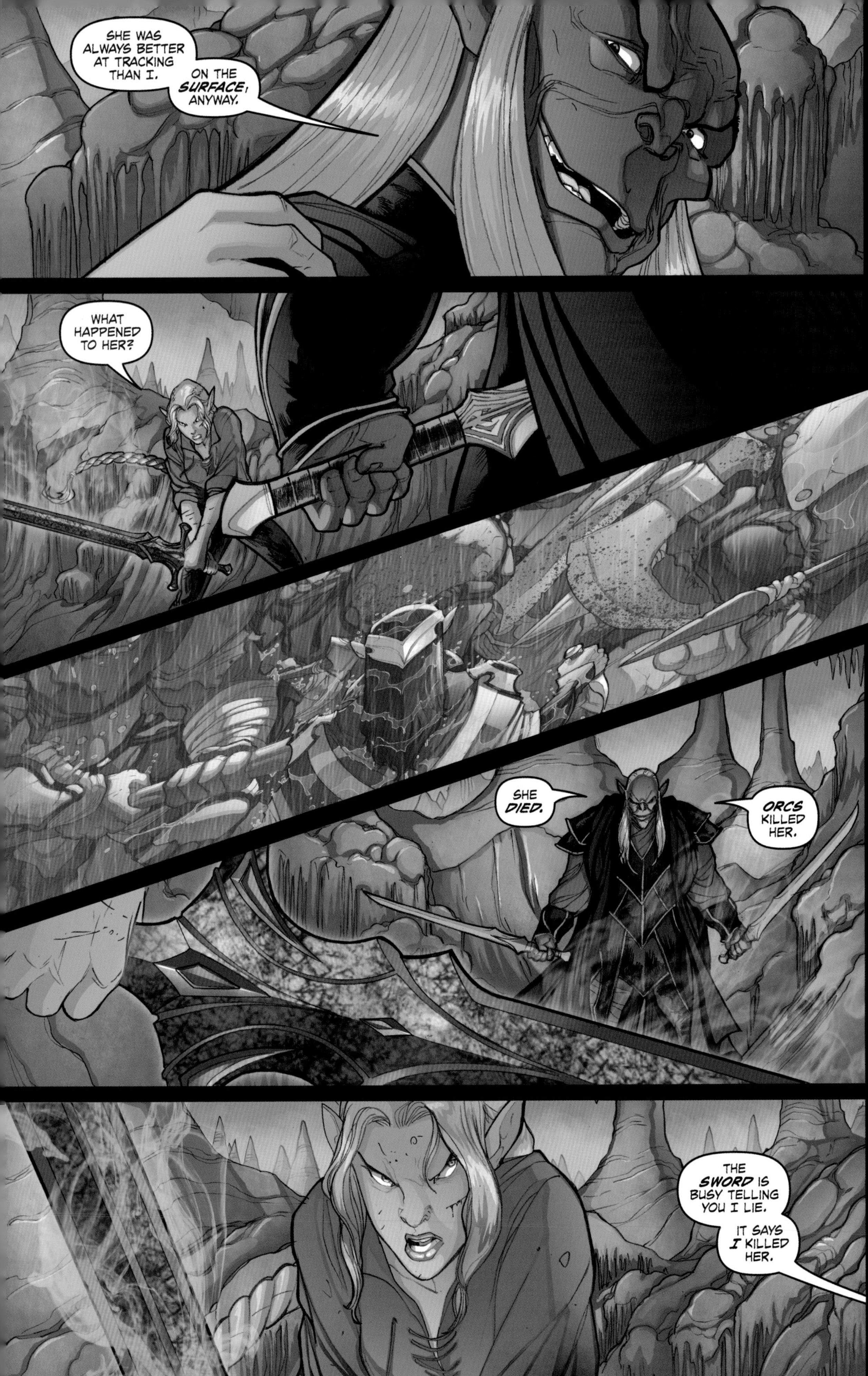

SHE WAS ALWAYS BETTER AT TRACKING THAN I.
ON THE SURFACE, ANYWAY.
WHAT HAPPENED TO HER?
SHE DIED.
ORCS KILLED HER.
THE SWORD IS BUSY TELLING YOU I LIE.
IT SAYS I KILLED HER.

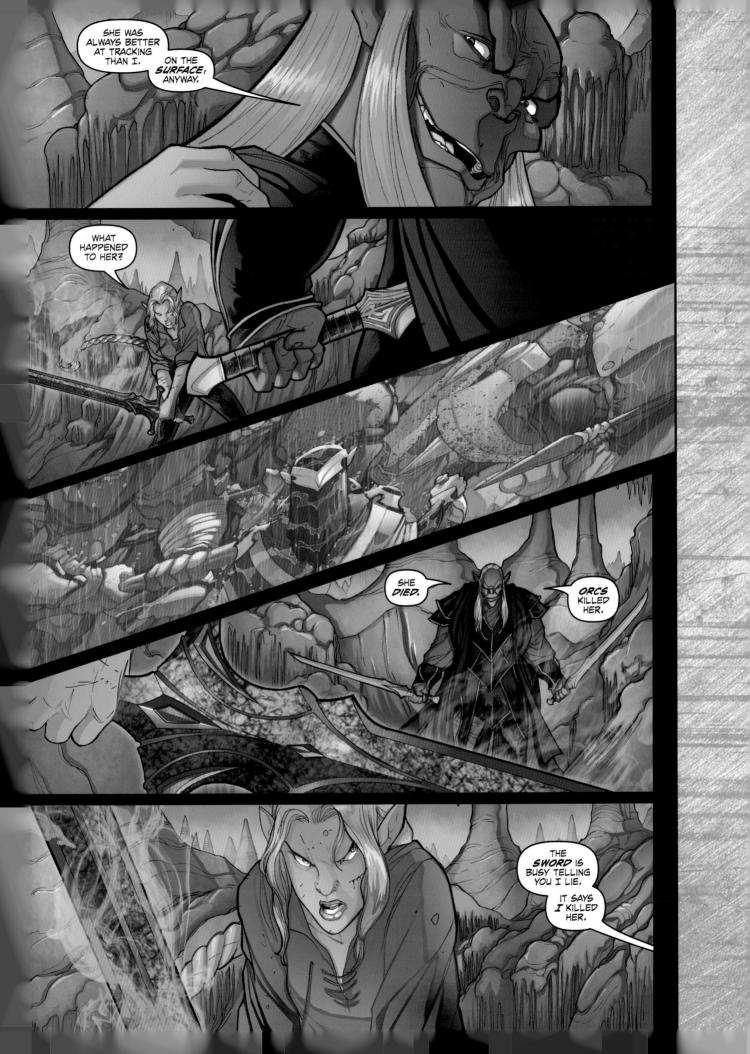

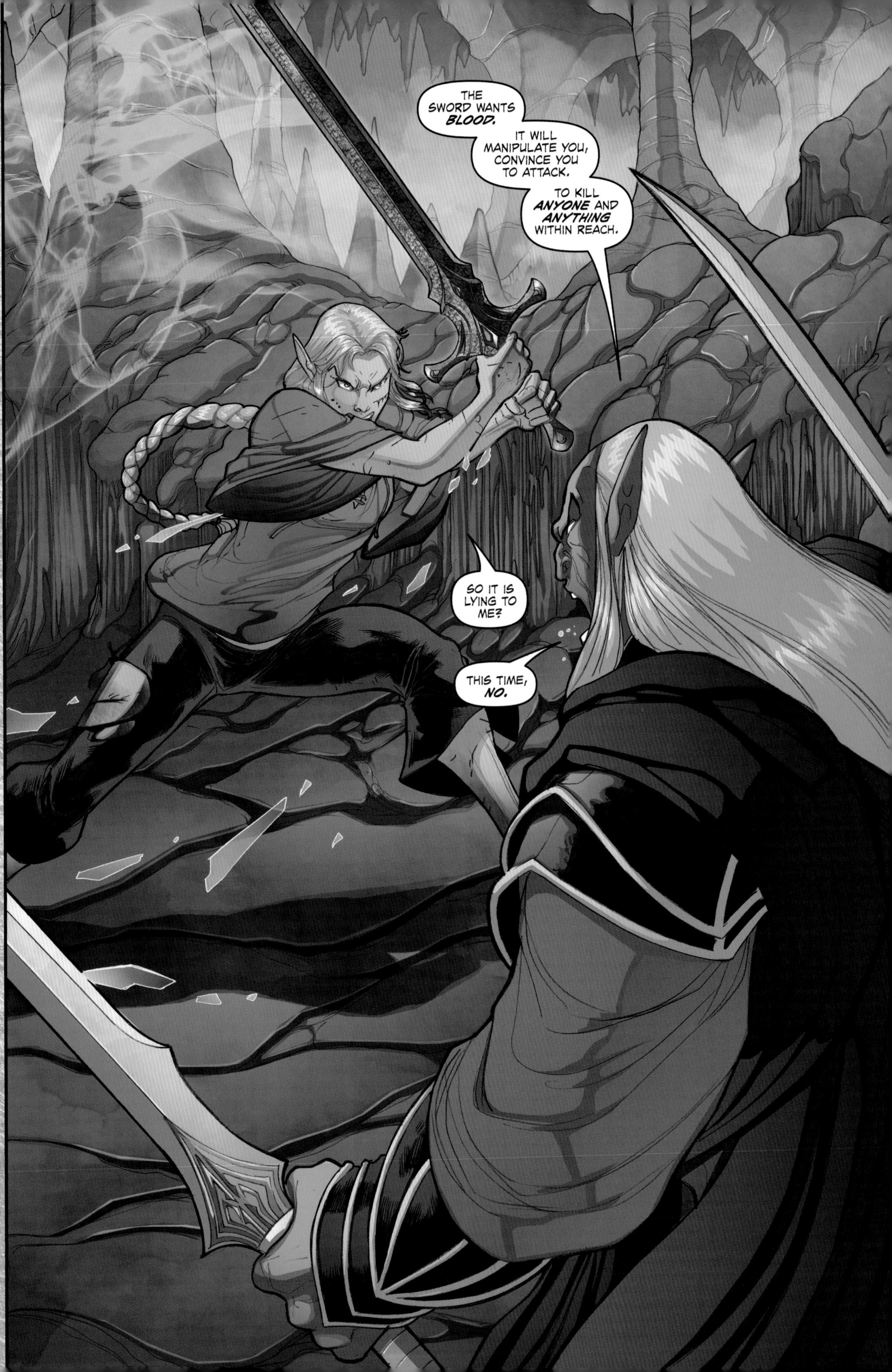
THE SWORD WANTS BLOOD.
IT WILL MANIPULATE YOU, CONVINCE YOU TO ATTACK.
TO KILL ANYONE AND ANYTHING WITHIN REACH.
SO IT IS LYING TO ME?
THIS TIME, NO.

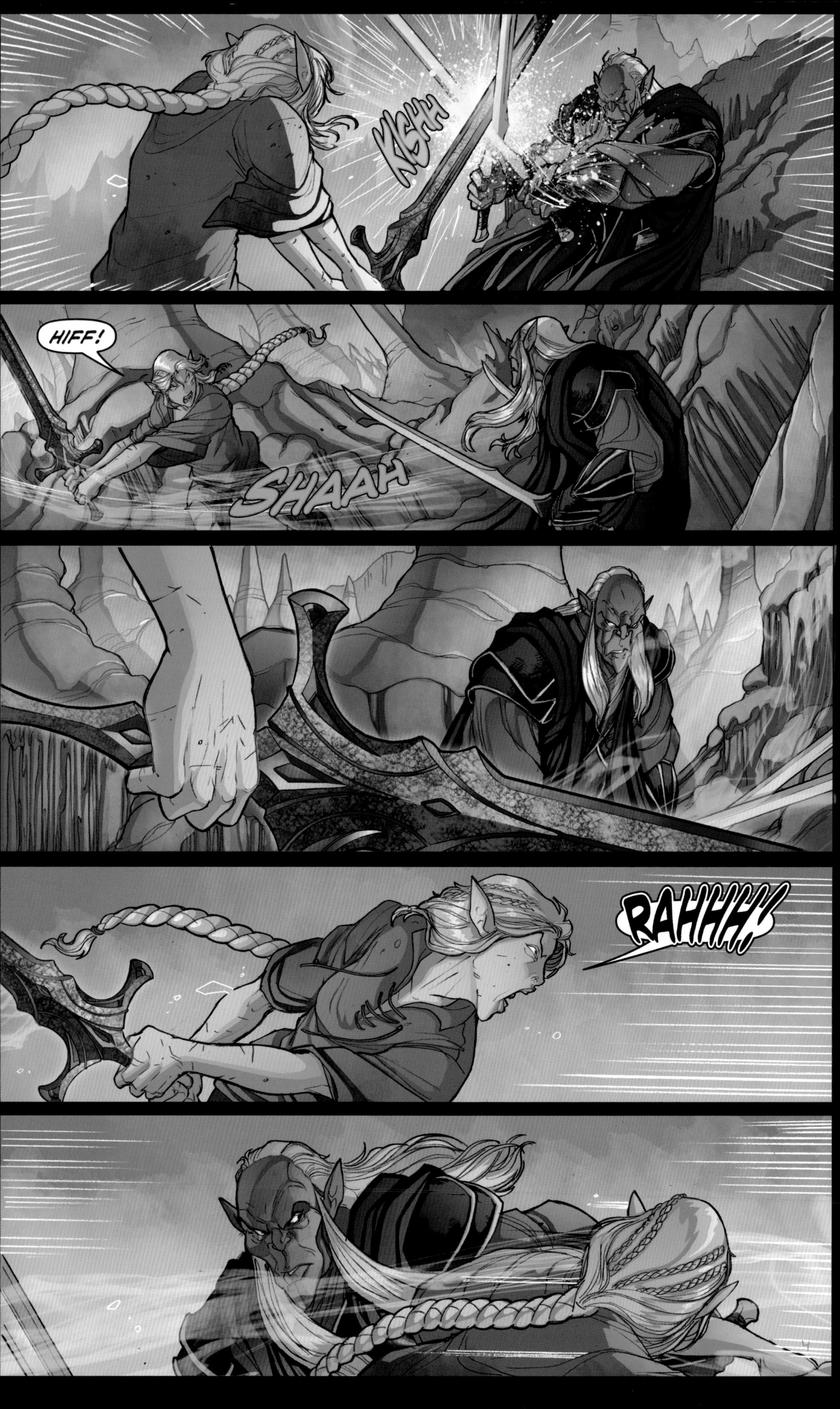
KISHH
HIFF!
SHAAH
RAHHH!

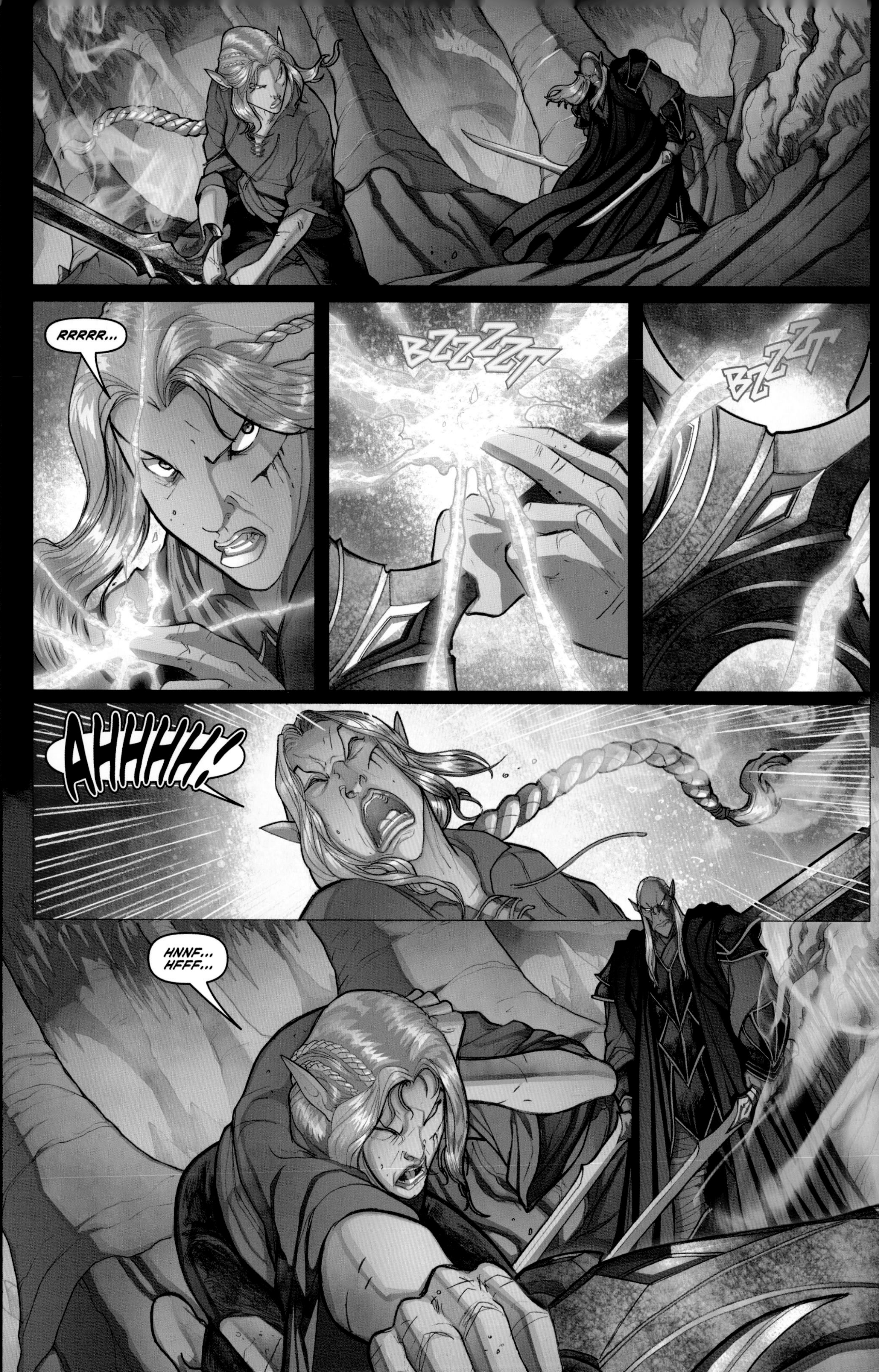
RRRRR...
BZZZZT
BZZZT
AHHHH!
HNNF...
HFFF...

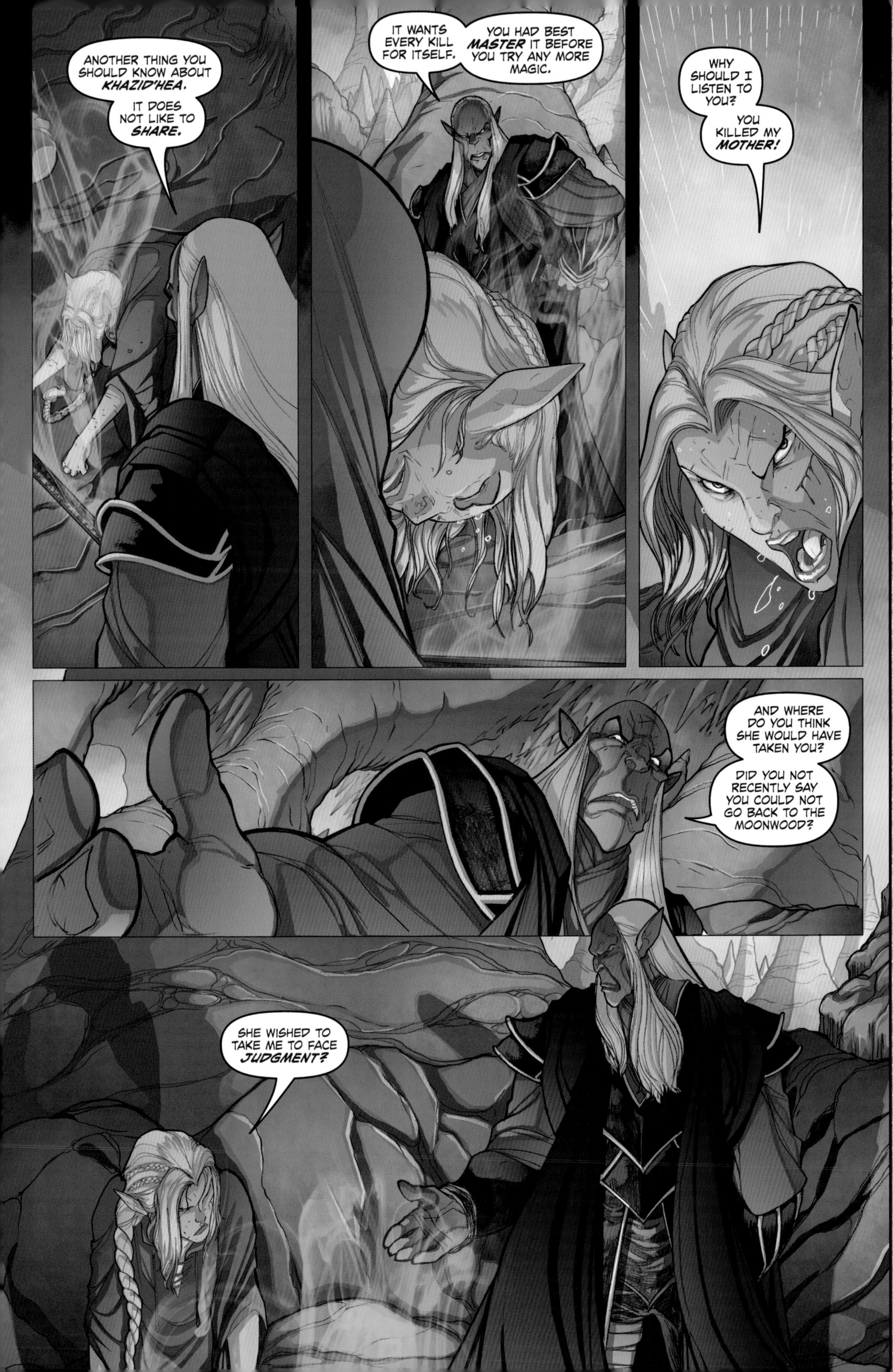
ANOTHER THING YOU SHOULD KNOW ABOUT KHAZID'HEA.
IT DOES NOT LIKE TO SHARE.
IT WANTS EVERY KILL FOR ITSELF.
YOU HAD BEST MASTER IT BEFORE YOU TRY ANY MORE MAGIC.
WHY SHOULD I LISTEN TO YOU?
YOU KILLED MY MOTHER!
AND WHERE DO YOU THINK SHE WOULD HAVE TAKEN YOU?
DID YOU NOT RECENTLY SAY YOU COULD NOT GO BACK TO THE MOONWOOD?
SHE WISHED TO TAKE ME TO FACE JUDGMENT?

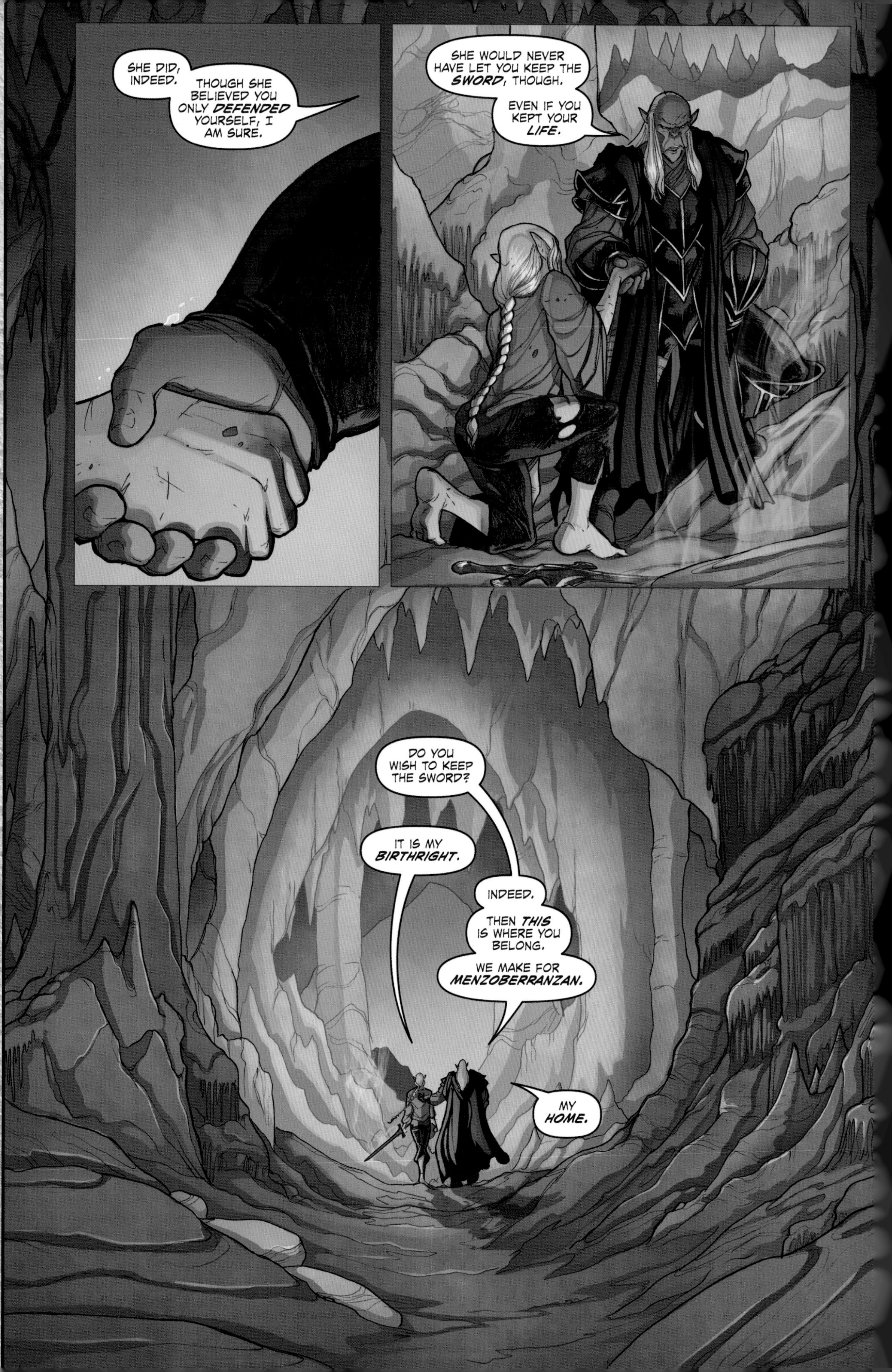
SHE DID, INDEED.
THOUGH SHE BELIEVED YOU ONLY DEFENDED YOURSELF, I AM SURE.
SHE WOULD NEVER HAVE LET YOU KEEP THE SWORD, THOUGH.
EVEN IF YOU KEPT YOUR LIFE.
DO YOU WISH TO KEEP THE SWORD?
IT IS MY BIRTHRIGHT.
INDEED.
THEN THIS IS WHERE YOU BELONG.
WE MAKE FOR MENZOBERRANZAN.
MY HOME.

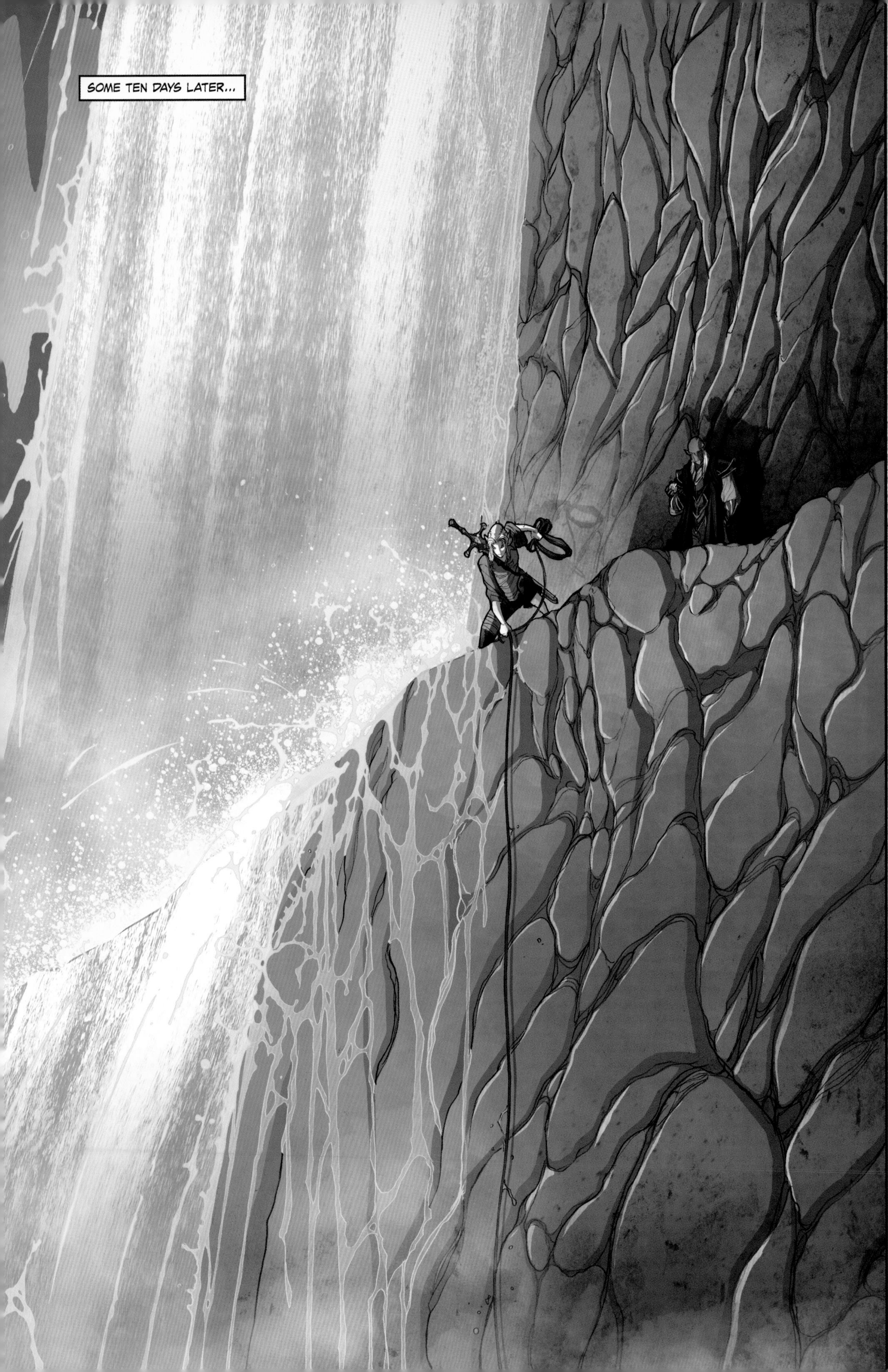
SOME TEN DAYS LATER...

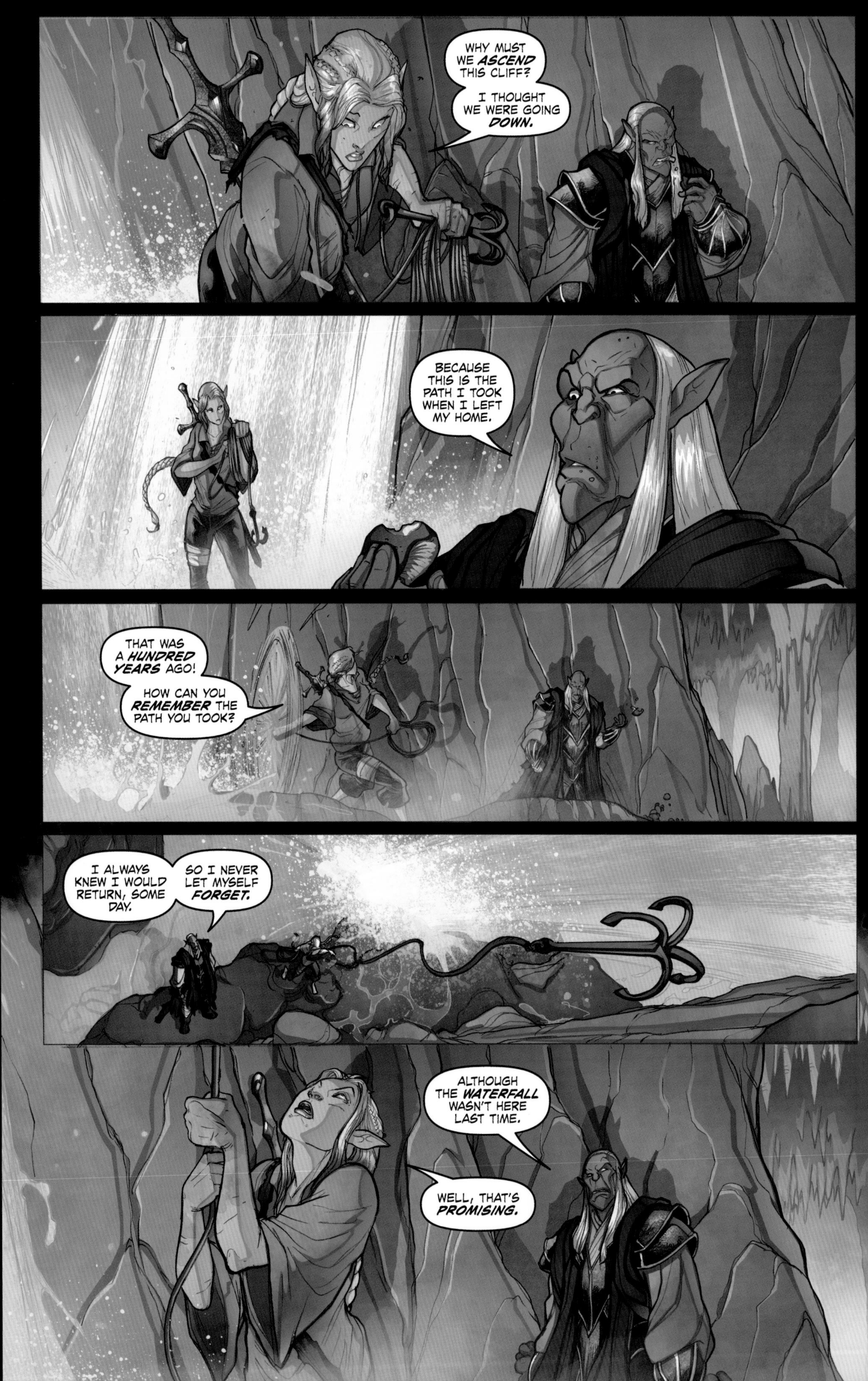
WHY MUST WE ASCEND THIS CLIFF?
I THOUGHT WE WERE GOING DOWN.
BECAUSE THIS IS THE PATH I TOOK WHEN I LEFT MY HOME.
THAT WAS A HUNDRED YEARS AGO!
HOW CAN YOU REMEMBER THE PATH YOU TOOK?
I ALWAYS KNEW I WOULD RETURN, SOME DAY.
SO I NEVER LET MYSELF FORGET.
ALTHOUGH THE WATERFALL WASN'T HERE LAST TIME.
WELL, THAT'S PROMISING.

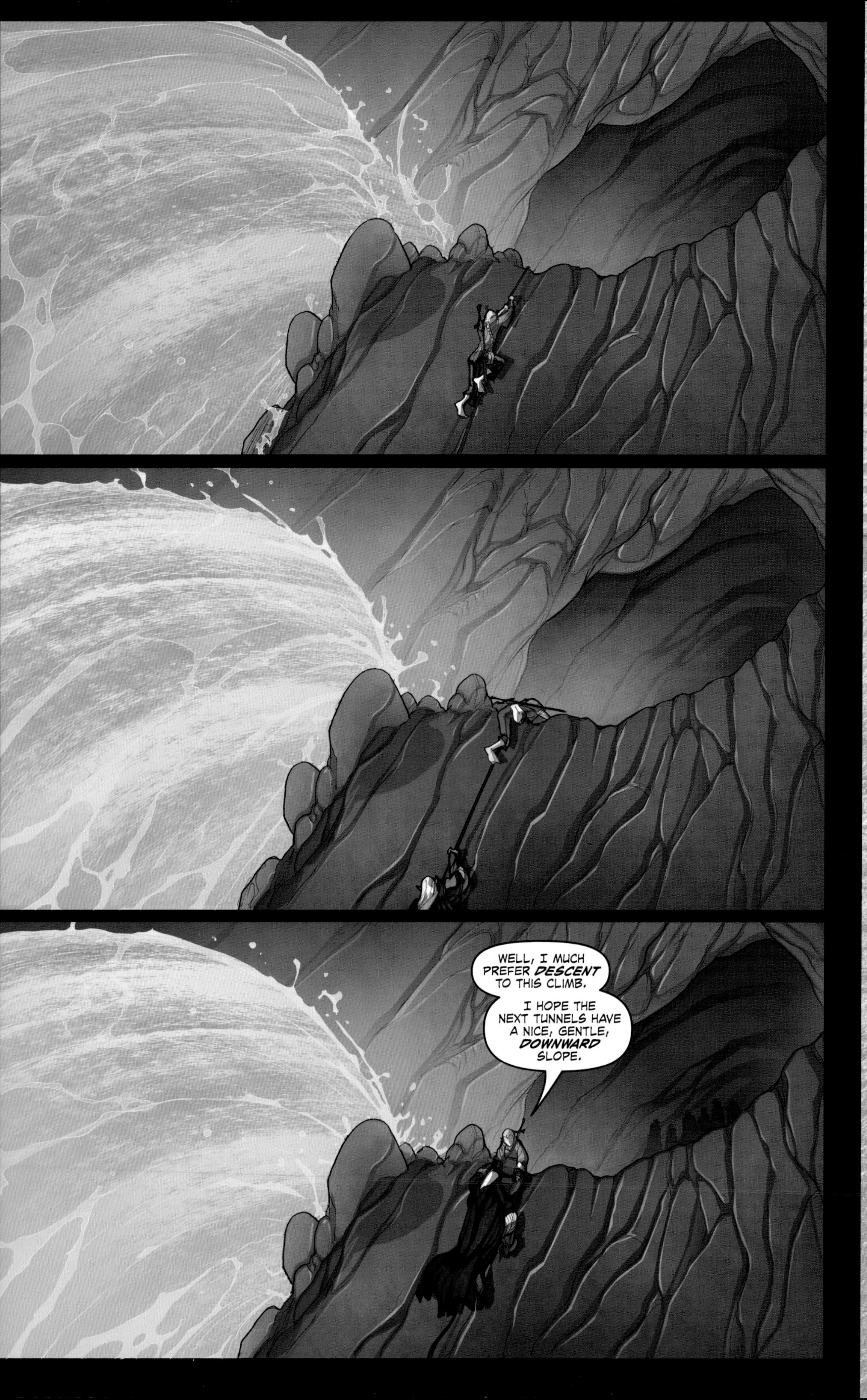
WELL, I MUCH PREFER DESCENT TO THIS CLIMB.
I HOPE THE NEXT TUNNELS HAVE A NICE, GENTLE, DOWNWARD SLOPE.

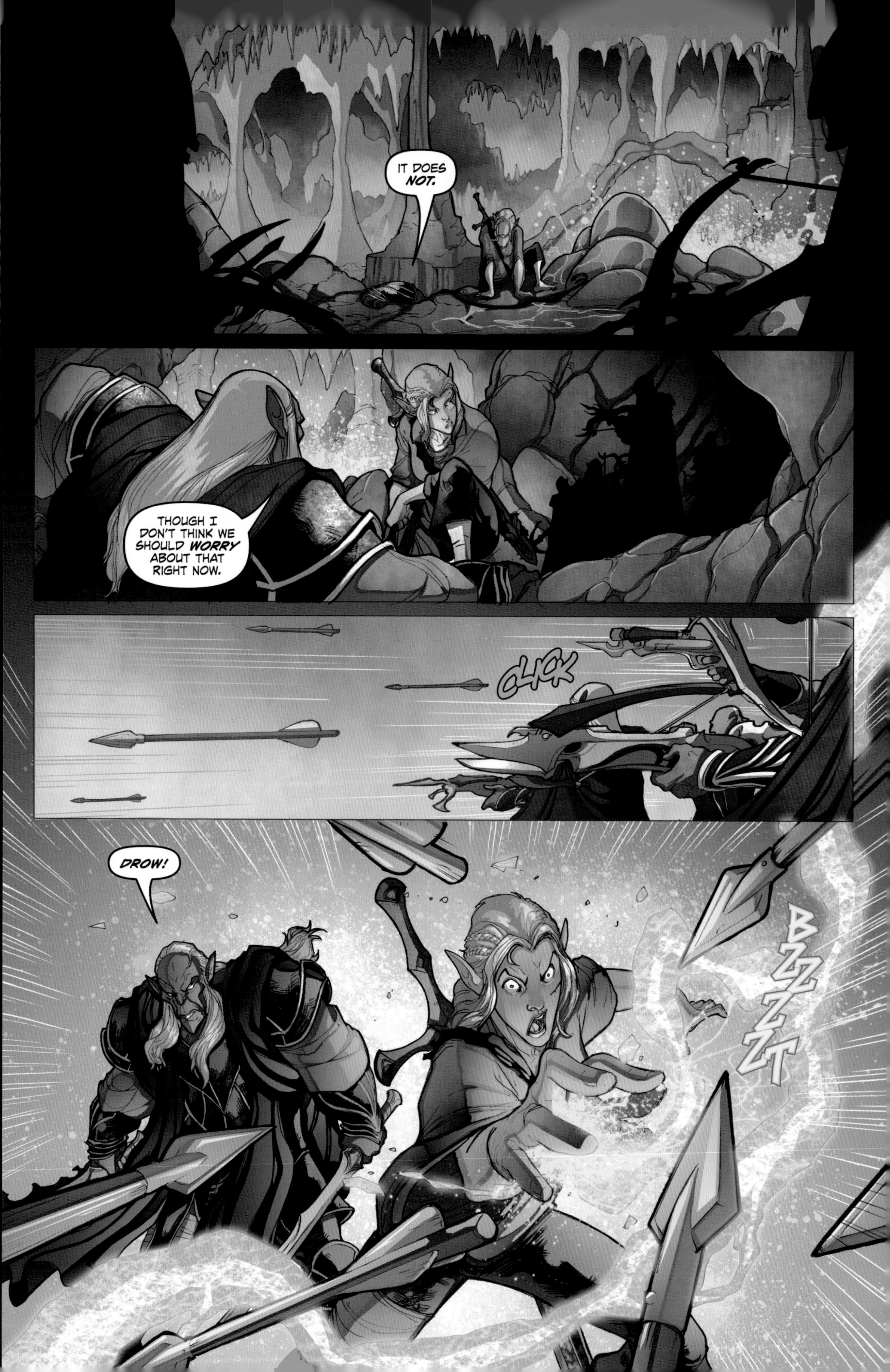

IT DOES NOT.
THOUGH I DON'T THINK WE SHOULD WORRY ABOUT THAT RIGHT NOW.
CLICK
DROW!
BZZZZT

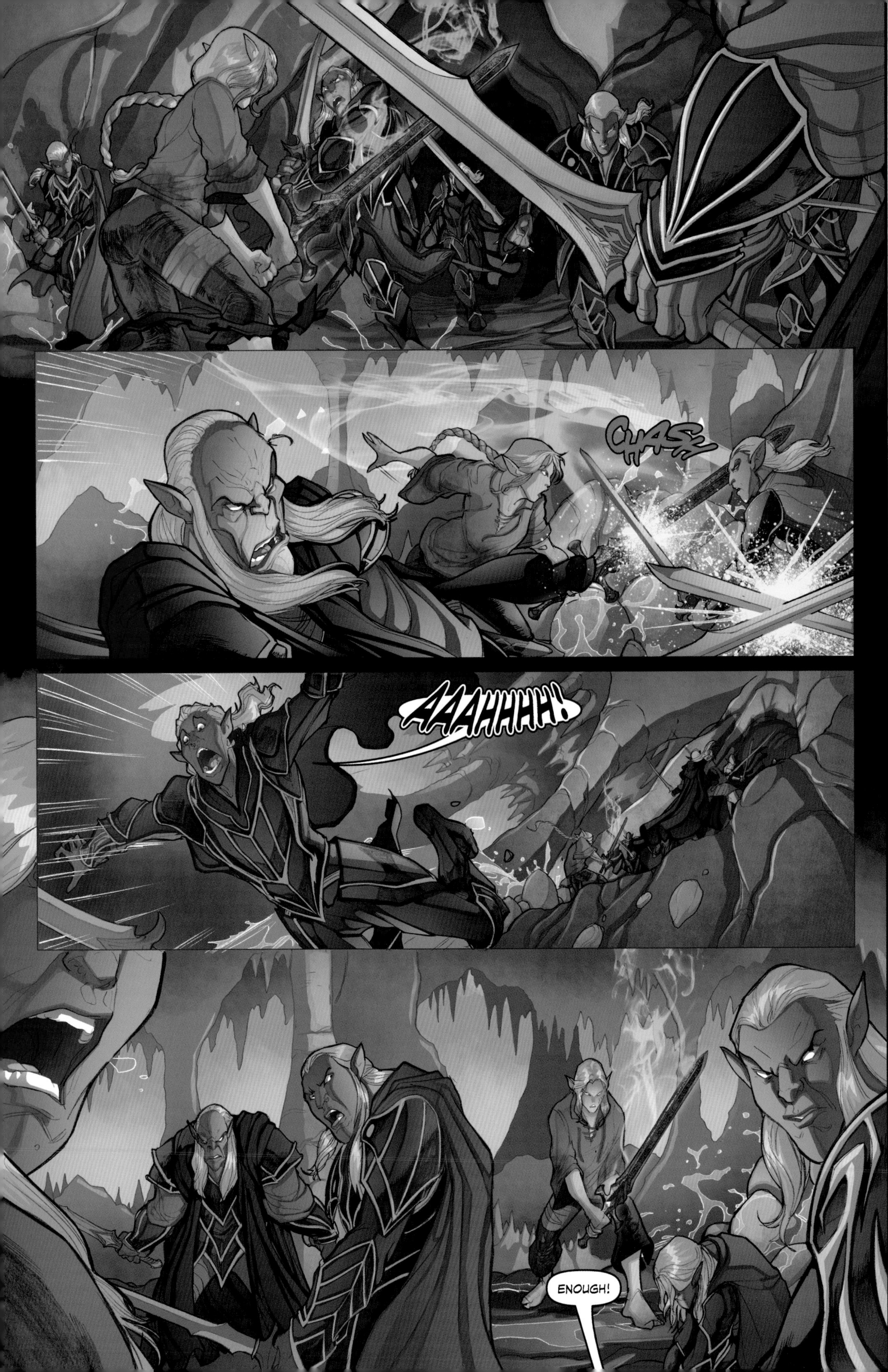
CHASH
AAAHHHH!
ENOUGH!

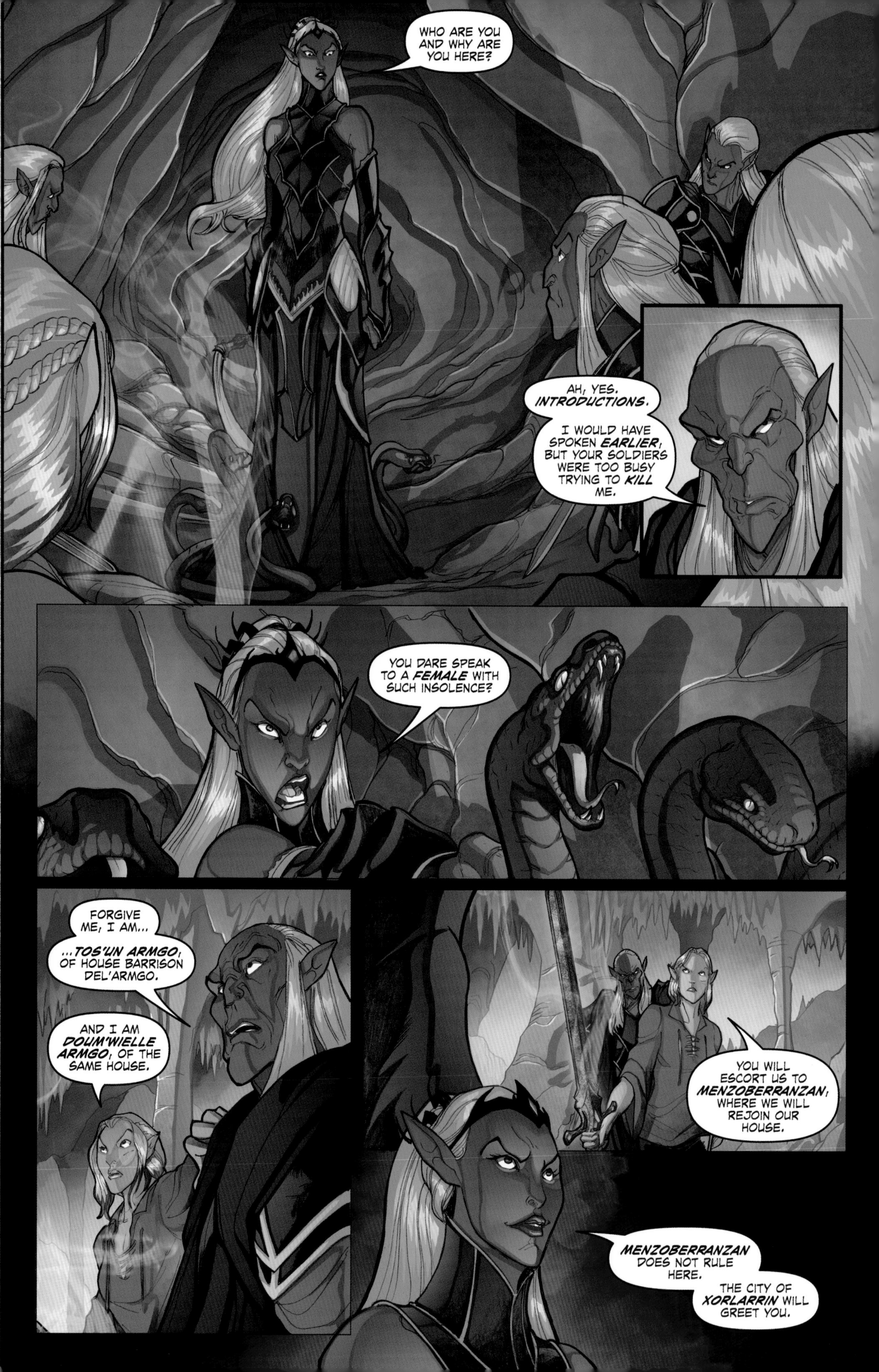
WHO ARE YOU AND WHY ARE YOU HERE?
AH, YES. INTRODUCTIONS.
I WOULD HAVE SPOKEN EARLIER, BUT YOUR SOLDIERS WERE TOO BUSY TRYING TO KILL ME.
YOU DARE SPEAK TO A FEMALE WITH SUCH INSOLENCE?
FORGIVE ME, I AM...
...TOS'UN ARMGO, OF HOUSE BARRISON DEL'ARMGO.
AND I AM DOUM'WIELLE ARMGO, OF THE SAME HOUSE.
YOU WILL ESCORT US TO MENZOBERRANZAN, WHERE WE WILL REJOIN OUR HOUSE.
MENZOBERRANZAN DOES NOT RULE HERE.
THE CITY OF XORLARRIN WILL GREET YOU.

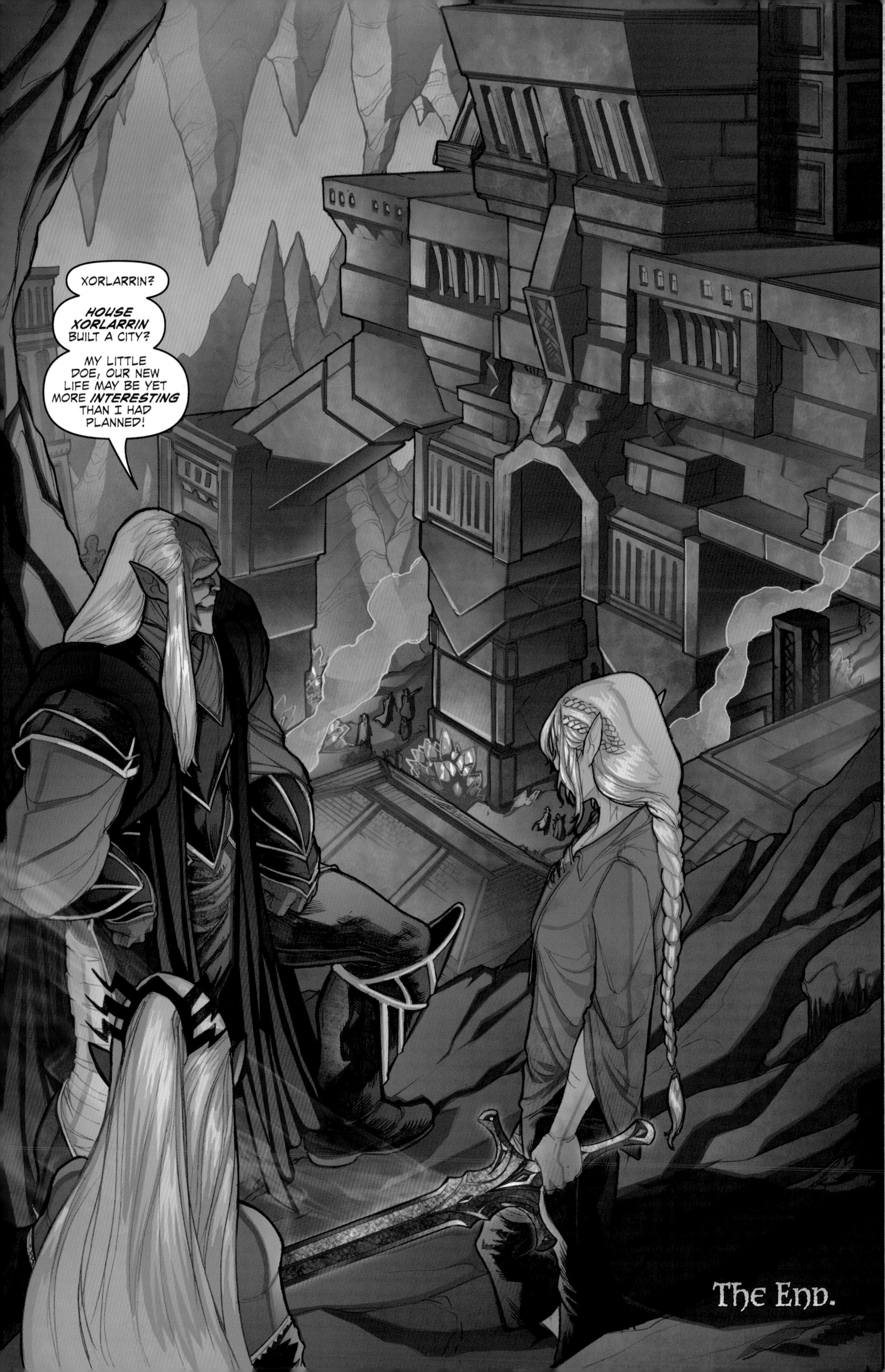
XORLARRIN?
HOUSE XORLARRIN BUILT A CITY?
MY LITTLE DOE, OUR NEW LIFE MAY BE YET MORE INTERESTING THAN I HAD PLANNED!
The End.

Art by David Baldeon
Colors by David Garcia Cruz

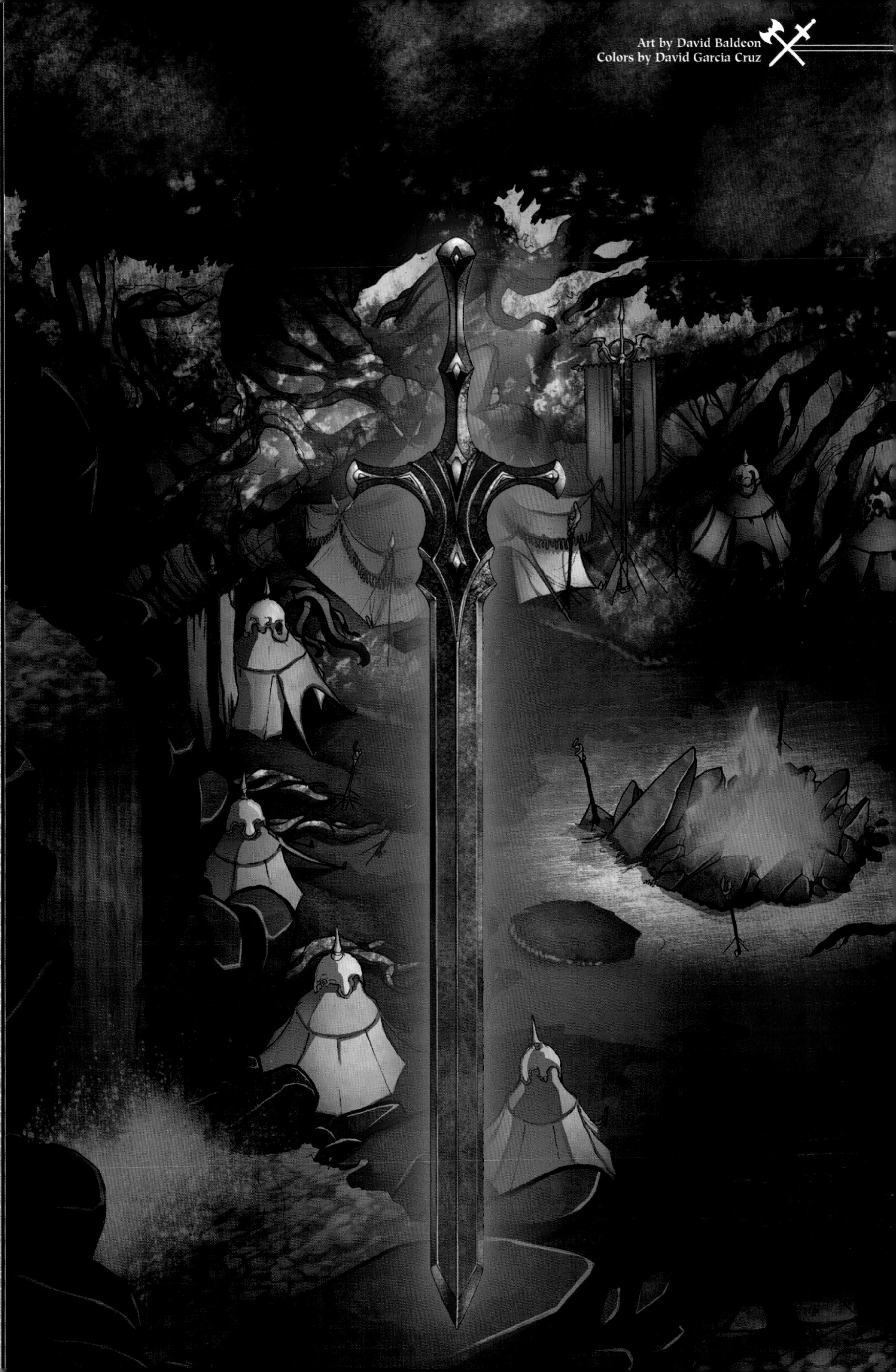

DUNGEONS & DRAGONS

Get your fantasy fix with these other adventures!

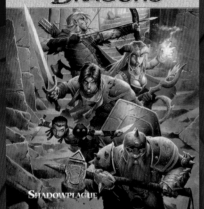

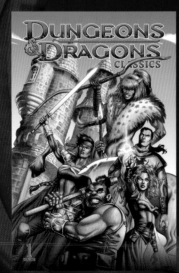